SACRED MYSTERIES

Sacramental Principles and Liturgical Practice

DENNIS C. SMOLARSKI, S.J.

PAULIST PRESS
NEW YORK/MAHWAH, N.J.

IMPRIMI POTEST
September 12, 1994
Very Rev. John A. Privett, S.J., Provincial
California Province, Society of Jesus

Library of Congress Cataloging-in-Publication Data

Smolarski, Dennis Chester, 1947–
    Sacred mysteries : sacramental principles and liturgical practice
 / Dennis C. Smolarski.
      p.   cm.
    Includes bibliographical references and index.
    ISBN 0-8091-3551-5
    1. Sacraments—Catholic Church.   2. Catholic Church—Liturgy—
 History—20th century.   I. Title.
    BX2200.S57   1995
    264'.0208—dc20   94-41024
                                                        CIP

Published by Paulist Press
997 Macarthur Boulevard
Mahwah, New Jersey 07430

Printed and bound in the
United States of America

CONTENTS

Preface   1

Chapter 1—*Liturgia Semper Reformanda*   7

Chapter 2—From Principles to Practice   12

Chapter 3—The Foundational Mysteries in the Church's Worship   17

Chapter 4—The Great Mystery of Baptism   33

Chapter 5—The Great Mystery of Confirmation   52

Chapter 6—The Great Mystery of the Eucharist   64

Chapter 7—The Great Mystery of Penance   85

Chapter 8—The Great Mystery of Anointing   96

Chapter 9—The Great Mystery of Marriage   105

Chapter 10—The Great Mystery of Order   126

Chapter 11—The Mystery of Death and the Rites for the Dead   138

Chapter 12—The Mystery of Blessings   156

Chapter 13—Obfuscating the Mystery   161

Postscript   179

Notes   180

References and Reading List   201

Index   209

To the memory of Popes
Pius XII, John XXIII, and Paul VI

Pius XII: who in 1947 published the encyclical *Mediator Dei* supporting the Liturgical Movement, and who in 1955 authorized the revision of the liturgy of the Sacred Triduum;

John XXIII: who in 1959 convoked the Second Vatican Council;

Paul VI: who continued the Second Vatican Council and in 1963 promulgated its first document, *Sacrosanctum Concilium,* the *Constitution on the Sacred Liturgy,* and subsequently promulgated the revised *Roman Missal* and other revised sacramental and liturgical rites.

PREFACE

Sacred Mysteries—In the prayer before communion in the Byzantine eucharistic liturgy, the assembly prays: "O Lord, . . . grant that I may, without condemnation, share your *sacred mysteries* for the remission of sins and for eternal life." The sacred mysteries of the eucharist provide us with a glimpse of the divine wonder of the ultimate sacred mystery, "God's mystery, that is, Christ himself" (COL 2:2), who, as St. Paul tells us, is the "mystery hidden for ages and generations but now made manifest to his saints" (COL 1:25–27).

What Western Christians term "sacraments," following the Latin *sacramentum*, Eastern Christians call "mysteries," following the Greek *mysterion*.[1] Eastern Christians speak about the "mystery of baptism" or the "mystery of anointing." Yet the various liturgical rites called *sacraments* or *mysteries* only mirror the ultimate mystery of Christ and his sacrificial life, death, and resurrection. And, in a sense, whatever mirrors the presence of Christ and the power of God in our world can be considered a *sacred mystery*, whether it is a sacred gesture, such as the imposition of hands, a sacred object, such as an icon, or a sacred activity, such as proclaiming the word.

Eastern Christian authors are not always comfortable with the Western practice that neatly places religious activities and rites into tidy ecclesial categories. As Father Thomas Hopko writes:

> The practice of counting the sacraments was adopted in the Orthodox Church from the Roman Catholics. It is not an ancient practice of the Church and, in many ways, it tends to be misleading since it appears that there are just seven specific rites which are "sacraments" and that all other aspects of the life of the Church are essentially different from these particular actions. The more ancient and traditional practice of the Orthodox Church is to consider everything which is in and of the Church as sacramental or mystical.[2]

1

I would suggest that the word *mystery* is appropriate when referring to something that is more experienced through the emotions than comprehended with the intellect.[3] I am reminded of this distinction when I look at a wall hanging I received years ago. It bears the motto: "Life is a mystery to be lived—not a problem to be solved."

When people use the word *mystery* in common parlance, they use it in a way that suggests an intellectual problem or puzzle that begs for a solution. We speak about "murder mysteries" and expect that someone using careful deduction and some insight will be able to provide a solution. But there are other mysteries that are not meant to be solved but rather meant to be experienced, such as the mystery of love. We will never quite comprehend this mystery and will never quite "solve" it. With God's help, we may be able to experience it more deeply and live it more fully, and perhaps that is enough.

Similarly, the mystery of Christ and the various liturgical mysteries—the sacraments—we celebrate are to be experienced from the inside, rather than comprehended from the outside. Christ is the Word of God, spoken because "God so loved the world" (JN 3:16). Christ is the word of love and love needs to be experienced. The liturgical mysteries, each mirroring God's love made visible in Christ, are celebrations to be experienced, not things to be comprehended. They can be experienced as ways of delving more deeply into the mystery of who we are as a people loved by God and redeemed through the mystery of Christ's death and resurrection. An authentic experience of the mystery can lead us not only to ponder it but to live it, until it shines forth in our lives.

The first document approved by the Second Vatican Council was the *Constitution on the Sacred Liturgy, Sacrosanctum Concilium,* promulgated by Pope Paul VI on December 4, 1963. It is considered by many as the Magna Carta of liturgical renewal. This document gave birth to the initial revision of liturgy that immediately followed the Council and also guides the ongoing renewal that many hope will take place continually. Although the *Constitution* often uses the ecclesiastical terminology common before the 1960s, it does refer to *mystery* at several key points. In article 2 we read that "it is through the liturgy . . . that the faithful are enabled to express in their lives and manifest to others the mystery of Christ." In article 5, the *Constitution* refers to the passion and resurrection of Christ as the *Paschal Mystery,* and Chapter II is titled "The Most Sacred Mystery of the Eucharist." Speaking about faith, liturgy, and life in terms of *mystery* is not something new. If anything, it is an attempt to regain an older terminology that fell out of common use.

What follows are reflections on the liturgical mysteries that the Christian community experiences in its pilgrimage toward the heavenly Jerusalem. As the Church continues its journey, it needs on occasion to pause and reflect on the direction it is taking and to savor the nourishment it has received. Too often we have set our patterns of actions and speech in stone not "by deliberate choice" but rather "by unreflected evolution."[4] The health and life of the Christian community seems to call for some sort of regular evaluation of the Church's liturgical life.

Our world has changed much since the day on which Good Pope John announced his decision to convoke the ecumenical council. A quarter of a century has passed since that Council. During that time human beings have walked on the moon, the Vietnam War has ended, the Iraq-Kuwait War has been fought, Germany has been unified, the Soviet Union has been dissolved, AIDS has become a global epidemic, and unemployment has reached record numbers.

The years immediately following the Council saw great changes in the manner in which Catholics worshiped. Numerous books and documents were promulgated by the Holy See that have led to a revolution in Roman Catholic practice. The most obvious change was that the mass, the sacraments, and other liturgical rites could now be celebrated in vernacular languages. But in addition to introducing new languages for communal prayer, the Council authorized a revision of the actual ceremonies and prayers. For example, the altar was repositioned so that the priest could face the people. The book of readings for mass was completely revised to provide three biblical readings for Sundays and major feasts. This cycle of readings now spanned three years, not one.

Perhaps more important than these external and textual changes was the new mindset that gave rise to the revised rites. No longer were the liturgical rites considered to be something done by a priest and silently witnessed by a congregation. Instead, they were activities communally performed by God's people gathered together under the leadership of a priest. As the *Constitution* proclaims: "every liturgical celebration . . . is an action of Christ the Priest and of his Body, which is the Church" (art. 7). This approach is reinforced in later documents, such as the General Instruction of the Roman Missal, which states: "The celebration of the Mass [is] an action of Christ and the people of God" (n. 1), and, "In the Mass . . . the people of God are called together into one place where the priest presides" (n. 7). This ideal recaptured from the early Church enabled scholars to reflect further and discover other basic principles underlying Christian worship. This recaptured ideal also became a starting point for restructuring the liturgical rites. In response to this ideal, the Church has provided a set of revised rites, many in marked contrast to old editions of the rites.

In recent years, further revisions of liturgical books have appeared with regularity. Revision takes time and for many people is painfully slow, yet the results have been a significant improvement over the first generation of revised texts. In 1983, the English speaking world received a revised edition of the rites of anointing in *Pastoral Care of the Sick*. This was followed in 1988 by the definitive English translation of the *Rite of Christian Initiation of Adults*. This was followed in 1989 by the revised *Order of Christian Funerals*.

Although each of these three books focuses on a particular liturgical rite—anointing, initiation, funerals—what is novel is the collection of additional, related services that each book also contains. We have begun to see the sacraments and other rites in a broader context of being only one service among several that help expand the full meaning of what Christian celebrations are about. For instance, initiation is more than baptism, confirmation, and the eucharist: It begins with inquiry and continues past mystagogy into the future. The revised books no longer merely contain isolated rites. They provide an entire "order" and situate a celebration of sacramental mysteries within a whole array of services that enable ministers to pray with fellow Christians according to needs and circumstances.

The revision of liturgical books is not limited to a revision of translations and a rearrangement of texts. In 1983, the Italian bishops issued a second edition of the *Roman Missal*, which contained newly composed opening prayers for Sundays to match the three-year cycle of lectionary readings. In 1989, Rome issued a revised edition of the *Ordination of Bishops, Priests, and Deacons*, followed in 1990 by a revised edition of the *Rite of Marriage*. In 1991, the hierarchy of England and Wales worked on revising the British marriage ritual, incorporating aspects of the old Sarum rite.

The International Commission on English in the Liturgy (ICEL) has responsibility for providing the English translations of liturgical texts and, for several years, has been working on the revision of the texts of the *Sacramentary*. Publication of the revised *Sacramentary* is due in the late 1990s. The next project for ICEL will be a revision of two of the rites of Christian initiation of children (that is, the rites of infant baptism and of confirmation). Meanwhile, in Rome the Congregation for Divine Worship and the Sacraments has been working on a supplementary volume for the *Liturgy of the Hours* and has also been discussing a third edition of the *Roman Missal*.[5]

The revisions of the Latin editions and vernacular translations of various liturgical books offer us a challenge. These revisions hint that now may be an appropriate time to pause, renew, recommit and reenergize ourselves according to the spirit and vision of the Council. Now may be an appropriate time to reflect on and to savor the experience of the *sacred mysteries* that are our liturgical rites. We can once again reflect on the mandate of the *Constitution on the Sacred Liturgy*, to encourage knowing, active, and fruitful participation by the faithful[6] and to provide liturgical rites worthy of divine worship that inspire and build up the faith of the Christian community. This vision of the

Council still rings true. Our task is to reflect on how best to use the heritage of the Roman tradition as we face the twenty-first century.

This book is an attempt to take advantange of the opportunity provided by recent revisions of liturgical books. Perhaps it can help the assembly of Christians, especially priests who will be presiding, toward a more fruitful celebration of all sacred mysteries of life. Of course, we cannot do this unless we know something about the history of the liturgical rites. We need to begin with a healthy appreciation and reverence for the ideal celebrations of the rites that are presented in our official books. We need to know which parts are primary and which are secondary, and also how to adapt the rites to our own situations. At the same time, we need to avoid the pitfalls that can turn the experience of mysteries into mere problems to solve.

My thanks go to all those who helped in the preparation of this book, in particular to Sr. Mary Constance, OCD, Rev. Michael Gilligan, Paul Halmos, Edward McFadden, SJ, Michael Moynahan, SJ, J.J. Mueller, SJ, J-Glenn Murray, SJ, Rev. George Remm, and Rev. Thomas Royer. A special word of thanks goes to Peter Mazar for his insightful suggestions and his editorial skills. I am also indebted to the scholars who by their writings have influenced my thoughts on and appreciation of the liturgy. I am particularly indebted to the many devoted priests I have known who by their example have shown me how to turn theory into practice, how to respect tradition, and how to remain mindful of the needs of God's faithful.

Chapter 1

LITURGIA SEMPER REFORMANDA

The phrase *Ecclesia semper reformanda*, "the Church always needs to be reformed," has been used by some contemporary Catholic authors to capture an ancient tradition highlighted in this century in the words of the *Decree on Ecumenism* of the Second Vatican Council: "Christ summons the Church . . . to that continual reformation of which she always has need."[1] Constant reform of lives and hearts is basic to Christian belief. In St. Mark's gospel, Jesus begins his ministry by announcing the kingdom of God and proclaiming *metanoia*—reform, change of heart. Unless reformation is always present in the Christian spirit, we unconsciously and imperceptibly harden our hearts and neglect the voice of the life-giving Spirit.

The Church teaches that the essentials of Christian belief do not change.[2] Yet, as human knowledge develops and the ways we live in our world change, our mode of understanding our faith and the ways we express our faith should always be under scrutiny, if only to safeguard the underlying unchanging truths. It is a perennial human temptation to idolize the words rather than the truth underlying the words. But the gospels remind us that Christ calls us to look beyond the letter of the texts in order to preserve the heart of the message.

The *Constitution on the Sacred Liturgy* proclaims a vision of the interrelationship between the Church and the liturgy.[3] In an often quoted sentence, we read that "the liturgy is the summit toward which the activity of the Church is directed; it is also the fount from which all her power flows."[4] Thus, in a sense, the Church ever in need of reform means that the Church's liturgy also needs continual reform and renewal. The liturgy must adjust to the world in which we live, yet preserve the sacred trust of faith in God's presence through Jesus, the Word made flesh. *Ecclesia semper reformanda* goes hand in hand with *liturgia semper reformanda*. The *Constitution on the Sacred Liturgy* suggests as much when it states:

For the liturgy is made up of unchangeable elements divinely instituted, and of elements subject to change. These latter not only may
be changed but ought to be changed with the passage of time.[5]

In many ways, this statement reflects the common human experience
that life means growth and growth means change. It also hints that change
and continuity can occur together, as suggested by the French proverb: *Plus ça
change, plus c'est la même chose*, "the more things change, the more things
stay the same."

Change and adaptation are inevitable and, at times, necessary and good.
And here is the paradox: In order for our expressions of faith to remain
grounded in the fundamental truths, they must continue to change. In other
words, for our faith to reflect the relationship to God and to others that it was
meant to have, the expressions of faith must adapt to a changing world.

Of course, not everyone is agreeable to change, and those who are entrusted with the task of bringing about change or even making minor revisions
will almost always face opposition. It can be of some comfort that our ancestors
in the Christian community faced opposition. St. Jerome was aware of the
opposition he would arouse in revising the Latin text of the Bible, and so around
the year 383 he wrote to Pope Damasus to express his misgivings:

> You urge me to revise the Old Latin version, and, as it were, to sit in
> judgment on the copies of the Scriptures that are now scattered
> throughout the world; and, inasmuch as they differ from one an-
> other, you would have me decide which of them agree with the
> Greek original. The labor is one of love, but at the same time it is
> both perilous and presumptuous—for in judging others I must be
> content to be judged by all. Is there anyone learned or unlearned,
> who, having taken the volume in hand and perceiving that what one
> reads does not suit the reader's settled tastes, will not break out
> immediately into violent language and call me a forger and a pro-
> fane person for having had the audacity to add anything to the
> ancient books, or to make any changes or corrections therein?[6]

Jerome, in fact, was criticized for his work. A man not known for graciousness
under fire, he referred to his critics as "two-legged asses," "yelping dogs," and
persons who "think that ignorance is equivalent to holiness."[7] Jerome's experience offers encouragement (although maybe not the right vocabulary) to those
involved in the ongoing process of liturgical revision and renewal today. If a
task is well done, after the criticism comes the appreciation!

A monumental task was accomplished in the decade after the promulgation of the *Constitution on the Sacred Liturgy*. In the sixteenth century the

major liturgical books of the Roman rite of the Catholic Church had been standardized by decree of the Council of Trent and had remained virtually untouched for 400 years. And yet in a single, amazing decade, most of these liturgical books were revised, translated, and in some cases adapted to local customs and needs.

But the speed with which this task was accomplished turned out to be a blessing and a curse. It quickly provided Catholics with a renewed liturgy that many thought was only a dream a few years earlier. Yet, an inadequate amount of time elapsed between the post-Tridentine, Latin liturgy and the post-Vatican II, vernacular liturgy. Time is needed to discover authentic traditions and to evaluate approved experimentation. As a result, there was little opportunity for a more profound adaptation to present needs and different cultures. That the Latin *typica*, "normative," editions of the liturgical books might not be ideal for every culture was foreseen in the *Constitution on the Sacred Liturgy*, which opened the door to more fundamental adaptations to cultures and customs.[8]

The Second Vatican Council started a minor revolution in our understanding of the liturgy, the principles involved in human worship, and the ways we celebrate the sacraments. But all of that seems like ancient history to many people today. The experience of "Church" for those in their 20s is a vastly different experience than that of people in their 70s. Many people who are now young parents have no personal experience of Latin masses or of receiving communion on the tongue. Keep in mind that someone who was 21 years old in 1991 was born six years *after* the first stage of vernacular liturgies and perhaps celebrated first communion in 1977, the same year communion in the hand was introduced in the United States.

More than a quarter century has elapsed since the Council. There is less hesitation now about omitting secondary liturgical elements, many picked up as excess baggage over the centuries, and more concern about celebrating a liturgy that speaks to and reflects the concerns and values of the contemporary Christian community. This was a fundamental concern of the *Constitution on the Sacred Liturgy*. A second stage of liturgical renewal is potentially in our midst, in which we now can build upon the successes and failures of those many liturgical scholars and visionaries of the 1960s. They laid the foundation, some of which has been experienced as tentative and even inadequate, but much of which has been fruitful and well-received.

As noted in the preface, this passage of time has provided liturgical scholars, both in Rome and throughout the world, the opportunity to reflect on the revised liturgical rites and to begin to provide a second generation of texts for use by Western Catholics. In most cases, not much of substance has been changed in this second generation of rites, and the basic order of the services has been preserved.

As we have gained more experience in praying in our own tongues rather than in Latin, texts have been amended in response to the insights of biblical, doctrinal, and linguistic scholars.[9] Alternative prayers and orders of service have been created that are more sensitive to pastoral situations not envisioned in the 1960s. Beloved local traditions have been included that preserve the best of ethnic devotions. Pastoral notes have been added to help ministers come to a better understanding of the rites they celebrate. Some proposals debated by the post-conciliar liturgical commissions have been reevaluated in the hopes that the biases of the 1960s may dissolve in response to contemporary needs.

Yet confronted by societal, national, and global problems begging for solutions, there are people who question the relevance of liturgical rites. Some have suggested that we as a Church have become too comfortable with our interpretations of the revised rites. As a result we are no longer moved by their energy. Others have rejected even the revised rites as being too archaic to challenge and comfort men and women faced with the problems of unemployment, homelessness, hunger, and loneliness.

For many centuries Catholicism developed primarily in a European culture and proclaimed a vision of God often colored by European glasses. This is no longer the case. The Church is learning how to learn from the experience of peoples throughout the world. It is challenged to proclaim the truth of the gospel in cultures and societies that are far different from the Western culture often associated with Catholicism.

The new situations of our world and our Church place the liturgy in a new context. We have moved from a time when the Latin mass was celebrated the same way whether in Beijing, New Delhi, Durban, Rome, Chicago, or Quito. The revised liturgical books advise the priest to choose options appropriate to the local situation. Such regular accommodations may eventually lead to acculturation of the liturgy, in which local traditions supplant the Roman counterpart. But the ongoing challenge is a deeper inculturation, in which appropriate pre-Christian ritual elements in the local culture are identified, endowed with Christian meaning, and then become part of Christian worship.[10]

This process of ongoing adaptation presupposes a thorough knowledge of liturgy and of culture. We need to respect the precious inheritance that is found in the revised liturgical rites. We also need to understand the culture in which the liturgy is celebrated. That culture includes the global commercialism that entices people through fast food outlets and athletic shoe advertisements. Yet it also preserves hallowed ethnic traditions. It is easy to let contemporary culture water down the effectiveness of our rites in contrast to letting our rites stand in judgment of the culture in which we live. It is just as easy to ignore the sacredness of local values and devotions in favor of something imported from afar.

Many believe that the liturgy still has the power to soften hardened hearts, comfort the afflicted, and challenge the timid, even in the new context of our post-Cold War world. That this has not happened is not necessarily due to any defect in the liturgy itself. And so we might ask, why have we failed to understand and to make full use of the power of the liturgy? Perhaps this failure is reason enough for a second period of liturgical renewal. Mark Searle has written:

> We were ill-prepared for the reforms when they came. This lack of preparation manifested itself . . . in failures of implementation. Even now, the fundamental problems of the reform are still with us, and the renewal that the council hoped for remains elusive.[11]

Searle noted that the Council presupposed that for the reform to be successful, a significant educational effort directed at the clergy would be needed.[12] Unfortunately, in most places the education consisted of a few lectures about how to follow the new rubrics without any real effort at reorienting hearts, relearning a forgotten art-form, and recapturing lost attitudes about the experience of worship. For good or ill, most Catholics still experience the Church through the medium of the local parish and its priests, and the success or failure of renewal in the Church is intimately connected with how well or how poorly priests (and in more recent years, deacons and parish staff) are able to help the ongoing renewal take place.

We have learned that changing externals does not automatically lead to changed hearts. As the noted American Episcopalian liturgical historian Thomas Talley has phrased it: "Too many communities have already been brought to despair by the discovery that, having rearranged the furniture of the sanctuary and instituted an offertory procession, they still don't love one another."[13]

In our longing to understand the sacred mysteries we celebrate and experience, we should never fear to reflect and rethink our rites. Yet perhaps there is less need to change our ceremonies than to change our hearts.

Chapter 2

FROM PRINCIPLES TO PRACTICE

I teach mathematics to college students. One of my biggest frustrations as a teacher is in relating abstract theory to concrete applications. Sometimes, no matter how hard I try, my attempts to relate principles to practice seem to get nowhere. What seems to be grasped as abstract mathematical theory becomes forgotten, seems irrelevant, is misunderstood, or is ignored as if it didn't *really* apply in working out a specific problem.

The difficulty that some students experience is not in learning the *science* of mathematical rules and principles. Rather, the difficulty comes in developing the *art* of applying appropriate rules in appropriate ways.

I am not sure if the world of mathematics and the world of liturgy are all that different when it comes to moving *from principles to practice* or *from science to art*. Both worlds deal with well-accepted principles. Why is it, then, that so many practitioners fall short of applying these principles? Is it because the principles were never fully understood? Or is it because the practitioner fails to recognize the operative principles when faced with real-life situations?

The Council realized that a revision of the liturgy would require reeducation of those charged with leading the liturgy.[1] However, especially right after the Council, this "reeducation" of many of the ordained was limited to a comparison of old and new rubrics. The more important underlying vision was never emphasized. The rediscovered principles that underlie Christian worship were never presented. Too often the revised liturgy was presented as a *problem* to be solved, rather than as a *mystery* to be experienced through a renewed sense of the nature of Christian worship.

And what is the nature of worship? It is an experience of the mystery of God's love for us and our love for God. It is the Church giving praise, glory, and thanks to God (ROM 1:8; COL 3:17) through Christ our mediator (1 TIM 2:5) in the Holy Spirit (ROM 8:26; JUDE 20). It is an encounter with Christ, who himself is the image (in Greek, *ikon*) of the unseen God (COL 1:15). The liturgy challenges us to find God through Christ, a Christ who is present in the people gathered, in word and in sacrament, in the person of the priest

12

presiding over the worship,[2] and, indeed, present in all of creation since it was through him that all things were made (JN 1:3).

When Jesus was asked why he and his followers did not observe certain traditions, he replied that "new wine is for new wineskins" (MT 9:17). Christ's presence in our world demanded that men and women rethink their former customs and perceptions, something not particularly easy to do according to the Acts of the Apostles. Many significant events in human history have demanded a major rethinking of older practices and priorities.[3] The reformation in liturgy that has occurred since Vatican II similarly demands a reformation in our understanding of liturgical rites. We cannot celebrate the post-Vatican II liturgy with a pre-Vatican II mindset.

Understanding the new rites requires understanding the new principles. Using the new rites requires the ability to apply the new principles. An ongoing challenge is to make sure that the forms contained in our revised ritual books are given a life and a spirit by those who lead them.

But we cannot hope to give life and spirit to the rites, unless we have been first imbued with their mystery. Immersion into the spirit of the revised liturgy is a plunge into its mystery. Yet, the unfortunate reality is that many people have only received a light surface mist from the liturgy, rather than being totally immersed into its depths. The liturgical explanations prior to Vatican II emphasized the externals of worship and said little about why we did what we did. With deep faith, we believed that by saying the right Latin words and performing the right actions somehow people were brought closer to God. Since old habits die slowly, many Catholics still interact with the liturgy only on this surface level. They neglect to experience or even to become aware of the strong depths that exist in our contemporary revised rites.

Unfortunately, like my math students, presiders have not always been successful in penetrating the depths and grasping the principles, or in applying them to their own situations. Some dioceses have sponsored workshops on pastoral and liturgical questions. Dioceses also sponsor "clergy days," and other opportunities for continuing education. This is often done in conjunction with seminaries or Catholic universities. But, unlike the legal or medical professions, priests and deacons do not need a regularly renewed license to practice. Once they leave the seminary, there are no structures to ensure that the ordained are made aware of revisions in liturgical rites and of suggestions that can help them better celebrate the rites.

We need ongoing education in liturgical principles. But we also seem to need better skills at celebrating the rites appropriately. Why is it that certain people choose to ignore the principles and rubrics of the rites? Certainly there is a tension we try to balance between the community's right to participate in the liturgy of the universal Church and the community's right to adapt worship to its own situation. Some pastors truly believe that their own adapted rites, inspired by their personal vision, experience, and principles, are more appropriate for their local communities. But when are these adaptations authentic liturgy inspired by the best of our heritage and when are they not? One should not judge harshly every minor deviation from the printed rubrics, yet it has been observed that "pastoral adaptation" sometimes has become an excuse for out and out non-observance of liturgical law.[4] Further comments about the snare of "pastoral solutions" are included in Chapter 13.

Theresa Koernke suggests that there may be an "ethics of liturgical behavior" that we have too lightly embraced during the transition from the rigidity of the Tridentine liturgy to the adaptability of the Vatican II liturgy.[5] For the good of society, personal initiative and creativity need to be tempered by the accepted norms for interaction between individuals. This applies as much to liturgy as it does to any human endeavor.

It is said that "a little learning is a dangerous thing." I would also suggest that a little *freedom* is a dangerous thing. Too often liturgical ministers have become so caught up in their new-found knowledge of liturgy and the new-found freedom of the revised rites that some have forgotten the virtues of prudence, patience and humility. Instead of choosing options based on the good shepherding of the assembled flock, options were chosen based on personal taste and piety. In some parishes, a new form of "clericalism" has emerged, in which the idiosyncrasies of the presiding priest have overshadowed the rites.

Mark Searle warns us that "the liturgy has proved highly susceptible to the individualism of our culture, rather than becoming, as the promoters of the liturgical movement had hoped, a bulwark against it."[6] And liturgical ministers are not the only people imposing their personal tastes on communal worship. Sometimes it seems as if every member of the assembly has become a critic of some facet of liturgy, even criticizing options that are actually beneficial and are encouraged in official documents. For example, there are still some who complain that a priest is taking undue liberties if he includes a homily during a weekday mass.

Of course it is good that many people now have a better understanding of the principles and history of liturgy and no longer act as if they were slaves of the rubrics. However, basic knowledge is different from technical expertise, and the ability to make significant adaptations requires a level of expertise that most people in a parish do not possess. Most of us would agree that we do not have the medical skills to make our own decisions when we get sick. We consult those who are more knowledgable and ask their advice. But what is it about liturgy that seems to turn some people into self-proclaimed "experts"? Certain people act as if participation in liturgy alone provides them with all the expertise they need.

Perhaps some of this is the result of our notions of democracy, of giving

Rubric : a direction in a missal, hymnal, or other liturgical books

instruction

everyone a hearing. Some of this might even be born of some arrogance. Among certain people there is the real desire to engage the parish in active participation in the liturgy—which is then expanded to include participation in liturgical adaptation, as if everyone by right were a liturgical expert. All of us probably have some pet peeve when it comes to the ways we worship. There are those who want to bring back the pieties of the Tridentine mass. There are others who want worship to emphasize some particular moral, catechetical, or even political stance. We need to step back, pause and realize that God is the one who has called us together and God alone is the one we worship. We need to regain the humility that enables us to learn from others, from our tradition, and especially from the rites themselves.

One of the major challenges regarding the liturgical life of the Church is for pastors and faithful alike to let a science become an art in their lives. The "science" of music only becomes an art after hours and hours of painful practice and study. The "science" of ballet dancing becomes a true art, to be admired and applauded, only after hours and hours of meticulous practice and study. Perhaps in a similar way, the "science" of liturgy becomes an art only after an extensive practical experience and study. Liturgical rubrics—the "science"—are something like a recipe for fine pastry, or a playwright's stage directions, or a composer's notes for a symphony. The only people really capable of turning rubrics or recipes or notes into art are those who have dedicated themselves to nearly endless practice and study.

Another way to describe liturgy is with the images of prose and poetry. Much of the liturgical renewal since the Second Vatican Council has been on the level of prose, but the challenge is to drink deeply not of prose but of poetry. As Sister Kathleen Hughes, RSCJ has written:

> By 1974 our new liturgical library of revised rites was virtually complete. In a period of about five years we had had an instructional barrage of liturgical documents, one after another. We quickly tired of the work of catechesis. It's time for new efforts in the liturgical education of our communities. Now, however, I think we need less catechesis and more profound mystagogia. That means a new commitment to *doing* the rites well—the best form of teaching. The difference between catechesis and mystagogia is that catechesis is prose and mystagogia is poetry. Mystagogia deals less with teaching but rather unfolds the symbols of our celebration in a more poetic mode, gradually forming the deeper affections of our heart.[7]

In the past few years, several people, such as Archbishop Annibale Bugnini, CM and Dom Bernard Botte, OSB have had the courage to tell their stories of the post-conciliar days and the discussions, debates, false accusations, delays, compromises and papal interventions that went into the revisions of the liturgical books in the late 1960s and early 1970s.[8] We found out what many of us suspected, that many sound suggestions of liturgical experts were set aside because of compromises and individual idiosyncrasies. We learned that the hard work of scholars was attacked by some as heretical and even as the work of Freemasons!

Perhaps, now, twenty-five years after the Council, with less exaggeration and emotion we can evaluate what has happened, where we have come from, and where we want to go. Perhaps with less of a bias to conserve what is not helpful or, in contrast, to "throw the baby out with the bathwater," we can try to experience the full meaning of our *mysteries* and come to understand their underlying *principles*. Then we can attempt to incarnate our often imperfect scientific knowledge into a living *practice* of the worship of God that leads to service of our sisters and brothers.

SEE NOTE' ON '0-11

ON 1960 COUNCIL

P. 2-3

Chapter 3

CRITICISM

THE FOUNDATIONAL MYSTERIES IN THE CHURCH'S WORSHIP

AN AGREED UPON PATTERN OF MOVEMENT

Each of the great mysteries or sacraments of the Church consists of a ritual celebration involving a complex of gestures and words that together form the mystery being celebrated. Yet the various gestures and words can also be mysteries in themselves, even though they are building blocks from which is formed the structure of the larger celebration. Often these foundational mysteries are common, everyday gestures or words that receive added meaning because of the context in which they are used.

Jesus recognized the extraordinary significance of ordinary things: a simple touch, a gentle word, a shared meal. Throughout his ministry great significance was given to what may at first have seemed the most ordinary of gestures, objects, or words—and this transfiguration of the ordinary fills us with awe.

Before examining the various great mysteries of the Church, it is appropriate to reflect on some of the many foundational mysteries common to nearly all the sacraments. These foundational mysteries—such as placing a hand on a person's head, standing in reverence, walking in procession, greeting and responding, sensing the fragrance of incense or chrism—draw us deeper into the great sacramental mysteries we gather to celebrate. Since these gestures and words are so common in our ritual celebrations, we may tend to overlook their significance. Yet without them, the great mysteries evaporate into nothingness.

Touch and the Laying On of Hands

When Jesus was approached by a man with leprosy (MK 1:40 ff), the gospel tells us that Jesus stretched out his hand and touched the individual. Because of this simple gesture of human contact, the leprosy vanished. This seemingly insignificant gesture has immense meaning. Under Mosaic law, those with leprosy had to separate themselves from the community. Only after

17

their cure was verified by the priests could they reintegrate themselves into society. Jesus broke a social taboo by reaching out to someone who was forbidden to reach out to him. Through that simple touch, the healing power of divine life and love freed that unfortunate person from the illness that had burdened him.

Human communication mediated through touch is a mystery, part of the mystery of human flesh and spirit created in the image and likeness of God. The solemn biblical gesture of laying hands on someone is a simple extension of a natural, human gesture. In the Hebrew Scriptures, laying on hands expressed continuity with past generations as it signified the transmission of blessings, gifts, and leadership roles from one generation to the next (cf. GEN 48:13–16, NB 27:18–20, DEUT 34:9). This gesture also suggests affection and welcome, as when Jesus laid his hands on children (MK 10:16). The Acts of the Apostles and the letters of Paul tell us that persons were commissioned for ministry through prayer and the laying on of hands (cf. ACTS 6:6, 1 TIM 4:14).

In our liturgical tradition, this gesture has not only been used to communicate God's presence and power within individuals but also when giving thanks to God over sacred objects, such as the bread and wine at the eucharist.

Over the centuries, the meaning of the imposition of hands in liturgical rites became obscured and the importance of this gesture of human touch was overlooked. A conscious decision was made to reintroduce and reemphasize the extending and the laying on of hands in sacramental rites revised after Vatican II. Father Godfrey Diekmann, OSB was a member of some of the postconciliar Vatican committees that revised the various rites and has suggested that the imposition of hands is the basic sacramental rite.[1] Dominican theologian Yves Congar has said that the reintroduction of the importance of the imposition of hands into our liturgical rites may be one of the most important consequences of liturgical renewal.[2] Physical touch has become once again a foundational element in each of the seven sacraments.

In one of the oldest accounts of baptism, the *Apostolic Tradition* of Hippolytus of Rome (usually dated around the year 215), we read the following:

> When the individual has entered the water, the one who baptizes places his hands on the person's head and says to him: "Do you believe in God the Father Almighty?" The person being baptized replies: "I believe." The one baptizing then lays his hands on the person's head and baptizes him the first time.[3]

The original Latin text of the *Rite of Christian Initiation of Adults* states that when baptizing an adult by immersion, the celebrant should touch the candidate while immersing him or her.[4]

During confirmation, the bishop extends his hands over all to be confirmed and then individually touches the forehead of each person while anointing him or her with chrism.

During the eucharistic prayer while praying for the Spirit to make Christ's body and blood present, priests extend their hands over the bread and wine.

When celebrating the sacrament of penance, the priest is directed to extend his hands over a penitent as he says the absolution. (Old rituals used to label the rite of penance as the "laying on of hands for reconciliation.")[5]

The central gesture of the sacrament of orders is the bishop's imposition of hands on the head of each candidate to be ordained. This gesture takes place before the solemn prayer of consecration.

The laying on of hands prescribed during the celebration of the anointing of the sick finds its origin in the gospel of Mark.

The only sacrament in which the priestly imposition of hands does not play a central role is marriage. Yet, in this rite the bride and the groom join their right hands while exchanging consent and, in many places, the presiding minister extends his hands over the couple while he prays the nuptial blessing.

Even apart from the seven sacraments, the imposition of hands is an important component in other rites of the Church. For example, *Pastoral Care of the Sick* suggests that any pastoral visit of the sick conclude with an imposition of hands.[6] When a solemn blessing is used to conclude a liturgical rite, the bishop or priest is directed to extend his hands over the assembly. The *Book of Blessings* often directs that a priest or deacon extend hands over the person or object being blessed.

Contemporary Western English-speaking culture is a mixture of different and somewhat contradictory traditions. On the one hand, in some parts of the United States there is an informality that may seem brash to people from a European or Asian background. On the other hand, unlike many Europeans, many Americans are uncomfortable with greeting one another with a hug or kiss, or standing close to another person during a conversation. Many Americans put an exaggerated value on their own personal "space," so much so that some hesitate even to give someone the holy gift of Christ's peace.

In some sense, a touch is both a bond of commitment and an openness to vulnerability. No wonder so many people become flustered by another person's touch except in socially acceptable situations. This cultural taboo against closeness often influences the way that gestures are performed in our liturgical rites, particularly the imposition of hands, and also the way they are accepted by people.

Because of its biblical origin and rich, human meaning, the imposition of hands is a gesture of great power. If done with sureness, gentleness, in a relaxed and yet formal manner, it can become a sign of the gentle touch of a loving God. The mystery of human touch embodied in the laying on of hands is truly a foundational mystery in the celebration of Christian worship.

GREETINGS

The formal liturgical greeting signals the beginning of the interactive worship between a minister and the assembly. Father Thomas Krosnicki, SVD writes that "the specific function of the liturgical greeting is to mutually declare, affirm, and confess that the community has taken on a dimension bigger than itself."[7] This greeting, which is often a biblical verse, moves the community

> deeper into the mystery of its own being as a community of faith. . . . The act of gathering to worship is not the result of purely human initiative; it is the result of grace calling individuals to become the ecclesial Body. Having been gathered to worship, it has become Church.[8]

A greeting is also used at other points of the liturgy, such as before the gospel, at the beginning of the eucharistic prayer, as part of the rite of peace, and at the beginning of the concluding blessing. In each case, the greeting not only invokes God's presence but also reminds all present, who together form the liturgical assembly, that they are there because of the God who has called them. The priest declares and all affirm that because of the mystery of God's love they have been gathered together to experience the mystery of who they are as the body of Christ.

The one who greets has the awesome responsibility to remind the community of the divine presence in their midst. Amazingly, this is done with the simple words: "The Lord be with you." Unfortunately, the function of the sacred greeting is overlooked when it is replaced or supplemented by a casual impromptu greeting more appropriate for welcoming people at the doors of the church.

The liturgical greeting is, by nature, formal and repetitive. That does not mean that it is spoken mechanically. A biblical text can be warm and personal, yet pregnant with the presence of God. Adding a "Good morning" suggests that the scriptures and the liturgy are impersonal, or not personal enough, or somehow are not our common heritage.[9]

Father Robert Hovda pointed out the sacredness of the liturgical greeting, especially the initial greeting, and the inappropriateness of substituting or supplementing it with a casual greeting.

No "Good morning, sisters and brothers" is as worshipful an orientation after the opening song of the Sunday assembly as the sign of the cross and the scriptural greeting. The former spotlights the speaker; the latter the purpose of the gathering.[10]

Other liturgical writers, such as Ralph Keifer, Aidan Kavanagh, OSB, and James Challancin would agree with Hovda.[11] A few additional examples might help us also see what can happen when we modify the liturgical dialogue, even slightly.

Some presiders rephrase the greeting into a flat statement: "The Lord *is* with you." This changes the greeting into a piece of information and suggests that the assembly does not know that the Lord is in its midst.[12] Another adaptation is to turn the greeting into a wish: "*May* the Lord be with you." Although this might seem more personal, it waters down the intensity of the original. "Thy will be done" and "Long live the Queen!" are strong statements, but "May your will be done"and "May the Queen live long" seem to be hedging on the conviction of the desire.

Yet another adaptation changes the object: "The Lord be with *each and every one of you.*" Hovda suggests that this rephrasing of the greeting actually leads to greater fragmentation at a time when the "hunger at this moment . . . [is] to feel and be as one."[13] By emphasizing "each and every one," the presider seems to separate the united body of Christ into a group of individuals who just happen to be in the same place at the same time.

The liturgical greeting is repetitious, as is any greeting. It is also liturgical, in biblical language both stating a theological truth and serving the ritual function of unifying the assembly during the action of worship. Its function is to lead all present into the mystery of the body of Christ engaging in the praise of God.

Liturgical Interaction Between the Minister and the Assembly

There are two aspects of liturgical interaction that provide a foundation for celebrating the sacred mysteries. The first is the interaction that must take place between the liturgical ministers and the assembly. The second is the interaction between the individual minister and the individual members of the assembly; this person-to-person interaction occurs at the center of the sacramental experience.

The first type of interaction ideally takes place at every liturgical celebration, but is most often experienced at the Sunday eucharist. It is the interaction between the ministers, such as the priest, the deacon, the reader, or the

cantor, and a group of Christians gathered together for prayer. It is fostered by
liturgical dialogue between presider and assembly, by communal singing, and
by other acclamations of the assembly. The interaction unifies the gathering
and involves all present in the action of the mystical body of Christ, inspired
by the Spirit, giving praise and thanks to God.

Since such interaction is to be encouraged in worship, it is good to be
aware of those things that consciously or unconsciously mitigate against such
interaction. For instance, you might watch certain ministers during a liturgical service and notice the members of the assembly. It is not uncommon for
some people to act as if no one else were present or needed to be present.
Often, the same behavior is exhibited whether the person was trained before
or after the post-Vatican II reforms.

Some priests and readers walk in procession at a pace out of synch with
others in the procession. Some people speak prayers at their own pace, oblivious to the pace of the rest of the assembly. Some presiders speak their greetings
and then fail to pay attention to the assembly as it makes its response. These
are all signs that healthy interaction between the ministers and the assembly is
not taking place.

In some sense, the mass celebrated before the reforms of Vatican II often
fit an interactional model that we might liken to a stage performance. In this
model, it is usually proper that there be no interaction between the actors on
stage and the audience in the auditorium. Most worship spaces were designed
to match this model, with the sanctuary like a stage and the assembly's space
like an auditorium. Given the design of most churches, it is no surprise that,
despite the reforms, many people continue to act as spectators and not as
participants in the liturgy.

A new interactional model has emerged since the reforms of Vatican II.
The presiding priest can be likened to a conductor of a chorus or orchestra,
not in performance but in rehearsal. A conductor must interact with all those
present and coordinate the efforts of each. The members of a chorus or
orchestra must each play her or his own proper role, sensitive to other members' roles, as well as anticipating others' needs. This is not a band of soloists
(although at times certain individuals may perform their role solo) but instead
a united chorus or orchestra, whose joint efforts are coordinated by their
servant, the conductor.

In this interactional model of the liturgy, the foremost role is to be a
member of the assembly. The liturgical ministers—the readers, the presiding
priest, the ushers, the choir—may have their own parts to play, but they are
also members of the assembly. No one stands apart from this primary role.

Silence is a necessary companion to all prayer, individual as well as
communal. But one should not cite the proverb, *silence is golden*, to justify a
lack of vocal participation at mass. Nor should such lack of participation be

confused with a desire to be contemplative. Although quiet, contemplative prayer is appropriate for every Christian, liturgical services are, by nature, vocal and communal experiences. It makes as much sense for someone not to participate at mass as it would be for someone to attend a birthday party and not to speak to other guests or to run in a relay race and not pass the baton. The liturgy does recommend time for reflective, communal silence at appropriate moments (see comments in Chapter 6) and such moments are beneficial for all present. Yet, such silence must be a servant of the entire liturgy, which contains vocal moments of responses, acclamations, and hymns that demand participation of those present.

Our celebration of mystery is enhanced by a presider who interacts well with all present, and by Christians who are willing to bond together to form Christ's body and to interact with the presiding minister in prayer and praise of God. Few things are more upsetting at a liturgical gathering than a presider who changes the cues and gives mixed signals to the assembly. Sometimes unfamiliar signals may be a well-motivated attempt to avoid routine that can dull the appreciation of the mystery taking place. At other times, such signals may occur when, for example, a visiting priest's liturgical style differs from established local customs. The unfortunate result in either case is that people may fail to respond, and so the interaction that underlies a good liturgical celebration is inhibited.

Another type of liturgical interaction takes place between a minister and an individual Christian, sometimes at a distinctive point within a larger celebration. This type of interaction is different from the group interaction, and it has its own special importance.

In commenting on the personal nature of the interaction between a minister and an individual worshiper, Father Hovda made a few observations. (Here he comments on the sharing of communion, but his sentiments are applicable to core rituals of any liturgical action.)

> The personal sharing and transaction between minister and communicant is part of the symbolic action. . . . It is such a loss when that personal dimension is eliminated by . . . plates simply passed through a group. . . . The loss is not a minor one. It is a loss of personal eye contact, personal word, personal gesture, personal touch.
>
> The moment of communion is one that should be seized. . . . The eyes of the minister should meet the eyes of the communicant. The minister says the words of the formula *to* the person (not to the air). . . . In placing the holy bread on the palm of the communicant's hand, the minister will touch that hand. . . . *Eye contact, direct address, touching!* All are part of the experience of sharing.[14]

Hovda reemphasizes this individual, personal aspect within liturgical celebrations elsewhere. In every communal liturgical celebration, he writes,

> the presider relates not only to the congregation as a whole, but also, at certain moments, to individuals as individuals. . . . One may have a certain group style yet . . . fail to give undivided attention to individuals in moments when that is appropriate. Moments of direct, person-to-person confrontation are among the most precious in any liturgy. . . .
>
> Such a simple experience as sharing in holy communion . . . is an experience of the individual not in opposition to the collective but as attaining a new height both as person and as member. . . . Dormant feelings of faith and hope and love can be revived . . . if the presider and the other ministers appreciate the importance of the moment and the right of every member of that assembly to its full value.[15]

Hovda suggests that the important personal interaction can be lost in some adaptations that were, oddly enough, initiated to improve participation, such as passing the eucharistic elements through the assembly. As a result, he urges reflection on all possible effects of any adaptation.

Common to group interaction and individual interaction is the sacramental sign of the communication between God and the chosen people, between Christ and those he touched, healed, forgave. This holy sign must be personal, gentle, human, and grace-filled. It is a mirror of the qualities present in the mystery of God's self-communication with each of us. Anything that turns what can be a moment of personal human communication into mechanical ritualism clouds the wonders of the mystery of God among us.

THRESHOLD RITES

Victor W. Turner has written extensively on liminality and liminal rites from his perspective as an anthropologist of religion.[16] Rites at the *limen*, the threshold, are the observances in one's life that reflect significant moments of growth and of change of status in the community. At these liminal moments, individuals are between roles and the social structures that support those roles. For instance, one particularly intense liminal period is the awkward moment between childhood and adulthood. In many cultures, the moment of transition is marked by certain liminal rites to help the transition take place. In certain cultures, particularly in Africa, an adolescent male undergoes the tribal puberty rites with the adult males and, through these rites, he passes over the threshold, he travels through the "between-ness" of being neither child nor adult, and he achieves the new status of being accepted as an adult within his society.

Our culture still glorifies certain liminal traditions, such as when a groom carries his bride over a threshold on their honeymoon. The Church's liturgical celebrations include a number of liminal rites that, appropriately, are prescribed to be performed at the threshold of the church. In the *Rite of Baptism for Children*, in the *Rite of Marriage*, and at the beginning of the funeral mass, the celebrant is directed to meet worshipers at the door of the church, and there begin a rite that is, literally, a threshold experience for them. It is unfortunate when this prescription is ignored or overlooked, because the physical action of passing through the doorway of the church can be a powerfully symbolic, religious experience.

At a baptism, when the family of an infant enters the church building, they symbolically enter the community of the Church, on behalf of the child.[17] The child will leave the church a different person, now united to the Church through water and the Spirit.

At a wedding, by walking together over the church's threshold, two individuals come together to be united into one flesh. It is at the door of the church that the priest is to greet the couple "in a friendly manner, showing that the Church shares their joy."[18] A man and a woman enter the church as two individuals and leave as one couple united in the Lord.

At a funeral, the deceased is carried over the threshold a final time. It is at the door of the church that the initial greeting takes place, that the body is sprinkled with baptismal water, and that the coffin is clothed with the pall.[19] Here there is a solemn remembrance of the baptismal liminal experience and a prefigurement of the fullness of God's presence. When the body is taken from the church, we sing of our hope to enter paradise, to enter the new heaven and new earth.

There are other times in our liturgy when the rubrics prescribe moving over the threshold of the church or prescribing an action at the church doors. Processions of the entire assembly over the threshold are prescribed for Passion (Palm) Sunday and the Easter Vigil, and even suggested for the First Sunday of Lent.[20] On Good Friday, one option for carrying and showing the cross is for the priest or deacon to go to the church door and carry the unveiled cross through the assembly to the sanctuary. At the entrance of the church, the minister sings the invitation "This is the wood of the cross" the first time. Similarly at the Easter Vigil, after the Easter candle is lit and the procession moves from the outdoor bonfire to the church, the deacon stops at the church door and sings "Christ our light" a second time.

In so many ways, we are often at threshold experiences. The perennial temptation is to skip or simplify these rites at the church door, which often are not convenient or easy to accomplish. But these simple actions are too power-

ful to dismiss. They reflect the Church's self-understanding as a people travel-
ing to God's reign, as a people yearning for transfiguration.

PROCESSIONS

The image of God's people on a journey, on a pilgrimage, gives special
meaning to processions. One particularly significant biblical "procession" was
the movement of the people of Israel through the Red Sea during the Exodus
from Egypt. At the annual Jewish feasts, pilgrims formed processions en route
toward Jerusalem. Biblical scholars speculate that Psalms 120–134, each of
which has the title, "A song of ascents," were sung during the journey of these
pilgrims as they "went up" to Mount Zion. Jesus himself took part in one such
procession on the day now commonly called Palm Sunday.

Early Christian documents often mention processions in reference to
bearing the body of a deceased to its place of burial and during these processions psalms were sung. The procession was a journey into mystery—the
mystery of human death, the mystery of Christ's victory. Even in our contemporary society, the funeral procession is still a common occurrence and provides an opportunity for onlookers to pause, to pray, and to reflect.

Many are familiar with the major processions of the liturgical year that
occur on the Presentation of the Lord, on Passion (Palm) Sunday, after the
Mass of the Lord's Supper, at the beginning of the Easter Vigil, and, in some
places, on the Solemnity of the Body and Blood of Christ. The Easter Vigil
procession even includes a liminal rite at the door of the church. The earlier
liturgical books also mention a solemn procession on the Rogation Days
(immediately before Ascension Thursday) in which God was asked to bless the
year's harvest and to protect people from harm. Common during processions
is the singing of psalms and litanies.

Almost every liturgical celebration includes processions, although these
sometimes involve a limited number of people. At mass, processions occur at
the entrance, before the gospel, at the preparation of the gifts, during communion, and after the dismissal. During the celebration of baptism, there are
processions into the church after the liminal rite, from the place where the
liturgy of the word is celebrated to the baptismal font, and from the baptistry to
the altar. At the solemn celebration of evening prayer on Easter evening, a
procession to the font may take place.[21]

It is not easy to coordinate a procession, as anyone who has participated
in any political march can testify. It is not easy for hundreds of people to move
from one place to another. It is tempting to eliminate difficulties by avoiding
movement and omitting processions from our liturgy. But processions are
icons of the Church's mystical journey in this world and our liturgical rites
should reflect our spiritual pilgrimage. We cannot remain stationary. Journey

we must until, in procession and with all followers of the Lord, we reach the new and eternal Jerusalem.

GESTURE AND POSTURE

Throughout scripture we read about associations between prayer and body gestures or postures. The evening psalm, Psalm 141, speaks about the "lifting of my hands" at the evening sacrifice.[22] Other scriptures speak about other physical gestures associated with prayer, such as the imposition of hands, bowing (2 CHRON 7:3), kneeling (2 CHRON 6:13).

Certain gestures are still important in much of the English-speaking world. For example, it still is considered courteous to stand when meeting a guest or when a national anthem is sung. One sits at an orchestral concert or a movie where one is supposed to be passive. One stands in excitement at a sports competition when cheering a team on toward victory.

It is important to match parts of the liturgy with an appropriate posture that reinforces the liturgical activity taking place, while recognizing that certain postures can be a counter-sign. Although sitting can be a prayerful gesture, it is also a sign of passivity, for instance, when audiences sit during performances. "Body language" conveys certain messages. A man who stands in a "John Wayne" body posture, with arms folded in front of his chest, is giving certain signals whether he wants to or not. A woman who sits at the end of a performance when others are engaged in a standing ovation is also giving a signal, even if the reason is simply that her feet hurt.

We should also remember that the interpretation of certain postures and gestures is culturally determined. As an example, sitting can be a significantly active gesture in certain parts of India, Africa, and Japan. In the adaptation of the *Roman Missal* approved for Zaire, the assembly stands for the "Enthronement of the Gospel" and the accompanying acclamation but sits through the proclamation since sitting is considered the reverent posture for active listening to an important story.[23] In some places in India or Japan, the entire assembly sits throughout the liturgy, including the presiding priest who may sit before a low altar for the entire liturgy.

In contrast, in Zaire the entire assembly engages in a stationary rhythmic dance during the chanting of the *Gloria* and at other acclamations of the liturgy. Many Westerners, however, regard any form of liturgical dance with suspicion and would likely be uncomfortable communally dancing at worship.

The question really is not whether an assembly should be sitting, standing or kneeling at a certain point in the liturgy, or whether they should hold hands or lift them toward the heavens at the Our Father. The question, rather, is what is the meaning of these gestures or postures within the tradition of Judeo-Christian prayer and also within our local culture. If a certain posture seems to indicate passivity (such as sitting) or penitence or adoration (such as kneeling), that posture is probably inappropriate during a point of the liturgy that should resonate with activity and joy (such as the eucharistic prayer).

In our religion we hold dear that the divine became one with the human in the person of Jesus, and so we cannot separate the bodily aspects of worship from non-corporeal aspects. We worship God through the mystery of the fullness of who we are as human beings. We are not angels without bodies. We are women and men of flesh and blood and we meet God through our bodies. As Tertullian said so succinctly, *caro cardo salutis*, "flesh is the hinge of salvation."[24] The long tradition of Catholic and Orthodox worship has employed the mystery of material creation, including the mystery of communication through bodily gestures and postures, to help our spirits reach their Creator. This is another mystery on which our worship of God is built and on which it grows.

SENSORY ELEMENTS

The five senses are windows of human communication. In contrast to other cultures, in recent times we Westerners have tended to mistrust our senses. This mistrust is perhaps a legacy of the puritans, but it runs counter to our liturgical heritage that uses the senses as windows into heaven. Have we forgotten the fragrance of chrism, as rich as that of a fine perfume, whose scent gently, yet noticeably fills a church? Have we forgotten how flickering candles, glistening mosaics, and multi-colored windows can entrance a worshiper? In our drive toward efficiency, have we forgotten how delightful is the flavor and texture of freshly baked bread? No wonder the puritans distrusted their senses! Touch and taste and sight and sounds and fragrance can be intoxicating, enrapturing.

Since our rites are dominated by elements that involve our eyes, ears, tongue and hands, we often overlook the sense of smell and how fragrance may enhance our experience of mystery. There is a long tradition of using fragrances in worship, particularly through incense. What follows will focus on this traditional element in liturgical rites.

The evening psalm, Psalm 141, sings forth: "Let my prayer arise to you like incense." In the history of Christian worship, incense has had multiple meanings. The psalm indicates one symbolism given to the visible smoke rising toward the sky. It is a visible reminder of our prayers arising toward the God of the heavens.

Incense is also used as a mark of respect to honor Christ and to distinguish what is holy. At various times during the mass, for example, the altar, the cross, the gospel, the members of the assembly, and the eucharistic elements are honored with incense.

Incense has been used as a means of sanctification, and was especially common in older rites for blessing some object, for example in the former rite of blessing palms on Palm Sunday. In one sense, it still retains some of this meaning when incense is used around the remains of the deceased during the final commendation at the end of a funeral liturgy.

Incense, in particular, involves the sense of smell. Perhaps this important function is one that bears more reflection. Using various things in worship that stimulate the senses is a way of involving the whole person in the action of prayer. It is too easy to turn worship into a strictly verbal exercise, especially in our rationally-oriented Western culture. We hear words, we speak other words, we ponder these words and come to conclusions, and, for many people, this is the sum of their experience of worship. Unfortunately, what many people hear or say often does not affect their hearts. It remains on the level of their brains and does not touch them as whole persons.

The five senses, potent and enticing as they are, have the power to draw us beyond words and thoughts, to beauty, love, and even action. It is these very human sensations that open us to the foundational mysteries of our worship, because they are windows into the foundational mysteries of our lives as human beings.

Time

The mystery of time is the mystery of repetition and change. It is the mystery of sunrise and sunset, of winter and summer, of new moon and full moon, of work day and sabbath rest.

Christianity inherited from Judaism the practice of worshiping God according to times and seasons. The day, the week, the year all structure our common prayer. Each dawn the Church praises God for creation and resurrection. Each twilight the Church reflects on the redemption Christ won and gives thanks. Each Sunday, that is, each "Lord's Day" (REV 1:10), which is the first day as well as the eighth day, we remember Christ's victory over death and celebrate his eucharist of praise to our God. Each spring the first full moon heralds the annual remembrance of Christ's passover from this life to the next.

Many in our contemporary world experience a separation from the ebbs and flows generated by the rhythms of God's creation. There seems to be little difference between winter and summer except for the weather. Electric lights permit us to work before sunrise and after sunset. Job and production schedules mean that some people rest on Wednesdays while others work on Sundays.

In the midst of all this, our worship tradition says that remembering certain hours and days and dates is foundational to celebrating who we are. For instance, since the sacraments of initiation unite us to Christ in his death and resurrection, Sunday, the day of the resurrection, is the most appropriate day on which a person can experience baptism, confirmation, and first eucharist. Since Christ is associated with the "dawn from on high" (LK 1:78), then the sunrise is an appropriate moment for praising our Redeemer.

Ideally, celebrations reflect the liturgical "time" during which they occur and are scheduled appropriately. For instance, the Lord's resurrection should be the foundation for any liturgical celebration between Easter and Pentecost. Whether the community gathers for Mother's Day, for a graduation, or to honor Mary during May, respecting the liturgical "time" means remembering Christ's victory over death.

In our fast-paced society, scheduling is often based on practicality and convenience. In our Church, worship should be founded on mystery and symbol. Time and all that time includes—anniversaries, dates, days of the week, seasons—comprise another foundational mystery that support our celebrations of Christian worship.

RITUAL

In the tongue-in-cheek book, *A Stress Analysis of a Strapless Evening Gown*, a chapter written by Horace Miner is dedicated to the strange customs of a certain obscure tribe of human beings called the *Nacirema* ("American" spelled backwards). In this chapter, the author describes a ritual that one might mistake for a religious purification rite by members of an ancient cult. We read about domestic shrine rooms, sacred chests, fonts with sacred waters, and community elders who dispense herbs and liquids with special powers. The author notes that "the rituals associated with [the shrine room] are not family ceremonies but are private and secret. The rites are normally only discussed with children, and then only during the period when they are being initiated into these mysteries."[25]

The author is describing the activities that take place when people go to the bathroom and wash up in the morning, and then take their usual assortment of medicine and vitamins. Through this spoof, the author manages to highlight something basic to our lives that we often overlook, namely, that we all engage in ritual behavior even when we do not recognize it.

Certain human rituals are communal—a turkey dinner on Thanksgiving Day, blowing out candles on a birthday cake, standing for the playing of a national anthem. Other rituals may be more private, such as spouses exchanging gifts on their wedding anniversary, or parents saying goodnight to their children.

Repetition and ritual are part of the mystery of human life. By engaging in ritual behavior that follows a recognizable pattern, behavior that is repeated when similar gatherings take place, people can feel more comfortable with what they are doing and become more attuned to the ultimate reason why they are doing what they are doing.

Contemporary Western culture focuses on the immediate and the perceivable. Ritual, on the other hand, takes us beyond the limitations of our senses, something that goes against the direction of much in our culture. Margaret Mead even suggested that American culture lacked the capacity for ritual.[26]

Ritual establishes a rhythm and structures human behavior. It alleviates distracting uncertainty, thereby allowing participants to center their attention on values and meaning, on origins and goals. By the use of symbols and metaphors religious ritual, in particular, stimulates people to confront ultimate questions and to experience the God who calls them into greater intimacy. The formal, stylized activity that is ritual can enable human beings to step into a different dimension of human activity, leaving behind the impromptu and the unexpected. People are thus freed to focus on what is more important, on what transcends the day-to-day.[27]

Breaking out of ritual can be akin to jet lag. The body along with the psyche gets caught off guard and may fail to adjust. For example, people who are not used to Italian family meals in which the salad is served at the end are often uncomfortable with that custom. Being forced to endure unexpected change in expected patterns, like jet lag, usually results in uneasiness, discomfort and even surliness. Think about that the next time someone substitutes a cheerful "hello" for "the Lord be with you."

Thomas Talley suggests that the common failure to appreciate the value of ritual is a significant problem that is being ignored, with dire consequences for worship.

> One of the profound characteristics of any traditional cultic life is its ritual quality. . . . It is not something we devise, but that to which we give ourselves. . . . Certain that with a bit more planning [the liturgy] can be somehow "better" next Sunday than last, we deny the assembly one thing that it desperately needs: immersion in a ritual pattern whose authority, dimly understood but powerfully experienced, transcends our own ingenuity, erudition, and energy. . . . We need the insight and the faith to obey the rubrics. . . .
>
> As beautiful, as meaningful, and as impressive as our liturgical designs are, they need a deeper authority than our own. . . . Such authority resides in the ritual itself, and our best intentioned and best informed attempts to improve upon it had better be good, because the power they dissipate is great.
>
> Given the flexibility built into our liturgies today, this ritual sense can never become a straightjacket. But forgetfulness of it can

reduce our liturgies to mere performances. The reformation is not over, and by God's grace it never will be, but we should not suppose that everything is still up for grabs the way it was or seemed to be in the years just following the council.[28]

Talley's concern about reverencing the authority resident in ritual and having faith to obey the rubrics has also been raised by others. In one sense, the rubrics are merely the rules of behavior for the assembly and its servants. They are an attempt to structure human activity in response to some value or principle. They exist so that ritual celebration and communication between God and the assembled people can occur. Perhaps we do not realize the subtle yet significant role that rubrics play in our lives in supporting the rituals that we all participate in. Perhaps an unconscious anarchy has led us to abandon rubrical directives in the hope that personal creativity may produce better results.

Li Chi is a Chinese ritual book compiled in the first century of the Christian era. It warns: "the ruin of states, the destruction of families, and the perishing of individuals are always preceded by their abandonment of the rules of propriety."[29] Before individuals and communities tinker with their religious "rules of propriety," their rubrics, in the hope of finding something better, perhaps they should reexamine these guidelines and attempt to understand what they are trying to convey.

The mystery of human repetition and ritual is a foundational mystery for many different levels of human activity. Rituals are part of morning bathroom activities and formal dinner etiquette, they are exhibited at baseball games during the seventh inning or at the playing of the Hallelujah chorus during Handel's "Messiah," they are seen when greeting a friend with a handshake or waving goodbye to loved ones.

Through ritual, people communicate to others more than mere words. The ritual in many cases supplies its own profound level of meaning to an activity. As with so many other aspects of worship and human activity, the mystery of ritual stands as a foundation stone on which worship is built.

Chapter 4

THE GREAT MYSTERY
OF BAPTISM

Baptism incorporates us into Christ and forms us into God's people.
This first sacrament pardons all our sins, rescues us from the power
of darkness, and brings us to the dignity of adopted children, a new
creation through water and the Holy Spirit. Hence we are called
and are indeed the children of God. *(Christian Initiation: General
Introduction, n. 2)*

I. From Principles . . .

HISTORICAL OVERVIEW

The sacramental mystery of Christian baptism (a word derived from the
Greek word for *immersing*) finds its origin in the great commission recorded at
the end of Matthew's gospel, given by the risen Christ himself to the eleven
disciples. "Go, therefore, and make disciples of all nations, baptizing them in
the name of the Father, and of the Son, and of the holy Spirit" (MT 28:19).
The baptismal practices of the early Church are suggested throughout the
New Testament. We read, for example, about the massive group baptisms
after Peter's speech on Pentecost (ACTS 2:41) and the baptism of the Ethiopian
court official by Philip (ACTS 8:38).

In the writings of Paul we find the image of baptism as an immersion into
the paschal mystery of the death and resurrection of Christ (ROM 6:3–4) and
the image of baptism as "tomb," that is, being buried with Christ (COL 2:12).
Baptism is also seen as a way for someone to be publicly united with Christ
through union with the Christian community (1 COR 12:13, GAL 3:27).

In the gospel of Luke the Lord identifies "baptism" with a struggle involving suffering when he says, "There is a baptism with which I must be bap-

tized, and how great is my anguish until it is accomplished!" (LK 12:50). In the discourse with Nicodemus, the image of baptism as "womb" is evident when Jesus speaks about being born again in water and the Spirit (JN 3:3–8).

Christian tradition has also used images from the Hebrew Scriptures in reflecting on baptism. The waters of the primeval chaos, the waters of the flood, the waters of the Red Sea (cf. 1 COR 10:2), the waters flowing from the temple—all have been seen as prefiguring the waters of baptism and leading to the images of baptism as new creation and new exodus.

The central rite associated with Christian baptism, the washing with water, imitates traditional forms of ritual washings or purification rites found in Judaism and in pagan ascetical groups. The gospels state that John the Baptist performed a ritual washing of his followers, a ritual in which the Lord himself participated. Especially within the Jewish context, such religious washings were seen as a way for individuals to cleanse themselves from ritual impurities and moral imperfections. The cry of John the Baptist was, "Turn your lives around" (MT 3:2), and Mark's gospel describes John's ritual as a "baptism of repentance which led to the forgiveness of sins" (MK 1:4).

These several themes—new creation, new exodus, union with Christ, incorporation into the body of the Church, forgiveness of sins, ritual imitation of Christ's death and resurrection, the "womb," the "tomb"—are all woven together into the cloth that comprises Christian baptism.

EARLY DOCUMENTS

One of the earliest non-scriptural descriptions of baptism is that found in the *Didache*, the *Teaching of the Twelve Apostles*, which dates to about the beginning of the second century. This document prescribes that a person should be baptized in "living" (moving) water if possible. It also associates with this ritual activity the preparational practice of fasting, stating that the candidate, the minister, as well as the community should fast for a day or two before the rite.[1]

The description of baptism found in the *Apostolic Tradition* of Hippolytus of Rome was already mentioned in Chapter 3. It is in this document that we read of the prominence of the laying on of hands in various sacramental rites. The *Apostolic Tradition* describes the minister placing his hand on the head of the candidate and immersing the person into the water three times. During this triple immersion, the minister questions the candidate about his or her belief in God the Father, God the Son and God the Spirit.[2]

Other early documents describe a cooperation of different ministers in the total initiation process, with priests or deacons performing the ritual washing, and the bishop performing the anointing with chrism and presiding over the eucharist with the newly-baptized. In some places, female deacons took charge of the baptismal washing of women.

As Christianity grew and became legalized throughout the Greco-Roman world, the rites surrounding baptism developed in complexity. The water bath of baptism was one moment in what became a *process* of initiation. The total experience of being initiated fully into the Christian community included (and still includes) the three ritual stages of receiving baptism with water, being anointed with the oil of chrism, and fully participating in the celebration of the eucharist by giving thanks to God and sharing in the eucharistic bread and wine. But the initiation process was more than the celebration of the communal ritual elements. It also included a period of preparation in which the candidates were designated as "catechumens" and later as "elect," and a period of post-initiation instruction called "mystagogy." If our interpretation of the historical texts is correct, the process emphasized participation in a community and a way of life based on the gospels.

This process began with gatherings of adult candidates for prayer and instruction. These catechumenal gatherings sometimes continued over several years. When catechumens were judged ready for initiation, they were enrolled as "chosen ones" or "elect" and underwent a period of intense instruction during Lent in preparation for celebrating baptism during the Easter Vigil. When they joined the Christian assemblies for the liturgy of the word during this final period of preparation, there were special prayers of "scrutiny" and exorcism for the elect and they received an anointing with the oil of the catechumens. They were told the words of the Creed and the Lord's Prayer. They and the community together fasted and prayed for their separation from the world and their union to Christ and to his way of life. At the vigil of Easter, after hearing numerous readings about God's providence throughout history, culminating in Christ's resurrection, the candidates were baptized and anointed with chrism and then participated in celebrating the eucharist for the first time. After this experience, during the Easter season, the neophytes came together several times for the "mystagogy," an explanation of the rites they had experienced and further instructions in the Christian faith.

UNIFIED CELEBRATION OF INITIATION

One striking aspect of various historical texts is the unified vision of the initiation rites that they portray. Initiation is more than participating in the water bath of baptism. Initiation is a process in which the key celebration includes being washed, being anointed and participating in the eucharist. Certain aspects of the initiation rites complement others and the whole is as important as any one part. Such is the vision that is still portrayed in the

unified celebration of baptism, confirmation, and eucharist still practiced by
many of the Eastern Christian Churches.

The Western tradition of identifying baptism and confirmation as separate sacramental mysteries can lead us to misread historical tests and overlook
other traditions. Dom Burkhard Neunheuser, OSB notes:

> It is understandable that the Nestorians, for instance, hardly ever
> bothered their heads explicitly about the distinction between bap-
> tism and confirmation. This state of affairs is by no means a devia-
> tion, but rather an archaism . . . according to which "baptism,"
> considered as the entire process of initiation, imparts regeneration
> and the filling with the Spirit, without any exact distinction being
> made in detail.[3]

It is only in the seventeenth century that some Eastern Churches accepted the
Western enumeration of the seven sacraments and officially separated confirmation from baptism.[4]

When viewing baptism, confirmation and eucharist together, a person is
struck by the complementarity of images and symbols. For example, water-
baptism reminds us of the "Christic" dimension of initiation while confirmation is seen as the "Spirit" dimension of the initiation process. This imitates
the Lord's own experience when, after receiving water baptism at the hands of
John the Baptist, the Spirit descended upon Jesus and the Father's voice was
heard. In a similar way, a Christian is associated with God's presence through
the Spirit after baptism.

The water baptism vividly symbolizes cleansing and rebirth. It represents
a break with the past and the creation of a new future. The anointing symbolizes what the baptism leads to. The individual experiences God's presence in a
new way, through the Holy Spirit. Going into the font and its water is entering
the tomb and the waters of chaos. Rising from the font to receive the anointing is becoming a new creation and experiencing life in the Spirit. The waters
of the font remind us of the waters of the flood. The anointing reminds us of
the dove that signaled land. St. Cyril of Jerusalem states: "The water cleanses
the body, but the Spirit seals the soul."[5]

Through baptism, the baptized have been washed clean of attachments
to things of this world and raised to new life with Christ. Through confirmation, the confirmed acknowledge that the Spirit of the risen Christ is present to
them in their hearts, enabling them to respond to God and to pray as Jesus
himself has taught.

Dead to the old self, reborn in Christ, anointed as a "new Christ," alive
in the Spirit, we recognize who we are around the holy table. In truth, we are
the living Body of Christ, with the Spirit as our life-breath. And so we offer

our endless sacrifice of praise as the Body and Blood of Christ eternally giving thanks to the Father. In baptism, confirmation and eucharist, we are swept up into the life of the Trinity.

TRANSITION

As the Roman world became more and more Christianized, there were fewer adults who were not baptized, and the full initiation process for adults could not be used. The initiation rites associated with baptism became divorced from their original connection to the Easter Vigil and their integral union with confirmation and the eucharist.

These rites were then telescoped, abridged and adapted to be used almost exclusively for the baptism of infants. It was a descendant of these abridged baptismal rites that was included in the 1614 *Roman Ritual*, and used for baptizing infants, though not specifically designed for them. One odd result was that the minister had to address questions to the infant as if the infant could answer.

As a result of historical circumstances, the rites of baptism in common use before Vatican II, for adults or for infants, were liturgically ill-suited for the awe-inspiring role that they were to fill in uniting a human being to Christ in the Church.

STANDARDIZED RITES

In Western Christianity, baptism was usually conferred by a minister pouring water on the head of a candidate while reciting the declarative formula: "N., I baptize you in the name of the Father, and of the Son, and of the Holy Spirit." The rubrics prescribe that water be poured three times. Until the recent post-conciliar reforms, the ritual books also prescribed that the water be poured in the sign of the cross. Additional rites occurred both before and after the sacramental washing. These rites found their origin in the elongated process of Christian initiation of the early centuries. In the 1614 *Roman Ritual*, the pre-baptismal rites included an exorcism by blowing on the catechumen, additional prayers of exorcism, signing the catechumen with the cross, blessing salt and placing some on the tongue of the catechumen, the "Ephphetha" (the rite of touching the nostrils and ears with spittle and repeating the Lord's words: "Be opened"), and the anointing with the oil of the catechumens on the breast and on the upper back. The post-baptismal rites included anointing the newly baptized with chrism, the clothing with a white garment, and the giving of a candle.

In the Byzantine Churches of the East, baptism was usually conferred by immersion and the formula was in the passive voice: "The servant of God, N., is baptized in the name of the Father, and of the Son, and of the Holy Spirit." The rite usually includes a rather lengthy pre-baptismal renunciation of Satan and a profession of union to Christ, followed by an anointing with oil of the catechumens on the various senses. In the Eastern Churches, the unity of the rites of initiation did not disintegrate as happened in the West. As a result, it is still customary for the newly-baptized to receive confirmation after baptism. Finally, the newly-baptized is nourished by the eucharistic food within the same service, even if the individual is an infant.

II . . . to Practice

A Celebration of God's Love

The baptism of an adult catechumen or of an infant is a sacrament, and as such it is fundamentally a celebration of the mystery of God's faithful love, shown most vividly through the death and resurrection of Jesus. Because it is a sacrament, it is a public celebration of the entire people of God. This is the foundation on which any baptismal liturgy must be built.

Unfortunately in recent years there has been a tendency to try to "personalize" the baptismal liturgy to such an extent that it results in exclusive celebrations that lack the necessary universal or ecclesial dimension. In many churches, baptisms are still scheduled and celebrated as private affairs, disconnected from the parish and its liturgical life. Not only do such "private" celebrations keep the baptismal liturgy apart from the communal life of prayer, they also tend to express a theology inconsistent with the Church's teachings.

The contemporary celebration of baptism should be guided by the contemporary understanding of the ultimate meaning of this mystery. Part of its meaning can be found in recent ecclesial documents. For example, the General Introduction of *Christian Initiation* states the following:

> Baptism is the door to life and to the kingdom of God. . . . Baptism is therefore, above all, the sacrament of that faith by which men and women, enlightened by the Spirit's grace, respond to the Gospel of Christ. . . . Further, baptism is the sacrament by which men and women are incorporated into the Church, built up together in the Spirit into a house where God lives, into a holy nation and a royal priesthood. It is a sacramental bond of unity linking all who have been signed by it. . . . Baptism, the cleansing with water by the power of the living word, washes away every stain of sin, original and personal, makes us sharers in God's own life and his adopted

children. . . . Those who are baptized are united to Christ in a death like his. . . . For baptism recalls and effects the paschal mystery itself, because by means of it we pass from the death of sin into life.[6]

The General Instruction of the Liturgy of the Hours suggests similar thoughts when it states:

There is a special and very close bond between Christ and those whom he makes members of his Body, the Church, through the sacrament of rebirth. Thus, from the Head all the riches belonging to the Son flow throughout the whole Body: the communication of the Spirit, the truth, the life, and the participation in the divine sonship that Christ manifested in all his prayer when he dwelt among us.

Christ's priesthood is also shared by the whole Body of the Church, so that the baptized are consecrated as a spiritual temple and holy priesthood through the rebirth of baptism and the anointing by the Holy Spirit and are empowered to offer the worship of the New Covenant, a worship that derives not from our own powers but from Christ's merit and gift. . . .

The unity of the Church at prayer is brought about by the Holy Spirit, who is the same in Christ, in the whole Church, and in every baptized person.[7]

BAPTISM BY IMMERSION

It is often overlooked that the rubrics show a preference for baptism by immersion. The General Introduction of *Christian Initiation* states that immersion "is more suitable as a symbol of participation in the death and resurrection of Christ."[8] Baptism by immersion has been in use for centuries by Eastern Catholics, by Orthodox Christians, as well as by various Protestant denominations. When someone enters the waters of the font and becomes completely covered with water, the truth that baptism is an entry into the tomb with Christ as well as a bath for cleansing is conveyed quite dramatically to all present.

In practice, many places use a hybrid format, sometimes called "semi–immersion." A catechumen, wearing appropriate bathing attire and perhaps a gown, steps into the pool of water and can even kneel in it. The priest then pours water over the head while pronouncing the Trinitarian formula. Afterwards those who were baptized leave momentarily to dry themselves and change clothes. They return to celebrate the remaining rites.

Sacramental authenticity demands the use of a good amount of water, some of which might splash on those near the font. Thus, the priest or deacon is advised to remove watches, and to wear an alb and stole that allow freedom of movement and yet won't be stained if water should splash on them. In larger fonts, it might be possible or even necessary for the minister to enter the font with the one to be baptized although some commentators urge against this practice because it might seem to diminish the attention on the person being baptized.

The temperature of the water should be appropriate for bathing. This normally necessitates having both hot and cold running water near or at the font or having the font warmed. An alternative would be to add sufficient hot water to the water in the font immediately before or even during the blessing of the water.

Those who have witnessed or experienced baptism by immersion testify to the power that this way of celebrating the sacrament emits. Although immersion demands attention to several practical details, the benefits that flow to those present from such a celebration are well worth the effort.

VARIETY OF RITES

At present in the Roman rite, there are different baptismal formats for the different ages and circumstances of those being baptized.

The premier rite is the *Rite of Christian Initiation of Adults*, which is the paradigm for understanding all rites of initiation. The documents of the Council speak primarily about catechumenal formation and the baptism of adults and only secondarily about the baptism of infants.[9] Initiation into the mystery of Christ and the Church is an adherence to Christ with adult faith and a commitment to the community of Christians. The living out of an adult Christian life and the personal faith that is a necessary component of being a Christian are the goals toward which every Christian initiation tends, and they are most clearly seen in the initiation of adults.

Although it was revised first, the *Rite of Baptism for Children* is theologically derived from the adult rite. This format of infant baptism was, in fact, a new creation after the Second Vatican Council, since, as already mentioned, the former rite for baptizing infants was merely a telescoped version of the adult rite. In comparison to the former rite, the present texts never question the infant, even though there are a few points within the rite where the minister does address the infant directly.

These two formats provide the two basic patterns of initiation—one used for those who can respond, as in the case of adults, and the other used for those who cannot respond on their own, as in the case of infants. But in addition to these basic rites, the ritual books also contain adaptations for special circumstances.

The *Rite of Christian Initiation of Adults* presupposes that adults will follow the standard pattern of catechumnate of some length. This period of formation leads to the catechumens being chosen as "elect" at the beginning of Lent and being initiated at the Easter Vigil. Nevertheless, it does include a revised condensed version of the adult rite for use in special circumstances. Also included is a special collection of rites for the initiation of children who are of catechetical age. Since these children have reached the age of reason, the rites used for their initiation assume they are no longer infants, that they are now capable of receiving appropriate catechesis and that they can respond on their own during liturgical rites. Finally, there is a rite for receiving some- one baptized in another Christian denomination into full communion with the Catholic Church.

By including the Rite of Baptism for Several Children first, the *Rite of Baptism for Children* presupposes that the norm will be for several infants to be baptized at a common ceremony. Adapted rites are included for other situations, as when only one child is baptized or when a very large number of children are baptized together. There are also rites for celebrating the sacra- ment when a priest or deacon is not available, or for celebrating the word of God and the explanatory rites in case an infant was baptized in an emergency.

THE RITE OF CHRISTIAN INITIATION OF ADULTS

In 1962, the rite for adults found in the 1614 *Ritual* was revised slightly. In addition, the restoration of the catechumenate was permitted as well as the possibility of celebrating the initiation of adults in stages. The following year, the *Constitution on the Sacred Liturgy* authorized the full restoration of the catechumenate and the revision of the rites associated with the process of Christian initiation for adults. [10] The revised rite, entitled the *Rite of Christian Initiation of Adults* and commonly called the RCIA, was published in 1972. For over a decade, the English speaking world used a provisional translation. Finally, in 1988 the definitive English translation was approved by Rome.

The revision of this rite was based on sound scholarship that brought to light authentic insights into the meaning of the ancient rites. Yet the rite is not merely an archeological reconstruction but a new rite inspired by the best of liturgical and ritual history yet well-adapted to contemporary situations. Ide- ally, the various ritual celebrations of the catechumenate take place in several stages over a period of time, perhaps several years, and they culminate in the celebration of baptism, confirmation and eucharist at the Easter Vigil.

The rite envisions several stages that a person goes through on the journey to becoming a Christian. The initial stage is that of the Pre-Catechumenate or Period of Inquiry. After individuals become certain that they wish to become Christians, they may be accepted into the Order of Catechumens. While in this stage, a catechumen learns more about the faith, and this instruction is complemented by liturgical rites of exorcism, blessing, and anointing with the oil of the catechumens. The journey of formation and prayer should ideally culminate in a decision to be baptized. The normal time for baptism would be the Easter Vigil, and so at the beginning of Lent, some catechumens are chosen for the next stage, that of Election. During Lent, the rites of scrutiny take place with the "elect," and are ordinarily celebrated on Sundays in Lent. The scrutinies are moments of prayer for the elect, occurring after the liturgy of the word at mass, during which the presiding priest imposes hands on the elect and prays for God's strength and blessing for them.

The scrutinies and other liturgical rites for the catechumens and elect, such as the presentations of the Creed and Lord's Prayer, if they occur during mass, can end with the formal dismissal of the catechumens and elect before the liturgy of the eucharist. The catechumens and elect would leave the eucharistic assembly and go with their sponsors and catechists to a separate room to reflect on the readings and perhaps to receive some instruction. This action impresses upon all present the reality that baptism is an entrance into the eucharistic community. In fact, in the dismissal of the catechumens, we are all reminded that the presence of those who cannot communicate during the eucharist is really an anomaly. Those who have attended a eucharist celebrated in the Byzantine rite, for example in Russian Orthodox or Ukrainian Catholic churches, frequently remember the litany for the catechumens followed by the command of the deacon: "All catechumens depart. . . . Let not one of the catechumens remain!"

The central stage in this formation process is when the elect complete their initiation during the Easter Vigil. They are baptized and confirmed, and then they celebrate their first eucharist. The revised ritual books emphasize that, for adults, there should be no separation in the reception of the three sacraments. The priest, at any occasion when an adult is baptized, should also confirm the individual[11] and admit the newly baptized to full participation in the eucharist.

In celebrating the rites of baptism and confirmation, the symbols of the sacraments should be allowed to shine forth as fully as possible.

Baptism by immersion is symbolically richer and should be chosen whenever possible. But it does necessitate providing an appropriate private place for the newly baptized to dry themselves and change clothing before being confirmed. This slight delay and inconvenience is worth the effort to achieve greater ritual authenticity.

Whenever oil is used in church, it is most appropriate that the oil be visible in an appropriate vessel and not merely contained in a small stock stuffed with oil-soaked cotton. In using chrism to confirm the newly baptized, it should be obvious that the newly initiated are being generously anointed with a perfumed oil.

Appropriate white garments, such as albs, large cottas, or capes, should be available in which the newly initiated can be dressed.

The candle given to the newly initiated should be of appropriate size and decoration that it can be used as a reminder of baptism in the years ahead.

Ideally, during the Easter season the neophytes, that is, the newly baptized, participate in a final stage of formation, called the period of mystagogy. This is a period of further formation, explanation, and assistance in living out a Christian life. As a final liturgical moment in the initiation process of this journey of faith, it is recommended that near Pentecost, the neophytes gather together for the celebration of the eucharist, if possible with the bishop, particularly if he was unable to initiate them personally. Such a celebration with the bishop brings home to the neophytes that they have entered a Church wider than their own parish, a "catholic," universal Church overseen by the bishop.

Especially if one examines the Introduction and the explanatory pastoral notes contained in the revised rites for adults, one is struck by relatively little emphasis on sin. Instead, the thrust of adult initiation is on a way of life and on an initiation into a society based on the gospels. The catechumenate is as much a formation period to help catechumens reorder their values as it is a series of liturgical rites that are held to celebrate these values.

No longer should adults be baptized privately with only a sponsor and, perhaps, a spouse present. The ideal presented in the rites of Christian initiation is that the catechumenate is a community activity, in which the community supports the catechumens and also renews itself while helping the catechumens on their journey.

Part of the genius of the order of initiation is that most of the secondary rites are skeletal, with suggestions or models or some texts, but leaving the specifics to those in charge of the local situation. The result is that the *Rite of Christian Initiation of Adults* is more of a resource containing liturgical texts and ideas, rather than a book of detailed rubrics and obligatory ceremonies. As such, it can and should be used as appropriate, and it must be adapted both for the local Catholic community and for those seeking initiation into that community.

BAPTIZING INFANTS

The rite for adults has taken hold in many parts of the world, resulting in a new appreciation of what it should mean for someone to become a Christian. Through the *Rite of Christian Initiation of Adults*, many adults have come to realize that Catholicism is ultimately a way of life based on the teachings of Jesus. In contrast, in some places there are difficulties encountered when attempting to celebrate the baptism of infants according to the renewed vision of Christian initiation.

Quite often, infant baptisms are celebrated by families that have been nominally Catholic for generations, even if the family does not practice the faith. There is a tendency from the family's point of view to want a ceremony that mimics pre-Vatican II rites and the implied theology. So they may shy away from communal celebrations (the preferred rite according to liturgical books), or they may request a service that is not integrated with the celebration of mass. Any attempt for ritual authenticity (such as baptism by immersion, or delaying the clothing of the infant until after the baptismal washing) may also be met with objections, such as, "we never did it that way before!" Some families may even request that the baptism be celebrated at home so that the guests will not be inconvenienced by having to travel to and from the church.

Clergy, also, may not appreciate the theological and liturgical shift that occurred through the promulgation of the revised rite for baptizing infants and subsequent rites and documents. No longer is it acceptable for a priest to stand at the door of the church on Sundays at 2:00 PM baptizing any infant that is brought. No longer is it assumed that the mother will not be present at the baptism. Since the theory of unbaptized infants being banished to limbo is no longer taught by responsible teachers (and in fact never was a part of official Catholic doctrine), no longer should getting the infant baptized as soon as possible take precedence over liturgical authenticity. No longer is it possible to justify anything less than a well-celebrated communal service during which new members are welcomed into the local Christian community.

The ideal envisioned by the present rite is that of an active Christian community rejoicing over the birth of children and formally celebrating the union of these infants to Christ and to his Church through baptism. The Church's presupposition is that the parents are active in practicing their faith and knowledgeable about what membership in the Church means for them and for their new child. If such knowledge is lacking or deficient, then appropriate instruction, perhaps taking several sessions, should be provided for the new parents. These instructional sessions might begin before the child's birth with conferences with active parents in the parish who can both share their faith in Christ and also share practical hints in dealing with a newborn. The godparents are seen as those who will assist the parents and the infants, and should be models of faith themselves. The several movies entitled *The Godfather* have made people aware of the inconsistency of chosing godparents only to honor close relatives or special friends without any thought about their moral and spiritual qualifications for the role.

The ideal rite for celebrating adult initiation is in the context of the eucharist, particularly that of the Easter Vigil. Although infants do not receive communion at baptism in the Western Church, integrating the celebration of infant initiation into a eucharist is a vivid way of proclaiming to the assembly that baptism is the entrance into a eucharistic community.

The celebration of the baptism of infants is as much for the adults present as for the infants. Note that the rite permits the infants to be taken from the church during the liturgy of the word, so that the adults may be properly nourished by God's message. [12]

THE RITE OF BAPTISM FOR CHILDREN

The rite officially begins with the priest greeting the parents and infants, along with the godparents and friends, *at the door of the church*. This is a liminal rite, done at the threshold. It is meant to symbolize the transition taking place through the celebration of the rite. At the door of the church the priest asks the names of the children and asks what the parents wish from God's Church for their sons and daughters. The godparents are asked whether they will help the parents, and the priest, parents and godparents trace the cross on the foreheads of the infants to be baptized. Then all enter the church and go to a place where all can be seated for the celebration of the liturgy of the word. If the baptism of infants is integrated into the celebration of mass, then this preliminary questioning at the church door takes the place of the introductory rite of the mass and the infants and families are part of the entrance procession. The *Gloria* and opening prayer follow before celebrating the liturgy of the word.

One of the oddities of most of the liturgical rites in their pre-Vatican II format was the absence of any formal proclamation of scripture. Now, even in baptisms celebrated apart from mass, it is assumed that there will be the reading of some scripture. In most cases, a form of the liturgy of the word similar to that at mass will most often be used.

After a short homily and the general intercessions (which are combined with a litany of the saints), there is a prayer of exorcism and a pre-baptismal anointing on the breast with the oil of catechumens. In some countries, such as Poland, this anointing has been officially omitted. In the United States, it may be omitted when pastorally desirable. [13] When omitted, it is replaced by an imposition of hands. Since it can be confusing for those present to anoint infants once before baptism and then a second time afterwards (even though different oils are used), it probably is better to omit this anointing when permitted.

If the font is not near, a procession to the place of baptism occurs next.

During the Easter season, the baptismal water blessed at the Vigil should be used, and a "prayer of thanksgiving" is now prayed. During the rest of the year, fresh water should be blessed, and there are several possible texts that can be used. The ones that include a response by those present have the advantage of including the assembly in the action of blessing. After the water is blessed, the renunciation of satan and the profession of faith take place, which are concluded by the assent of the celebrant and the rest of the assembly.

The child is then baptized either by immersion or by pouring water over the head. When immersion is chosen, the rite directs the priest to immerse the child while reciting the Trinitarian formula with the mother or father lifting the child out of the font.[14] When pouring is used, the rite states that the child is held by its mother or father while the priest pours the water and recites the formula. In either case, the former custom of the godmother or godfather holding the child in place of a parent may be retained.

After the child is raised from the water and then towel-dried (perhaps with the assistance of a godparent), the explanatory rites take place. First, the crown of the head is anointed with chrism. The priest should dip his thumb in the container of chrism and generously anoint the infant with this sweet-smelling oil, marking the child as another "Christ," a name that means the "Anointed One."

Next, the child is clothed with a white garment. Ideally, this garment is the traditional baptismal gown, which up to this point the child should not be wearing. It makes little sense to clothe a child with the garment symbolic of its baptism before the baptism takes place. The child can be clothed only in a diaper before the baptism and wrapped in a blanket. If baptism is by immersion, only the diaper need be removed and a fresh one put on afterward. After the baptism and anointing, the child is dressed with the white garment.

It should be emphasized the former practice of clothing an infant in a baptismal garment before baptism is against the letter and spirit of the rubrics. In addition, liturgical authenticity advises against using a tiny piece of cloth (such as a purificator or bib) that is not a garment or using something like a mini-stole, improperly imitating the vesture of the ordained ministers.

The child is then presented with a burning flame lit from the Easter candle. This candle can be later used at birthday celebrations, and might especially be used at later religious celebrations.

Finally, the rite of the "Ephphetha" may be performed, in which the celebrant prays that the newly baptized will hear God's word and proclaim the faith. In the 1614 *Ritual*, this rite was performed before the baptism, but now has been placed at this point in the ceremony. In some countries this rite is always omitted or performed only at the discretion of the celebrant.

If baptism is celebrated during mass, children and their families now return to their places and the mass continues with the preparation of the gifts. Otherwise, there is a procession with the families and infants to the altar where the Lord's Prayer is prayed. In the introduction to the Lord's Prayer, the sample text relates baptism to the later celebration of confirmation and the eucharist.

To conclude the service, whether during or outside of mass, a solemn blessing is invoked over the mothers, the fathers and all others present. It is appropriate that the respective parent hold the infant during the corresponding segment of the blessing.

Since it is a communal rite, singing should be considered as a normal component of any baptismal liturgy. The assembly should sing during the standard moments for singing during liturgies, such as during the entrance procession and as part of the liturgy of the word. The intercessions and litany of the saints by their nature are meant to be sung. The centrality of the solemn prayer of blessing over the water and of the trinitarian baptismal formula suggests that it is appropriate they also be sung by the presiding priest or deacon. The rite itself advises that an acclamation be sung after the sacramental washing of each person.[15]

THE DAY OF CELEBRATION

The scriptural association of baptism with the death and resurrection of Christ implies that the ideal moment for celebrating initiation is during the major liturgical celebration of the paschal mystery, the Easter Vigil. When that is not possible, particularly in the case of infants, then the appropriate day for celebrating baptism is Sunday, the weekly commemoration of the Resurrection.[16] By celebrating baptism on a Sunday, the day itself becomes a symbol of the paschal mystery commemorated in the sacrament.

MULTIPLE CELEBRATIONS

The General Introduction of *Christian Initiation* states the following: "As far as possible, all recently born babies should be baptized at a common celebration on the same day. Except for a good reason, baptism should not be celebrated more than once on the same day in the same church." The first part is again repeated in the beginning rubric of the Rite of Baptism for Several Children.[17] This regulation is based on both ecclesial and liturgical reasons.

The Church is for everyone, the rich and poor, the well-known and overlooked, the healthy and the sick. In the Church's liturgy, individual preferences or conveniences give way to the common good. Our preferences cannot lead to fragmentation of the local community. When individuals are united to the Church, it is the local Church that should be celebrating rather than only the family and friends of the one being baptized. This general liturgical principle was enunciated in the *Constitution on the Sacred Liturgy*:

> Liturgical services are not private functions but are celebrations of
> the Church. . . . Therefore, liturgical services pertain to the whole
> Body of the Church. . . . It must be emphasized that rites which
> are meant to be celebrated in common, with the faithful present and
> actively participating, should as far as possible be celebrated in that
> way rather than by an individual and quasi-privately. . . . This
> applies with special force to the celebration of the Mass . . . and to
> the administration of the sacraments. [18]

Unless there are a large enough number of people present, it is difficult to
celebrate any liturgical rite authentically and properly, for example, with
communal singing. Usually this participation is not facilitated if only one
family is present. In addition, it would be unfair to suggest to the parochial
clergy that they should repeat a well-orchestrated baptismal ritual several
times on a Sunday. To ensure ? vibrant celebration, with the presence of
music ministers and well-trained readers, some parishes schedule a special
baptismal liturgy once a month. Such liturgies help to emphasize the reality
that baptism is primarily a celebration of the Church and is a sacramental
mystery that deserves careful preparation and appropriate resources no less
than any other communal celebration.

The Place of Celebration

The place for baptism raises some ecclesial questions. The Introduction
of the *Rite of Baptism for Children* declares that baptism "should normally be
celebrated in the parish church." [19] The reasoning given is that parish celebrations show that baptism is related to the faith of the Church and admittance
into the people of God. Hence, the Introduction prohibits celebrating baptism
in private houses or in hospitals, that is, in places that have no community
that gathers regularly to celebrate the eucharist. [20] It is also the right of the
parochial clergy (and the diocesan bishop) to preside at the celebration. [21]
Other priests may preside at a baptismal celebration only with the permission
of the local pastor and after verifying that appropriate parochial preparation
has taken place.

Unfortunately, exceptions are made to this and other general rules. For
example, baptisms are celebrated by non-parochial clergy. They may be celebrated in chapels associated with schools or religious communities (or in
private homes with the permission of the bishop[22]). The celebration of the
sacrament may be repeated in a church on a certain day.

Such exceptions can sometimes be disruptive to parish cohesion since
the exceptions often give the impression that certain families get preferential
treatment over others. In these situations, it is extremely important that the

presiding minister and those in charge take special precautions to avoid possible misconceptions about the nature of the sacrament.

It is important to emphasize that baptism unites an individual to the universal Church as well as to a specific community and that the specific community is the parish. Sometimes celebrations performed outside of a parochial context often give the impression that the Church is a global, amorphous reality without any local, concrete realization. This can emphasize a solitary relation with God, often called "Jesus and me." As a result, it can happen that people do not follow through in living out the communal Christianity they were baptized into. It is true that piety over the last few centuries has emphasized the individual and the personal relationship with God, but the biblical tradition emphasizes the communal. This personal kind of piety still is present in the consciousness of many Catholics, ordained and non-ordained, and it is bolstered by the individualism present in American culture. [23] This piety can and does influence the way we pray and the way we celebrate liturgies, including baptism and other sacramental rites. A 1992 statement by Catholic musicians includes the comment: "In the United States there is a tendency to overemphasize the individual, to the detriment of our collective consciousness. Redemption in the Judaeo-Christian tradition is a collective, not a private, reality." [24]

The basic principle of the *Constitution on the Sacred Liturgy* already mentioned is that "liturgical services are not private functions but are celebrations of the Church." [25] Together we form the Body of Christ and it is as members of the body that we praise God the Father and are filled with the Spirit. Communal celebrations emphasize the unity of the Church and the reality that we are all brothers and sisters in Christ, children of one God. It is this union to Christ and to each other that is celebrated in baptism and is symbolized better by communal services celebrated in the local parish church.

ADAPTATIONS

The core action of this rite is the sacramental washing of the candidate by a minister who contextualizes the action by pronouncing an acceptable formula. Occasionally, problems arise if this central action is adapted improperly. The 1614 *Roman Ritual* specifically mentioned: "The same person must both pour the water and pronounce the words." [26] The background for this rule is that the one who says "I baptize you . . . ." should in fact be doing something that corresponds to "baptizing," that is, immersing or washing or bathing the other individual. As mentioned above, ancient documents mention that the minister would hold his hand on a candidate and in this way immerse the candidate three times. When baptism is administered by pouring, the celebrant should physically pour the water, or if there is a steady waterfall, the celebrant should physically guide the candidate's head into the stream of water. One would have reason to doubt the validity of the sacrament if one person (e.g., the parent of a child) were to pour the water while a different person (e.g., the priest) pronounced the words.

There could also be a problem in adapting the traditional baptismal formula in responding to concerns about gender and naming God. The words "Father, Son and Holy Spirit" are literally from scripture and traditionally have been included in the baptismal formula. Many understand these biblical titles as naming the persons of the Trinity in terms of their relationship one to another. However, most theologians suggest that one proposed alternative, "Creator, Redeemer and Sanctifier," is a modalist formulation that identifies persons of the Trinity with specific functions. They argue that it is inappropriate and contrary to tradition to identify any person of the Godhead with one specific external activity.

Because of this and other concerns, most mainline Churches have significant problems with altering the traditional baptismal formula, even as they struggle with changing language in other services. They would question the validity of a baptismal rite in which an altered formula was used, and would require an individual initiated at such a service to be baptized again.[27]

Many places when instructing adults who wish to become Catholics, make little distinction between baptized and non-baptized candidates. The *Rite of Christian Initiation of Adults* is specifically for the non-baptized. The liturgical services specifically meant for the non-baptized should not be used for those validly baptized in other Christian denominations. There are signficant religious differences between, for instance, a Hindu and an Episcopalian. The latter is a Christian who already is a member of a Christian community and wishes to be admitted to communion in the Catholic Church. The former needs to come to know and accept Christ. Ecumenical sensitivity and respect demands that this distinction be preserved.

Probably more crucial in celebrating this sacrament is to put energy into ensuring a quality and well-balanced celebration rather than worrying about specialized adaptations. Such a celebration should normally include song and the participation of well-trained ministers. Too often more energy and effort is expended on secondary aspects of the rite than on what is central, that is, on the proclamation of God's word, the profession of faith, and the baptismal bath.[28] There are various ministries to be performed in the course of the service. If trained parish readers, cantors or musicians are among the relatives and other guests present, it would be appropriate for them to exercise their ministry. Others present should actively participate through joining in the hymns and responses.

In Conclusion

The first sacramental mystery that a person participates in is baptism. Through it a human being is united to Christ in the Church and gains entrance into the eucharistic community. Annually during Lent, as the Church joins in special prayers for the elect, it recalls the fundamental conversion to Christ's way of life that each baptized Christian must undergo. The Church recalls the joys and sorrows, the sufferings and rewards that being a follower of Christ entails.

Paul reminds us: "all of you who were baptized into Christ have clothed yourselves with Christ" (GAL 3:27). Being clothed in Christ should mean that others can recognize God's loving presence in our words and deeds, as they were seen in the words and deeds of Christ. Participation in the mystery of baptism is a sharing in the mystery that is Christ. Care must be taken that those who are baptized (or their parents and godparents) understand the implications of the great mystery in which they have been immersed.

Chapter 5

THE GREAT MYSTERY
OF CONFIRMATION

By signing us with the gift of the Spirit, confirmation makes us more
completely the image of the Lord and fills us with the Holy Spirit,
so that we may bear witness to him before all the world and work to
bring the Body of Christ to its fullness as soon as possible. *(Christian
Initiation: General Introduction, n. 2)*

I. From Principles . . .

HISTORICAL OVERVIEW

The early history of the mystery that Western Catholics call *confirmation*
and many Eastern Christians call *chrismation* is not as clear as the history of
some of the other sacraments.[1] Yet what is evident from early documents is
that the rites considered central to confirmation were part of the process of
initiating adults into Christianity. Thus the history of confirmation is intertwined with the history of the rites of baptism.[2]

There are several key themes that this history presents to us. One primary
theme is that this mystery is intimately connected with the celebration of the
first key moment in the initiation process of Christians, the water bath of baptism. The mystery of confirmation is considered as a second key moment in this
process, a sacramental process that reaches its culmination in the celebration of
the eucharist. We see this format explicitly mentioned in the *Apostolic Tradition* of Hippolytus.[3] The placement of confirmation between baptism and the
eucharist is the traditional order assumed in Church documents throughout the
ages. Thus it is no surprise that this is the order assumed by the *Constitution on
the Sacred Liturgy* and mandated by the revised *Rite of Confirmation* itself and
other rites depending on it, such as the *Rite of Christian Initiation of Adults*.[4]

A second key theme is that confirmation is associated with making explicit the presence of the Holy Spirit in the person confirmed. As such, this mystery attempts to bring to consciousness in the individual and in the community that the life of a Christian is a Spirit-filled life, a life of sensitivity to the presence of divine life at the core of each person's being. Within this theme, the mystery of confirmation recalls the giving of the Spirit by God to Jesus after his baptism, decending as a dove hovering over him (cf. MT 3:16), the giving of the Spirit to the apostles by Jesus himself on Easter (cf. JN 20:22), and the giving of the Spirit by the apostles to new converts through the laying on of hands (cf. ACTS 8:17). John's gospel, in particular, associates the Spirit as a gift from Jesus. Jesus says about believers that "from within them rivers of living water shall flow," and so that we do not miss the point, the evangelist adds, "Here [Jesus] was referring to the Spirit, whom those that came to believe in him were to receive" (JN 7:38–39). In the last discourse, Jesus mentions that both the Father and he will send the Spirit (JN 14:26, 16:7), and finally in death Jesus hands over the Spirit (JN 19:30).

A third key theme is that confirmation has been associated with an anointing with perfumed oil. In Acts 10:38, Peter sees the appearance of the Spirit at Christ's baptism as an "anointing" when he proclaims in a speech: "You know . . . how God anointed Jesus of Nazareth with the holy Spirit and power." This connection between the reception of the Spirit and anointing is also hinted at in the scene of Jesus in the synagogue at Nazareth where he quotes a passage from Isaiah: "The Spirit of the Lord is upon me, because the Lord has anointed me."

It is not inconceivable that Middle Eastern bathing customs, which often included applying perfumed oil after a water bath (cf. EZ 16:4, 9), were taken over by early Christianity and given a specific meaning. Thus the anointing, which has its own scriptural authority for representing the conferral of the Holy Spirit, replaced an earlier tradition of merely laying on hands, as recorded elsewhere in Acts. This anointing is commonly performed by the minister tracing a cross on the forehead of the candidate with the perfumed oil, a sign that is referred to as the "stamp" or "seal." The vocabulary of "seal" is a reference to Ephesians 1:13, where Paul writes: "In [Christ] you also . . . were marked with the seal of the promised Holy Spirit."

The theme of the presence of the Holy Spirit in the believer is one that is particularly highlighted in the contemporary celebration of the sacrament. The revised central formula of the sacrament was borrowed from that used in the Byzantine liturgy for centuries, and proclaims that through the sacrament the one confirmed is "sealed with the Gift of the Holy Spirit." The prayer now used in the Roman liturgy during the extending of hands over those to be confirmed borrows a list of "gifts" of the Spirit from Isaiah 11—wisdom, understanding, counsel, strength, knowledge, piety, fear of the Lord. However, it should be emphasized that the sacrament is a celebration of the presence of the Spirit, the gift of God the Father, and not only the reception of the gifts of the Spirit.

Documents from the early centuries of Christianity that describe the initiation of catechumens usually mention the presidency of the bishop over the initiation rites. Even if the bishop did not personally baptize the catechumens, he did anoint them with oil after their water bath.[5] Because of this, there arose an early tradition associating confirmation with the bishop. The way this association was concretized varied, however. In the East, the bishop was associated with confirmation by demanding that the sacred oil used, called *chrism* or *myron* (myrrh), was always consecrated by the bishop. The ancient order of administration was observed, however, in that confirmation was administered immediately after the baptismal bath even when baptizing an infant and even if a priest was the presiding minister at the celebration. In the West, the custom arose that associated confirmation with the bishop by requiring that the bishop be the usual minister of this sacrament. Only in the danger of death could a priest administer confirmation, and only if he were the pastor of the adult who was near death.

Because the administration of confirmation was reserved to a bishop in the West, in practice its celebration was usually separated from baptism, often by several years. Thus, its relation to baptism became less and less obvious. Consequently, other meanings were given as reasons for celebrating the sacrament. The history and popular interpretation of the sacrament became more confused when Pope Pius x in 1910 (through the decree *Quam singulari*) permitted communion to be administered to children around the age of seven. In many parts of the world, this caused an inversion in the order of celebrating the sacraments, putting the reception of confirmation several years *after* first communion. This was done even in spite of the fact that the 1917 *Code of Canon Law* explicitly permitted confirmation of infants in certain cases. It also stated that confirmation is "delayed until around the age of seven,"[6] suggesting that confirmation closer to baptism was still an ideal. As a result of early communion, delayed confirmation, and other factors, we have the odd situation that in many places, contrary to history, the actual liturgical texts, canon law, and conciliar decrees, the culmination, finale, and high point of Christian initiation is often seen to be the celebration of confirmation rather than full participation in the celebration of the eucharist.

COMPETING SCHOOLS OF THOUGHT AND PRACTICE

A cloudy history has led to two different practices when confirmation is administered among Roman rite Catholics. The two practices are intertwined with two different and somewhat opposing theologies. These two approaches may be termed "confirmation as initiation" and "confirmation as commitment." In many places, we have the schizophrenic situation of using one theology of confirmation when dealing with unbaptized adults and another when dealing with children baptized in infancy.

When observing the prescriptions of the *Rite of Christian Initiation of Adults* and celebrating the complete rites of initiation for adults, we baptize, then confirm, and finally share the eucharist to complete the initiation. In this case, confirmation is part of the initiation process and is seen according to the more ancient order as a step between baptism and the completion of initiation through full participation in the celebration of the eucharist.

On the other hand, when dealing with children baptized as infants, it has been common to admit them to "first communion" around age seven, and then confirm them later at around ages thirteen through eighteen. In this case, confirmation is seen as a celebration of maturity and commitment. As a result it, rather than the eucharist, is seen as the "completion" of initiation, implying that the eucharist is a step on the road to confirmation, rather than the other way around.[7]

Perhaps a few comments about these two theologies and approaches are appropriate before discussing the celebration of the sacramental rite.

In the Eastern Churches, which in general have retained the ancient sequence of baptism-chrismation-eucharist, baptism and chrismation are administered together in one ceremony, even for infants. After a child has been initiated through baptism and chrismation, the child may receive communion, even though only an infant in arms. As mentioned in Chapter 4, confirmation is seen as a ritually explicit way to emphasize the presence of God's Spirit in the newly baptized, and in a real sense is celebrated as an integral part of the entire baptismal ceremony.

In common Eastern practice, confirmation is separated from baptism only if a person was baptized in an emergency by someone other than a priest or bishop. Because of the ritual history among Eastern Christians, there is no thought of considering confirmation as anything other than a sacrament of initiation celebrated between baptism and eucharist and always in the context of the baptismal rites. As noted earlier, some Eastern Churches only relatively recently have considered confirmation as a separate sacrament.

In Western Churches, the practice of reserving the administration of confirmation to a bishop, its separation from the rites of baptism, and its delay until at least the age of reason has led people to invent explanations that help make sense of its role in the life of a Christian. These explanations have led to the common interpretation of confirmation as a sacrament of maturity and commitment, and advocates of this position insist that it should be celebrated as a rite of transition from childhood to adolescence or from adolescence to adulthood. Some of these advocates suggest that the original meaning of this

sacrament has changed and it must be adapted to contemporary circumstances
and needs.[8]

As many others have pointed out, "confirmation as commitment" raises
significant problems for classical sacramental theology. One of the great liturgical scholars associated with the post-Vatican II reform of liturgical rites, Dom
Bernard Botte, OSB, argued that the essence of a sacrament should not be
altered, and that any theory that confirmation is a sacrament of adolescence or
commitment is not based on theology or religious history, but rather on
psychology.[9]

In many places confirmation has been turned into a kind of graduation
ceremony. Those preparing for confirmation are required to enroll in classes
that include, for instance, community service projects. Opponents have suggested that many confirmation preparation programs are more rigorous than
pre-marriage programs or even the catechumenate itself. The celebration of
the sacrament seems to mark the end of a person's demonstrated religious
education and, in some cases, the end of a person's religious practice. As
many a critic has pointed out, confirmation for adolescents often is a celebration of full initiation out of, rather than into, the Church.

On a positive note, people point out that community service projects are
well received by many adolescents, and the discussion of faith and values and
related issues that are on the minds of adolescents can be profitable for students and teachers alike. But sacraments are not prizes handed out at the end
of a series of successful tasks and discussions. No sacrament—including baptism and marriage—should appear to be the reward or goal of any preparation
program. In any case, as many have insisted, all baptized people have a
fundamental right to confirmation and the eucharist.

Most sacraments celebrate the presence of God's power that will bear
fruit in the future. For example, the eucharist is God's nourishment for our
journey. The anointing of the sick is God's healing strength in time of illness.
However, many sacramental preparation programs often seem to require people to have faith and perform works that should be the *fruit* of the sacrament
and not a prerequisite. In the case of confirmation, sometimes the cart (faith
and good works) is being put before the horse (the gift of the Holy Spirit).

Delayed confirmation for those baptized as Catholics in infancy presents
a strange situation. If a child of catechetical age is initiated, according to the
rites of Christian initiation, that child is baptized, confirmed and admitted to
communion all in the course of the same ceremony.[10] Thus a non-Christian
ten-year-old can receive the sacrament of confirmation, while a ten-year-old
who was baptized as a Catholic and raised as one must wait, in many dioceses,
until mid- or late adolescence.

The Church faces a challenge to respond to a perceived need among
religious educators and pastors. The need is to help people baptized as infants

ritually reaffirm the faith and their personal commitment to Christ. Some argue that a solemn, public commitment is not really necessary for everyone. In individual cases, perhaps a special celebration of the sacrament of penance is the right occasion for such a baptismal recommitment. However, others point out that almost every society has some rite of transition (such as the Jewish bar-mitzvah or bat-mitzvah) from adolescence to adulthood or from childhood to adolescence. Some have suggested that confirmation can serve this function. (But, in fact, there is still no agreement, as one would expect, as to what age is best for any proposed rite of transition.)

Perhaps, in the Western Catholic Church more thought should be given to introducing young people to various ministries in the church, both liturgical ministries, such as that of reader or eucharistic minister, or other service ministries, and have a solemn blessing of these types of ministries in lieu of trying to force confirmation to fit this purpose. Perhaps more emphasis should be placed on the eucharist as the third sacrament of initiation that is repeated week after week and how participation in the eucharist is a commitment to living a Christian life. Perhaps more should be made of celebrating the Easter Triduum by those already baptized so that, when catechumens are initiated at the Easter Vigil, all present may regain a sense of renewed faith and commitment.

The age at which Christians are confirmed and the underlying vision of what confirmation is about both affect the way the celebration is planned and executed. The discussions regarding the appropriate age for celebrating confirmation for Roman rite Catholics and the corresponding meaning of the sacrament will not disappear tomorrow. A variation in the ages of candidates will continue to exist for many years to come. Although this discussion and variation will continue, it is also appropriate to reflect on certain considerations to help individuals plan and celebrate the sacrament in a manner ritually appropriate and authentic to the ancient tradition and meaning associated with the rite.

- The traditional images associated with confirmation complement those of baptism. Through baptism a catechumen enters Christ's Church. Through confirmation a person is signed as a new "Christ," a name that means "Anointed One." The gifts of the Spirit who descended upon Jesus after his baptism are shared with those anointed with chrism. The tomb of the font leads to the life of the Spirit. The cleansing of the body leads to the sealing of the soul. As a member of the body of Christ and sharing the Spirit of Jesus, the confirmed Christian can fully participate in the eucharist of praise and thanks to God. Every celebration of confirmation should acknowledge this interrelationship between baptism, confirmation and the eucharist and the complementarity of the various images and symbols.

- The prayer texts of the sacramental rite and of the mass all speak about the presence of the Spirit. There is no mention about "completing" initiation or "adulthood" or about becoming "soldiers of Christ." The celebration of the eucharist is the traditional final step in Christian initiation and should be considered to be its "completion."[11] Delayed confirmation can be considered to "complete" initiation only in the secondary sense of filling in a step in the traditional initiation process that had been skipped.

- Some dioceses and countries have moved to an earlier age for confirmation, combining it with the celebration of first communion. This ritual order makes eminent sense, but still leaves a ritual "gap" for the emotional, spiritual, and physical transition into adolescence and adulthood. However, this shift to a younger age may allow religious educators to develop programs that fit the needs of children, of teens, and of young adults without turning the sacrament into the reward for successful completion of a religious education program.

II . . . to Practice

VARIOUS AGES AND SITUATIONS OF CANDIDATES

At the present time throughout the world, there are six different patterns of confirmation. Each pattern involves different age ranges and different reasons for receiving the sacrament.

- In some Spanish-speaking countries, infants and small children are regularly presented to the bishop for confirmation. The local parish priest celebrates baptism in the parish, and the bishop of the diocese celebrates confirmation in the cathedral. This custom keeps alive the bond between the local parish and the diocesan bishop, it preserves the bishop's traditional role as the minister of confirmation, and it also preserves the traditional order of baptism, confirmation, and eucharist.

- In some dioceses and countries, bishops confirm children around the age of reason and admit the children to first communion in the same celebration. This scenario has challenged many people to rethink their ideas about the nature of confirmation. It also requires religious educators to restructure some catechetical programs. However, in many ways, it may be the best arrangement since it corresponds to the norms provided in canon law and also preserves the traditional order.

- In many dioceses, bishops confirm children at some point during adolescence. Some places do this in early adolescence and other places later. This placement sees confirmation as a sacrament of commitment.

- Confirmation is mandated as part of the rites of initiating unbaptized adults into the faith. In this scenario, whether it occurs during the Easter Vigil or at some other time, the entire rite is integrated into the celebration of initiation, which culminates in the eucharist. In this case, the minister of the sacrament is ordinarily the parish priest.

- There is also the situation when someone who was validly baptized in another Christian community desires to enter into full communion with the Catholic Church. Except for the case of Orthodox Christians, the Catholic Church would not recognize the validity of a previous "confirmation" rite celebrated in those churches. As a result, the rite for receiving a baptized Christian into full communion usually consists of the profession of faith, celebration of confirmation, and the eucharist. In this case also, the minister of the sacrament is ordinarily the parish priest.

- There is also the situation in which unconfirmed adult Catholics present themselves for confirmation. Sometimes the prospect of marriage recommends that they be confirmed.[12] Sometimes individuals have not practiced their faith for years and then wish to return to a regular practice. There is no provision for a "private" celebration of confirmation by the parish priest for adults baptized as Catholics in infancy. Such individuals are usually invited to join the next celebration of confirmation by a bishop that occurs in the parish. Unfortunately, since such celebrations usually involve children or adolescents, the adults present may feel out of place.

Because of the various groups and types of individuals who are confirmed, the celebration of confirmation must be carefully adapted to each group, particularly through the readings and homily. Yet there are some things that can be mentioned that are of common value to any celebration of this mystery.

A Celebration of Initiation

The *Constitution on the Sacred Liturgy* mandated that the reform of the rite of confirmation should show its connection with the whole of Christian initiation and that the candidates should "renew their baptismal promises just before they are confirmed."[13] A formal renewal of baptismal promises was not part of the pre-Vatican II confirmation rite, although it was permitted in later years even though no set text was prescribed. Unfortunately, too often the connection between confirmation and baptism is conveyed only through more words added to the liturgy rather than making use of symbols that people are familiar with. For example, it might be appropriate to use the rite of blessing and sprinkling water as the opening rite to begin the entire celebration with a link to baptism. An alternative would be to sprinkle the assembly after the renewal of baptismal promises as on Easter.

If it is not already the ordinary parish practice at every eucharist, during the confirmation mass the newly confirmed and all present should receive communion under both kinds—the culmination and finale of initiation into the Christian community. Communion under both kinds should be available whether those confirmed are children, adolescents, or adults.[14]

LAYING ON OF HANDS

As mentioned in Chapter 3, one of the core gestures associated with sacramental rites has been the laying on of hands. Among some Western Christian communities, for example, in much of the Anglican communion, confirmation has been administered for centuries only with an imposition of hands by a bishop and without any oil. In recent years, some national churches in the Anglican communion have reintroduced the use of chrism in administering confirmation.

In the former rite for confirmation, the bishop was required to make an awkward gesture to administer the sacrament. The rubrics required him to place his hand on the head of the person receiving confirmation. Then, while keeping the fingers of his hand on the person's head, he was to make the sign of the cross on the person's forehead with his thumb (which had been dipped in chrism). While doing this, he pronounced the sacramental formula. In the revised ritual, this awkward gesture has been changed.

The present ritual requires the celebrant of this sacrament to proclaim a preparatory prayer with both hands extended over all those to be confirmed. If there are concelebrating bishops or priests *who will also anoint individuals*, they also extend their hands but do not join in reciting the words of the prayer. Other bishops and priests present do *not* extend their hands during this prayer. This constitutes the *first* laying on of hands over those to be confirmed. But, as the ritual itself declares, this extension of hands, though important, does not pertain to the validity of the sacrament.[15]

The central ritual action of the sacrament consists of the celebrant trac-ing a cross on the forehead of each candidate with his thumb, which has been dipped in chrism, meanwhile reciting the formula. This action of the minister touching a Christian on the person's forehead is construed as the second extension or laying on of hands and is considered to be an essential part of the sacrament, along with the use of chrism and the prescribed formula.

There is yet another "laying on of hands" during the rite, often overlooked. This one is done by each candidate's *sponsor*. While a candidate is being confirmed, the sponsor or person who presents the candidate to the bishop places his or her right hand on the shoulder of the candidate.

As the Introduction of the *Rite of Confirmation* states, it is desirable that the sponsor for confirmation be the candidate's baptismal godparent.[16] Another sponsor may be chosen, but this is not encouraged. If the baptismal godparent or other sponsor cannot be physically present, a parent may *present* a child to the bishop, but in this case is not to be considered the actual confirmation "sponsor."

ANOINTING WITH CHRISM

The anointing of a person's forehead with chrism while the words are pronounced, "N., be sealed with the Gift of the Holy Spirit," is now seen as the central action of this great mystery. When celebrating this sacrament, a bishop normally wears the miter and holds his pastoral staff with his left hand while anointing the candidates with his right.

The rite then continues with the bishop immediately wishing peace to the one just anointed. According to John's gospel (JN 20:21–22), the bestowal of the Spirit is associated with the greeting of peace by the risen Lord. The Lord appears to his disciples, wishes them peace, and then breathes on them saying, "Receive the Holy Spirit."

THE CARE OF THE CHRISM

Both in this mystery and in the mystery of anointing the sick, the central part of the sacramental rite involves the use of oil. Because oil is so key to this sacrament, some thought should be given to its display and use within the rite.[17] All holy oils are commonly kept in "oil stocks" with cotton to help avoid spillage if a priest needs to take the oil with him. However, there is no real necessity to use cotton in the bowl or oil stock during a celebration in a church. It might even be possible to use containers such as clear glass bowls that make the oil apparent to everyone gathered. The chrism might be kept in a special large glass flask that could be carried in the entrance procession by one of those to be confirmed and then placed in a prominent place in the sanctuary, for example, on a pillar with a lit candle nearby. (An appropriate

location would be near the ambo and the Easter candle.) Then, after the
prayer over those to be confirmed, the chrism can be poured into smaller
containers for use by the bishop and assisting priests who will perform the
anointings.

The use of oil in this sacrament should reflect the generosity of God's
love and mercy through the gift that is the Holy Spirit, a gift evident in
scripture. It should also be used in a natural way of using perfume or oil. In
the pre-Vatican II rite, the rubrics directed that a person who was confirmed
should have a linen band of cloth wrapped across his or her forehead (like a
sweat band), to absorb the oil. Some pictures engraved in *Pontificals* from
earlier centuries depicted the newly confirmed wearing these headbands. If
the use of the linen band was not customary, then the oil was wiped off with
cotton moments after it was applied. The cotton was then burned. All this was
to avoid the sacred chrism being touched by non-consecrated hands. Such
exaggerated reverence for chrism borders on the superstitious and is anachronistic when it is a common practice for people to receive the eucharistic bread
in their hands. The suggestion offered by a pastoral note in the present edition
of the *Pastoral Care of the Sick* is also applicable to the celebration of confirmation. That note reminds the priest:

> If the anointing is to be an effective sacramental symbol, there
> should be a generous use of oil so that it will be seen and felt by the
> sick person as a sign of the Spirit's healing and strengthening pres-
> ence. For the same reason, it is not desirable to wipe off the oil after
> the anointing. [18]

Chrism is a *perfumed* oil. Some people, especially Eastern Christians,
would argue that chrism should be considered to be primarily a perfume that
has been diluted by the addition of oil. [19] Those who prepare the chrism each
year for its consecration before Easter should be mindful of this tradition. It
can be a powerful sensual experience for all present if the entire assembly
smells the gentle, yet noticeable aroma of the chrism after candidates receive
the holy anointing and return to their places.

Unfortunately, in many places, chrism is so lightly scented that one has
to sniff carefully to realize that it really is a different oil than the oil of the sick
or the oil of the catechumens. Cathedral officials should be generous in
adding fragrances to the oil when preparing it for consecration as chrism in
Lent. Any perfume loses its aroma unless it is sealed tightly. If the parish
supply of chrism has lost its aroma, it would be desirable to obtain new chrism
for sacramental use. The sensual experience of smelling a sweet fragrance is a
dimension of this sacramental experience that needs to be enhanced.

In Conclusion

The mystery of confirmation is the mystery of Pentecost, the mystery of the presence of God's life-giving Spirit empowering Christians to witness to Christ. It is the mystery of being able to call upon God as Jesus did, using the intimate, endearing word: "*Abba*, Father" (GAL 4:6, ROM 8:15).

Confirmation is a celebration that God speaks to us in our hearts, and that we recognize the presence of God in creation, in other people, and in a particular way in the depths of our being, for "the Spirit itself makes intercession for us with groanings that cannot be expressed in speech" (ROM 8:26).

Confirmation is a celebration of divine faithfulness and intimacy with every Christian, an intimacy that is a gift of the risen Lord, an intimacy that empowers us to witness to Christ and to pray to the Father through him. It is a celebration of the mystery of Divine Love, the bond of unity between the Father and the Son.

After our rebirth in "water and Spirit" (JN 3:5), an experience that unites us to our Triune God and to the community of fellow believers, we are led to an intimate experience of God's presence through the outpouring of the Spirit. This enables us to be full members of God's household and partakers in the eucharistic banquet whether we are eight, eighteen, or eighty years old. As with every great mystery, confirmation is a shining glimmer of the ultimate mystery of Christ and his Church.

Chapter 6

THE GREAT MYSTERY
OF THE EUCHARIST

At the Last Supper, on the night he was betrayed, our Savior instituted the eucharistic sacrifice of his Body and Blood. This he did in
order to perpetuate the sacrifice of the Cross throughout the ages
until he should come again, and so to entrust to his beloved Spouse,
the Church, a memorial of his death and resurrection: a sacrament
of love, a sign of unity, a bond of charity, a paschal banquet in
which Christ is consumed, the mind is filled with grace, and a
pledge of future glory is given to us. *(Constitution on the Sacred
Liturgy, art. 47)*

I. From Principles . . .

HISTORICAL OVERVIEW

The eucharistic celebration has been at the center of the life of the
Church since apostolic times. The Acts of the Apostles seems to refer to the
eucharistic action when it mentions that Christians met in their homes for the
"breaking of the bread" (ACTS 2:42, 46). Although the ceremonies surrounding
the eucharist have varied and developed through the centuries and even now
are far from uniform in the Catholic world, a certain constancy has remained
in the celebration of the eucharistic mystery. Throughout the years and
throughout the world, the Christian community gathers in prayer, under the
presidency of a bishop or priest, to hear the proclamation of God's word and
thankfully to remember the death and resurrection of the Lord Jesus, sealing
their participation by partaking of the sanctified bread and wine that in faith
have become the body and blood of Christ.

The eucharistic ritual finds its origins in the customs associated with

Jewish meals. Food, particularly bread, is taken and God is praised and "blessed" for sustaining the human race. After a meal, a longer "grace after meals," the *birkat ha-mazon*, is recited. Through this prayer those present give thanks to God and intercede on behalf of all of Israel. Many scholars suggest that the *birkat ha-mazon* is the ancestor of the Christian eucharistic prayer.[1]

Another source for the Christian eucharistic ritual is the Jewish passover meal—the seder. During the meal, unleavened bread is shared among those present and cups of wine are poured and drunk. After the father of a family pronounces the prescribed blessings, those present eat the various ritual foods, while sometimes the father offers interpretive comments.

On the night before he died, Jesus gathered his followers together for a final meal, the Last Supper. The passover was near and the synoptic gospels suggest that this meal was, in fact, the passover meal. The evangelists suggest various thrusts in what Jesus said—service, unity, the fulfillment of the kingdom. In this context, Jesus gave thanks to God over bread and wine, probably using the standard Jewish meal prayers. He then interpreted the bread, associated with the hasty flight from Egypt and with God's nourishment in the desert, as his body broken for the many. He interpreted the wine, associated with sorrow and joy, as his blood shed for the forgiveness of sins.

Early Christian documents describe eucharistic gatherings in words that suggest a general structure similar to what we presently use. The community gathers, scripture is read, the president interprets the readings, and then intercessory prayers are offered. Next, bread and wine are brought to the table, a prayer of thanksgiving is offered to God through Christ in the Spirit, the bread is broken, and the broken bread and sacred cup are shared among those present. After this the community is dismissed and some of the holy food taken to those absent.[2]

Some scholars have suggested that this order has roots in the gospels and in Paul's first letter to the Corinthians. In these scripture passages, both in the institution narratives and in descriptions about the multiplication of loaves and fishes, there is a repeated use of four verbs: *take, bless, break* and *give*. These four activities are related to the ritual of the eucharistic gathering.[3] After the scriptures have been proclaimed and common prayers offered, the elements of bread and wine are brought to the altar, corresponding to Jesus *taking* bread and wine. Then the great eucharistic prayer is proclaimed, corresponding to the *blessing* prayers referred to in scripture. Next, the bread is *broken* as both a practical necessity and a symbolic statement of the unity expressed in sharing common food. In fact, the importance of this action led to the title "the breaking of the bread" as found in scripture. Finally, the eucharistic bread and wine are *given* and shared among those present.

Since the eucharistic celebration finds its origin in the family meal, at its root it is a very friendly and interactive occasion. Such interaction and enthusiasm appears to have been commonplace during the early centuries of the Christian era. Paul's admonition to the people of Corinth (1 COR 11) may have been necessary because people became too enthusiastic at eucharistic gatherings and were forgetting the reason for assembling—recognizing the body of Christ.

After the legalization of Christianity in the early fourth century, the Church in Rome flourished. St. Jerome (who died around 420) mentions that the Amen concluding the eucharistic prayer thundered in the churches of Rome and caused pagan temples to tremble. Elsewhere in the Christian world participation by those present at the eucharist became so exuberant that some presiders, for example St. John Chrysostom in Constantinople, had to call assemblies to order during homilies. The diary of the fourth-century nun Egeria records the enthusiasm of the people at services in Jerusalem during her visit.[4]

As the centuries progressed, the celebration of the eucharist was affected by various influences—the local culture, a growing clericalism, a diminished sense of worthiness among members of the assembly, the use of ancient languages no longer commonly understood. As a result, the eucharist developed into something that bore only a vague resemblance to its origins. Instead of being a highly interactive celebration in which the bishop or priest was the coordinator of diverse ministries and the animator of the community's prayer, the eucharistic celebration became in many places a solo activity of a priest separated from the majority of the people who silently watched from afar.

THE MASS BEFORE VATICAN II

The universal Church has never had one standard form of celebrating the mass. Various Eastern Churches, such as the Byzantine, Coptic, Armenian, Maronite, and others, all celebrated the eucharist in styles different in great and small ways from what was common in the West, each using the local languages. Even in the West, some religious orders, such as the Carmelites and the Dominicans, until recent times retained some of their ancient usages that predated the standardization of the Roman mass after the Council of Trent. In addition, certain cities retained the use of their ancient liturgies, for example, the Ambrosian rite of Milan, Italy, and the Mozarabic rite of Toledo, Spain.

At the time of the Council of Trent, there were differences in missals used throughout Europe. In order to standardize the ceremonies of the mass and as one means of reform in the face of the Protestant Reformation, the Council of Trent authorized the publication of a revised missal to be used by all Western Catholics. First published in 1570, this *Roman Missal* is often called the Tridentine missal after the Council of Trent. It was in use, with a few modifications, for nearly four centuries, until the revision following the Second Vatican Council.

The Order of Mass found in this missal included numerous additions and embellishments to the simpler rites described in early Christian documents. Devotional practices that originated as personal prayers for the ministers became prescribed for all liturgies, such as the recitation of Psalm 43 as part of the "prayers at the foot of the altar," or the recitation of the prologue of St. John's gospel as a "last gospel" said after the dismissal and blessing of the people. Certain ancient practices were not included since they had long before disappeared, for example, the general intercessions after the creed, retained only for the Good Friday liturgy, or communion under both kinds for all in the assembly. Numerous silent prayers were included that reflected the pieties of the Middle Ages rather than a sound insight into the nature of the liturgy, such as the "offertory" prayers or the prayers during the incensations.

If the mass was to be sung, the priest sang certain parts and a choir sang the prescribed chants and responses. But the rubrics also required the priest to recite quietly all the texts that were sung by the choir, as if to suggest that even the choir's role was dispensable and the priest could perform the mass solo.

On the one hand the Tridentine mass was a mess from a liturgical perspective. Yet on the other hand it held the piety of the people and established an ambience of prayer, awe, and mystery through practices many contemporary Catholics have all but forgotten. For example, the language of the mass was Latin and it was often recited so quietly that for most of the mass even the altar servers did not hear much of it. This contributed to a sense of awe and reverence. The altar was built like a shelf against the wall and elevated normally by three or five steps; the priest for the most part did not face the people and was separated from them by a sanctuary rail; the sense of reverence was heightened through the practice of the people kneeling throughout the mass (except for the gospel). Most present did not receive communion and those who did received communion on the tongue. In many cases, what occupied people's attention the most were things that were secondary to the liturgy, such as the use of bells during the eucharistic prayer and before communion, the music, the artistry in the church (such as stained glass windows or statues), or devotional items (such as votive candles).

In the rubrics, the role of the people had been mostly ignored. The communion of others present was mentioned in the rubrics as an afterthought. It was assumed that no one other than the priest would receive communion. Yet some parishes did encourage participation through congregational singing of the Latin mass texts or by means of the "dialogue mass" in which all present recited the Latin responses normally said only by the servers. Other parishes continued the Northern and East European traditions of congregational singing of vernacular hymns. In still other places, the services were always done with dignity and care that encouraged attentiveness and attendance. Such parishes, however, were relatively rare and so in most places it was common during mass for the people present to say the rosary, light vigil candles, or quietly recite private prayers while a choir sang hymns or an organist played instrumental music.

Popular piety that surrounded the Tridentine mass went hand in hand with a clericalism that pre-dated the Council of Trent. Only clerics could perform certain tasks prescribed by the liturgical books and so even those men and women who wished to participate more actively in the liturgy were very limited in what they could do. This situation sometimes led to attitudes by the clergy and pastors that inhibited renewal and participation when permitted. Although things have changed immensely in the last few decades, popular piety and clerical attitudes still are significant influences in how well or how poorly liturgy is celebrated.

VATICAN II AND THE REVISION OF THE MASS

The vision embraced by the Second Vatican Council was intended to regain the spirit of the early Church's liturgical celebrations. Documents from the early centuries of the Christian era indicate active communities imbued with the spirit of the gospels and liturgical celebrations in which all present actively participated in the worship of God. Regaining the spirit of the early Church is not so much an exercise in antiquarianism as it is a hope that a renewal of the liturgy will help recover the vitality of faith in God as well as love and service of our neighbors.

The Council Fathers declared that active and conscious participation by all present should be the norm for the liturgy, even if that meant changing the centuries-old prohibition against using vernacular languages in the Roman rite. As with all liturgical rites, the eucharistic celebration was to be revised to eliminate duplication and irrelevant ritual accretions. Part of the general revision involved composing a new lectionary that included three scripture readings for Sundays and major feast days and that spread out the biblical proclamation over a three year cycle based on the three synoptic gospels. Weekdays were assigned two readings, the first of which during Ordinary Time alternated between even and odd numbered years.

Perhaps more important than the textual revisions and additions were the ritual revisions that were based on a renewed vision of what the eucharistic celebration was meant to be. Instead of a priest doing everything by himself at the altar, the revised vision calls for a coordination of ministries and for the liturgy to take place at different points in the church, that is, at the chair, the ambo, and the altar, locations appropriate to the particular rite.

In the 1950s, some aspects of contemporary eucharistic practice that have become commonplace were only wishful thinking on the part of bishops and scholars. They dreamed of reestablishing authentic traditions that had been abandoned over the course of the centuries—for example, communion in the hand, communion under both kinds, concelebration, the singing of integral texts of the liturgy (rather than merely singing hymns "during mass"). Before 1960, the central prayer of the mass, the eucharistic prayer, was recited inaudibly after the *Sanctus*, and there was only one text found in the missal. Now the eucharistic prayer is proclaimed aloud in its entirety, and there are in many vernacular missals ten texts from which the presiding priest may choose.[5] At least in the official texts and rubrics of the *Roman Missal*, what should be considered important has been officially highlighted and secondary elements have been downplayed.

THE MISSAL OF PAUL VI

The revised Order of Mass, first published in 1969 and included as part of the complete *Roman Missal* of 1970, summarized several of the intermediate changes that became part of the mass between 1963 and 1969 and introduced a number of other significant changes. The most obvious included the language of the liturgy and the posture of the priest, now standing at an altar, which, in imitation of the ancient Roman basilicas, should be designed so that the priest can face most of the assembly.

In comparing the 1970 missal of Paul VI with the earlier 1570 missal of the Council of Trent, one comes face to face with significant differences in fundamental presuppositions, which are embodied in the rubrical instructions and in the rite itself. In the old missal, the people's presence was mostly ignored. Now the emphasis is on the communal celebration by the entire assembly, on full and active participation, on praying the mass rather than merely praying during the mass. In the old missal, all texts—the prayers for the priests, the readings for readers and deacons, the chants for the choir— were all contained in one book. Now, readings are contained in the *Lectionary* and presidential prayers are contained in the *Sacramentary*.

Some accretions to the mass have been dropped, such as the prayers at the foot of the altar and the last gospel. Most other secondary actions have truly become secondary, thereby streamlining the entire service. For example, the prayers and complex gestures formerly prescribed during incensation have been eliminated to let the symbol stand on its own. There is a certain real flexibility built into the rite now. Various options are available in the missal itself, such as the choice of the opening rite or of the eucharistic prayer. Other options, such as the choice of hymns, are left to the discretion of those who prepare and coordinate the liturgy.

Perhaps an important though often overlooked feature of the 1969 Order of Mass has nothing to do with the texts but rather with the new choreography for worship that it prescribes. This choreography suggests a new understanding of the action taking place. There are now three physical focal points for worship. According to the previous missal, the priest always was at the altar, unless he needed to sit to rest. In the present Order of Mass, the priest leads the introductory and concluding rites from the presidential chair, the symbol of his leadership in the community. He may also preach the homily from the chair, and stands there for the creed and general intercessions. For the proclamation of scripture, the various ministers (readers, psalmist, deacon, preacher, and the person who delivers the general intercessions) use the ambo, the structurally prominent place reserved for God's holy word. Only for the actual eucharistic rites do the priest and deacon move to the altar, although it is reverenced during the introductory rites.

The General Instruction of the Roman Missal (GIRM), the introductory document that summarizes the rubrical directions, is significantly different from its predecessor in the Tridentine missal. The General Instruction presents a pastoral and theological explanation while also describing the manner of celebrating mass and the duties of the various ministers involved in the celebration. It permits and describes practices such as communion under both kinds for members of the assembly and concelebration, both practices forbidden before the Second Vatican Council. Along with describing details, such as when incense may be used, it also tries to offer motivation for better liturgical practice, and it also gives explanations to help us to understand *why* certain things should be done in certain ways.

The revised mass is more than a collection of new texts for an old mindset. The revised liturgy springs primarily from a new mindset, a recaptured vision, and a renewed understanding of what it means to celebrate the eucharist. This new outlook is what is presented to us in the revised *Roman Missal*, in addition to a collection of appropriate rubrics and liturgical texts, some old, some new, to help bring that vision to birth.

II . . . to Practice

EUCHARIST AND INITIATION

The process of Christian initiation reaches a high point at the Easter Vigil in the celebration of baptism and confirmation. But the mysteries of baptism and confirmation lead the neophyte to the full participation in the eucharist, the "culminating point in their Christian initiation," according to the *Rite of Christian Initiation of Adults*. The General Introduction of *Chris-*

tian Initiation refers to the eucharist as the last of the three sacraments of initiation and says: "Finally, coming to the table of the eucharist, we eat the flesh and drink the blood of the Son of Man so that we may have eternal life and show forth the unity of God's people."[6]

To become a Christian means to enter a community that celebrates the eucharist. To be a Christian means to participate in the eucharist fully. In a real sense, participation in the eucharist is a celebration of our life-long initiation into the mystery of Christ and of his Church. Each eucharist offers us the opportunity of recommitting ourselves to the way of life accepted at baptism.

EUCHARIST AND CHURCH

If our reading of the Acts of the Apostles and early Christian writings is correct, from the earliest days Christians gathered to celebrate the eucharist. Thus, in one sense, to be the Church is to celebrate the eucharist. Father David Power, in his contemporary reflection on the eucharist, writes:

> The Eucharist makes the church. It makes it as God's covenant people. It makes it in the memory of Christ's suffering, into which the memory of all human suffering is to be gathered. It makes it as a witness, in the midst of the collapse of the human, to God's fidelity and love.[7]

The eucharist is the family banquet of all who constitute the Church. It is the meal at which all are fed, at which no one is a foreigner. Rich and poor, powerful and powerless, old and young, landowners and the homeless are all welcome at the one table at which Christ once again feeds his people.

The intimate interconnection between Church and eucharist is a dynamic, active relationship. The differences between the old missal and the new all point to the reality that the eucharist is not primarily the static elements reserved in the tabernacle but rather the active celebration of giving thanks in memory of the death and resurrection of Jesus. This dynamic celebration of memory-filled thanksgiving by the assembly of Christians is the core of what "eucharist" is about. It is in gathering for the eucharist that individual Christians become the Church.

The inter-relationship between Church and eucharist has been a constant theme in the writings and thought of Eastern Christians. As Father Alexander Schmemann, a noted Orthodox liturgical theologian, has asserted, "For the early church the real question was: what happens to the *Church* in the Eucharist?"[8] Putting it in different terms, he states: "The mystery of the Eucharistic transformation is thus the mystery of the Church herself, of her belonging to the new age and to the new life—in the Holy Spirit."[9]

This ancient truth, rediscovered and reemphasized recently, is why many are concerned by the recent development of "communion services" in place of the full celebration of the eucharist. These services are conducted when priests are not available on Sunday. Since the full celebration of the eucharist is what "makes" the Church, anything less than a full celebration, such as a liturgy of the word followed by the distribution of the reserved elements, in the long run, may do damage to Christians' self-understanding.

God's Word, Broken and Shared

There has been a significant renewal in the life of Roman rite Catholics over the last 30 years or so. Each Sunday we hear the scripture proclaimed in our own language and then hear someone reflect on that word and offer some thoughts on how it might apply to our lives. In new ways, many Catholics have begun to appreciate the riches of the Bible and to reclaim scripture as a living part of their tradition.

Years ago, it was not uncommon for Catholics to be woefully ignorant of the treasures to be found in scripture. This unfortunate situation was understandable given that the biblical readings were publicly proclaimed at mass in a language that few understood. In the revised *Lectionary for Mass* published in 1970, the several year cycles of readings now provide Catholics with an overview of the major writings in both Hebrew and Christian scriptures and also provide enough variety to keep the scriptures ever fresh in the hearing of the people. This lectionary, based on old traditions, has been so successful that, with only minor modifications, it has been accepted by various Protestant denominations, especially in the United States, for use in their own eucharistic services.

Although the renewed use of scripture is probably most evident in the celebration of the eucharist, a liturgy of the word is prescribed in all the revised liturgical rites, even in the private celebration of the sacrament of penance, albeit in a truncated and optional form. The liturgical rites themselves proclaim that the Christian community is based in God's written word and only in the context of hearing that word can we celebrate the various sacramental mysteries. One of the oddities of the sacramental rites found in the 1614 *Roman Ritual* was that the proclamation of scripture was notably absent in the liturgical texts. Happily, this has now been corrected. In addition, whether at mass or during the celebration of one of the other liturgical rites, it is always assumed that a proclamation of the word may be followed by at least a brief homily.

Whereas in the previous missal, the sermon was often disconnected from the scripture proclamation and was mentioned in the rubrics seemingly as an afterthought, the present regulations prescribe that a homily be given on

Sundays and other days of obligation, and recommend that one be given on other days.[10] Although a big step forward has been taken in renewing the liturgy of the word and in emphasizing the homily, the results have not always been ideal.

In some churches the readings are poorly proclaimed, with the reader reading too fast or not using the microphones properly. In addition, silence is frequently non-existent after the readings, and the musical texts—the psalm after the first reading and the Alleluia or acclamation before the gospel—are sometimes recited rather than being sung.

There are also problems with the homily. Some priests had a seminary education that did not emphasize scriptural study or scripture-based homiletic techniques. In some parishes, a significant number of parishioners are professional people with more years of education than the priests on the parish staff. All this leads to the possibility of a less than ideal homily in the eyes of some parishioners. When Bishop John Cummins of Oakland, California, was chair of the Bishops' Committee on the Liturgy, he remarked at a 1984 meeting that homilizing "has often enough evidenced a mediocre practice."[11]

The quantity of publications available in recent years to assist homilists is a good sign that the quality of preaching is of concern and is improving. Priests and deacons are making efforts to develop their talents in breaking the bread of the word of God and in sharing its riches and nourishment with their sisters and brothers. Preachers are learning that the homily is not so much exegesis as it is a proclamation of God's works and an exposition of how God's love challenges and sustains us in our lives. Through the homily the faithful learn how biblical messages can shed light on contemporary problems and opportunities.

When one reads the great homilies of the early doctors of the Church, one sees prayer-filled texts, based on scripture, in which the authors have woven together various biblical references. These classical homilies are often stirring and uplifting works of literature. It is no wonder that priests who celebrate the Byzantine liturgy still repeat the fourth-century Easter homily of St. John Chrysostom, rather than compose a new homily themselves. Such homiletic tradition, based in reflective and prayer-filled contemplation of the scripture readings and of the feast, needs to be regained, renewed, encouraged, and fostered in the contemporary Church.

RENEWED CELEBRATION

As with much in our lives, repetition can often lead to rote rather than ritual, and a "celebration" devoid of enthusiasm and life is a contradiction in terms, whether the "celebration" is a secular event such as a birthday party, or the eucharist of the Christian community.[12]

On the one hand, a parish community should not be content with poor Sunday liturgies, that is, those without singing, with poor readers, with communal or individual recitation of texts that make prayers sound like want ads in the daily newspaper. Parishes and other communities should continually reflect on how the celebration of the liturgy they experience compares to the ideal presented in the General Instruction of the Roman Missal. There can be a continual process of determining where and how improvements can be made.

On the other hand, one need not reinvent the liturgical wheel each week. When a parish is comfortable with a certain level of "good" liturgy in which the community sings forth God's praise, participates actively, knowingly and consciously, is nourished with the broken bread of God's word and of Christ's body and blood, then the community should give thanks that they have responded well to the implications of the renewed liturgy and can focus their energies elsewhere. Nevertheless, no community should neglect reflecting on their liturgical life. Some liturgical vesture may now be as outdated as ultra-thin ties. What seemed to be musically novel in 1990 may be considered hopelessly banal in 2000. There is a steady influx of new ministers all in need of training and formation. The challenge that faces each community is to keep the celebration of the eucharist faithful to the best of our tradition while always improving what needs to be fine-tuned.

The challenge of one parish may be to revamp their worship space. The challenge of another may be to improve its musical repertory. The challenge of yet another parish may be to move toward providing communion under both kinds. The challenge of still another may be to move to home-baked eucharistic bread. There may be a pressing need to improve reader training, or cantor training, or usher training, or of incorporating infant baptisms into the Sunday eucharist, or of improving participation in weddings and funerals or wakes. There may be a need to restore the Church's official morning and evening prayer to a parish's schedule of prayer, so that the eucharist is not seen as the only way that Catholics worship God. While not ignoring local accomplishments, sometimes achieved at significant personal and monetary costs, those who oversee the celebration of the eucharist in parish or other communities should never take their duty for granted.

THE FUTURE

From our present perspective, the 1969 Order of Mass seems something of a compromise. Other changes were proposed by the Consilium entrusted with the revision, but Pope Paul vi modified some of the proposals lest the 1969 Order be seen as too different from the 1570 Order in the Tridentine missal.[13] Today, various groups, from liturgical scholars to national episcopal conferences and even to the curial offices of the Holy See, are pondering additional changes for a new edition of the *Roman Missal*.[14]

The Consilium charged with the revision of the mass initially proposed that either a penitential rite or the *Gloria* be part of the opening rite, but not both. It also suggested making the washing of hands optional and abolishing the *Orate, fratres*, "Pray, my brothers and sisters," before the prayer over the gifts. Pope Paul VI specifically requested that these proposals not be implemented. However, after promulgation of subsequent rites, such as the revised *Rite of Marriage*, or of various vernacular sacramentaries, such as the German *Messbuch*, some of the reservations of the 1960s now seem relatively uncontroversial. As we ponder possible developments in our eucharistic ritual and propose new options in future editions and revisions of the sacramentary, it will be helpful to reflect on what already is being done by other nations.

As one example, let us look at the sign of the cross with which the priest begins his interaction with the assembly. Liturgical scholars have argued that the initial sign of the cross with the congregational Amen is a modern innovation and duplicates the simple scriptural greeting that follows it. They point out that historically the first words of the presider were "The Lord be with you" (or "Peace be with you" if a bishop was presiding). Although the English sacramentary has this initial greeting (after the sign of the cross) in a format identical to the Latin text, other vernacular sacramentaries have adapted the order slightly. In the most recent editions of the French sacramentary the text of the sign of the cross is in italics, which is used for texts said inaudibly by the priest. Even though everyone makes the sign of the cross, the first audible words of the priest are the scriptural greeting. In the German sacramentary the priest says the text of the sign of the cross audibly, but he alone says Amen, so that the first response of the assembly is to the scriptural greeting of the priest.

Other examples are numerous. The penitential rite is an adaptation of the "prayers at the foot of the altar" in the Tridentine missal, which were private prayers said by the priest and the ministers. It was never considered to be a public rite, and the "private" aspect was particularly evident when the mass was sung according to the 1570 missal. Some might argue that the *Kyrie, eleison* is a penitential litany, but *Kyrie, eleison* is the standard response used in the Byzantine liturgy for most intercessory litanies. One might even more appropriately consider it to be a cry of praise and an acclamation of hope. The invocations of the third form of the penitential rite are, in fact, acclamations of praise to Christ and not requests for pardon.

Because the penitential rite is an innovation, and because it may be considered incongruous at certain celebrations, some people have argued that on certain occasions, particularly joyous ones, the presiding priest should be permitted to omit it. In fact, this is one of the underlying reasons why the *Ceremonial of Bishops* states "on Sunday, it is commendable that the rite of blessing and sprinkling water replace the usual penitential rite."[15] In the revised *Rite of Marriage*, the rubrics now prescribe an introduction in lieu of any penitential rite and offer some sample texts. The German *Messbuch* permits the omission of the entire penitential rite when a particularly solemn celebration occurs or of the concluding absolution when the opening prayer itself is penitential.[16]

Although including the *Orate, fratres* in the traditional form, the German sacramentary also gives a simple "Let us pray" as an alternative. Thus, in the German sacramentary, all three major presidential prayers can consistently be introduced with "Let us pray."

The 1988 approbation of the *Roman Missal for the Dioceses of Zaire* gave official approval to even more profound changes in the 1969 Order of Mass. It introduced African customs such as a stationary dance by the assembly during the *Gloria*, the commemoration of ancestors, and the assistance of an animator. The most recent Dutch and Italian sacramentaries have included three newly composed opening prayers that match the scriptural readings for Sundays and some solemnities. The Polish and German sacramentaries have included interpolations in the post-Sanctus sections of eucharistic prayers II and III for Sundays and major feasts and also alternative opening sentences for the prayer for peace after the Lord's Prayer. The revised Spanish *texto único* provides six general scripturally inspired greetings for the opening rites and four additional seasonal greetings for Advent, Christmas, Lent and Easter. Many recently-revised European sacramentaries include a brief biography for each saint's celebration, indicating such things as when and where the saint lived and what he or she was noted for. The Congregation for Divine Worship and the Sacraments[17] and the various national hierarchies or international bodies entrusted with common translations are presently looking at ways of fine-tuning the 1970 *Roman Missal* to aid the process of inculturation.

All these variations of the Latin edition show that the reception and accommodation of the *Roman Missal* are never-ending processes. The days are long gone when one could assume that the mass is the same or should be the same all over the world. Translation is a difficult process and is more complicated than finding a word by word equivalent between two languages. Translation requires knowledge of cultural idioms and the ability to convey the core meaning inherent in the original. Sometimes the manner of expression must change from one language to another in order to preserve the meaning. But translation also needs to go beyond words to the ritual itself and this more profound translation is the present concern of many bishops and pastors throughout the world.

THE FORMAT OF THE SACRAMENTARY
AND THE LECTIONARY

The variety of options and variations from language to language may also affect the way liturgical texts are published. Since the early 1970s, Catholic parishes in the United States and Canada were fortunate in having one book for the altar and another for the ambo. However, that is not the case in all countries. Because the complete sacramentary can be such a formidable volume, some language groups, such as the French and Germans, have issued versions in two volumes, for ease of use at the altar and chair, and to prolong the life. The original Latin lectionary was published in several volumes. In Poland, the lectionary was printed in seven volumes.

A one volume book can be helpful, but it can have its drawbacks. Contemporary lectionaries are often printed in sense-lines to aid the reader in reading and in making appropriate pauses. Because of this less can be printed on each page. As a result, putting all the readings—for Sundays, weekdays, feasts, and special liturgies—into one volume could result in a book too large and too heavy to carry or use easily.

It is probable that future lectionaries will be issued in at least two volumes—one for Sundays and feasts, and another for weekdays. The second edition of the Canadian lectionary was published in four volumes, one for Sundays, two for weekdays, and one for ritual and other masses. It is also planned that the next version of the English sacramentary will be issued as two volumes—one volume for Sundays, the Easter Triduum, and solemnities, and the other volume for weekdays, saints' days, and ritual masses. These books will necessitate review before use to make sure the correct volume is at hand, but they will provide books that, because each segment has texts only for what is needed (Sundays or weekdays), in the end will be easier to use in the liturgy.

FOCAL POINTS FOR CONTINUING IMPROVEMENT

Although much has been done over the last thirty years to transform how Catholics worship, there remain challenges ahead in trying to come to grips with the vision of the Council and the implications of the missal of Paul VI. Perhaps the fundamental challenge is for priests and other liturgical ministers to exhibit a genuine care and reverence as they celebrate the liturgy. Even if there is limited success in making major strides with the resources available in the community, the concern and respect for the ritual and for those assembled can themselves lead to transformation in the community.

A few specific points regarding the ritual are also worth considering: 1.

Choreography, 2. Penitential Rite (Third Form), 3. Silence, 4. Preparation of the Gifts, 5. Communion, and 6. Music.

Choreography: Some Greek doctors of the Church used the Greek word *perichoresis* (dancing) to describe the inner activity of the Trinity. This image is striking. It suggests, among other things, gracefulness, activity, unity of purpose, coordination, complementarity, and beauty—appropriate images for our Triune God. The Trinity is not three static persons, but three persons joined together in coordinated action, as it were, overflowing with beauty and grace. When two people are dancing, each person must observe the choreography of the dance in order to coordinate with the other. Neither can usurp the movements of the other or else the dance is flawed. The Trinity is dancing the ultimate dance of perfection and holiness.

By applying the term choreography to liturgy, I am suggesting a sense of location and movement appropriate to the moment in the liturgy and to the role of the minister as well as a sense of coordination of duties. This movement supports the sung and spoken word in giving rise to a service of beauty and grace. The Tridentine missal prescribed that the celebrant of mass should always stand at the altar (after the prayers at the foot of the altar) and should read all the texts (even those sung by a deacon, subdeacon, or choir). In contrast, the *Constitution on the Sacred Liturgy* wisely advised that each person at a liturgy should do all of and yet only those things required in his or her ministry. Thus, the priest should avoid taking upon himself a task that is proper to another (such as reading the first reading).[18] One might say that a sense of proper choreography was restored to the liturgy.

The revised *Roman Missal* extended this principle to liturgical space as well. A renewed choreography now involves attending to *who* does something and to *where* something is done. The altar is used to hold the eucharistic elements, and so it is appropriate that the priest be at the altar only for the liturgy of the eucharist, when the bread and cup are there. The ambo is sacred because God's word is proclaimed there, and using the ambo for other purposes confuses its purpose. The places for the people, the cantor and the choir, the assisting ministers and the presiding priest should assist them in exercising their proper roles during the liturgy.

The Order of Mass envisions a distinctly different choreography from what was found in the Tridentine missal. Unfortunately, especially in some older worship spaces, the choreography still seems to mimic that found in the 1570 *Roman Missal*. For example, the priest may stay at the altar for the opening and concluding rites and use the presidential chair only as a place to sit during the readings. The chair is used like the sedilia in the former rite, that is, as a place to rest rather than as a locus for presiding over prayer and for preaching.

There needs to be an ongoing effort to arrange the worship space appropriately according to the vision of the revised liturgical rites, and to make sure the choreography of the ministers (priest, readers, cantors) respects the purpose of the various locations. Some places may be struggling with architectural questions, for example, finding a location for the Blessed Sacrament or the baptismal font that is prayerful yet appropriately distinct. Other places may be dealing with questions of decoration and environment. Still others may need to examine the placement and use of ambo, altar, and chair.[19]

The revised missal presents an ideal, that the mass is more than the mere recitation of prescribed texts by the priest. It is the sacred gathering of God's people at which God's presence is manifested in word and sacrament, in which ministries are coordinated, and during which all things, from vestments to vessels to gestures to the placement of the sacred furnishings to the choreography of the people performing the rites, together contribute to the Church's sacrifice of praise.

Penitential Rite (Third Form): The pattern for this option given in the *Roman Missal,* and the additional patterns provided in various vernacular sacramentaries are carefully worded so that this litany is always directed to Christ, focuses on Christ's mercy toward the human race (rather than on human sinfulness), and is in the form of a litany of praise rather than a list of sins of those present.

By seeing this expansion of the *Kyrie* as a litany of praise, it might be possible that a sung version could substitute for the *Gloria.* During penitential times, it may be better to use either the *Confiteor,* "I confess," or the more or less overlooked second penitential rite.[20]

Silence: Many of us tend to be uncomfortable with silence. The walkmans and other electronic devices plugged into our ears proclaim that we crave audio stimulation and may even have become addicted to it. In contrast, the Christian tradition holds fast to the practice of quiet, meditative prayer, and the religious need for individual and communal silence. In the face of our society's omnipresent noise, communal silence in liturgy feels strange and will continue to feel strange until it becomes our own habit, a comfortable way in which we worship.

The General Instruction of the Roman Missal suggests that silence is appropriate at several points of the liturgy.[21] In many parishes, however, the only regular time of extended silence observed is after communion. There often is a token silence at the beginning of the penitential rite and after the words "Let us pray", before the presidential prayers, but unfortunately such brief moments are too short to have their intended effect. Instead of being used as times of genuine prayer, they tend to be used to focus people's attention, like a teacher waiting for the rumble to die down before beginning a lecture.

In particular, the General Instruction of the Roman Missal as well as the

Introduction to the *Lectionary* suggests that silence needs to be a regular part of the liturgy of the word.

> The dialogue between God and his people taking place through the Holy Spirit demands short intervals of silence, suited to the assembly, as an opportunity to take the word of God to heart and to prepare a response to it in prayer.[22]

The introduction to the *Lectionary* suggests that silence should be observed after each of the readings. It also suggests that there be a moment of silence before the readings begin as well as after the homily.

In many assemblies, introducing moments of quietness may at first make some people uncomfortable, but the benefit to the community is worth the effort. Remember the beautiful story of the prophet Elijah (1 KINGS 19:12) who found the presence of God not in fire or wind or earthquake, but in a quiet whisper. Sometimes it is only in often scary silence that we can hear the voice of God.

Preparation of the Gifts: The piety of earlier centuries and the theological misinformation based on that piety was found in some books of explanation about the mass. An older understanding of this point of the mass saw it as the moment of sacrificial offering, in which the elements for the sacrifice are brought to the altar and there offered up. But "offertory" means, quite simply, "a carrying up." And that is all that should take place at this point in the eucharistic liturgy. The gifts are carried up and placed on the altar. The Tridentine missal reinterpreted this simple action as part of the sacrificial offering. The bread and wine were held at eye level or higher and the priest's prayers spoke of the offering of sacrifice.

Of course, the eucharistic prayer is the real offering of sacrifice, made verbally explicit during the *anamnesis* after the institution narrative ("Remembering your Son's death and resurrection, we offer you . . ."). The present Order of Mass makes this clear once again. Gone are most of the medieval accretions of the Tridentine liturgy that duplicated the sentiments of the eucharistic prayer.

The new pattern of the liturgy of the eucharist is related to the four verbs in the institution narratives, *take, bless, break,* and *give.* The "preparation of the altar and the gifts" corresponds to the verb "take." The bread and wine are taken up and placed on the altar, an action that must necessarily come before blessing, breaking and giving. Of these four verbs, only one indicates words— the verb "bless" to which the eucharistic prayer corresponds. The other three verbs are actions, and the corresponding sections of the liturgy of the eucharist—preparation, breaking of the bread, communion—should be seen primarily as actions as well.

In the present Order of Mass, the rubrics appropriately state that the bread and wine are only to be held "slightly" above the altar (much lower than at eye level). A careful reading of the rubrics suggests that the central focus is on placing the plate with the bread and the cup with the wine on the altar, and not on the prayers (which ordinarily are to be said inaudibly). Once the plate and the cup have made physical contact with the altar, the preparation is over.

But, unfortunately, the preparation rite in the revised Order of Mass is not totally satisfactory. There are still vestiges of the language of offering as well as new texts that duplicate the purpose of the eucharistic prayer.

Some consider that the *berakah* prayers ("Blessed are you, Lord, God of all creation. . . ."), though reminiscent of Hebrew meal prayers, are unfortunate additions that inappropriately anticipate the praise and thanksgiving proper to the eucharistic prayer. They should not be the focal point of this simple rite since they are not significant in themselves. They should always be said inaudibly at masses with music during the preparation rite and it may often be better to say the prayers inaudibly even when there is no music. The only traditional prayer of this point of the mass is the prayer over the gifts. It is now said aloud, but in the Tridentine mass it was called the "secret" because it was said inaudibly except for the last phrase of the conclusion (". . . *per omnia sæcula sæculorum*").

Priests who continue to hold the plate and cup high, or who insist on saying all the prayers aloud (even when there is singing by the assembly), or who place the bread and wine on the altar only to pick them up again to say the prayers (thereby suggesting the prayers are more important than the bread and wine making contact with the altar), are not following the Roman rite. Rather than using inappropriate gestures or audible prayers during this secondary rite, attention can be gently focused on the bread and wine through careful handling of the plate and cup and, perhaps, by reverently incensing them during this preparation rite.

Communion: The culmination of taking, blessing and breaking is the giving of the consecrated bread and wine through the action of communion. Much has changed for the better since the Council with regard to the communion rite—receiving the eucharistic bread in one's hands and drinking from the cup are two of the more significant changes. Yet there are aspects of the communion rite as practiced in some places that can still be improved.

The General Instruction of the Roman Missal states that the "nature of the sign demands that the material for the eucharistic celebration truly have the appearance of food. Accordingly, . . . the eucharistic bread should be made in such a way that . . . the priest is able actually to break the host into parts and distribute them to at least some of the faithful."[23] It is unfortunate that the wafer bread commonly used at mass is so unlike the bread we usually eat. Much of the richness of the symbolism of food and nourishment is absent when a person has difficulty recognizing the host as bread. Much of the richness of the Pauline image of many people sharing one loaf (1 COR 10:17) is lost when the bread used barely feeds a couple of persons. There are ways of baking altar bread with only flour and water that produce loaves that look like bread rather than like pieces of plastic and there are parishes that regularly involve individuals in the service of baking bread for the community's eucharistic banquet.

Arguments against this practice often make little sense when examining the practice of Orthodox and Byzantine Catholic Churches in which "home-baked" bread has been the norm for centuries. Unfortunately, many of us have been so accustomed to sacramental minimalism that trying to regain a sense of the ideal, or even of the expected, can be a painstaking process.

The purpose of the tabernacle is primarily for communion of the sick and for private devotion apart from mass.[24] Unfortunately, there are still many communities in which a significant amount of eucharistic bread is shared at mass that is taken from the tabernacle. This violates the intent of exhortations that date back almost a century encouraging the practice in which the assembly shares in communion from the elements consecrated at that celebration. Those involved in preparing the liturgy should set aside at each mass enough bread and wine to suffice for the communion of those present. Many parishes are doing this well—excuses for not doing this simply do not hold up any longer.

Particularly in the writings of Luke, that is, his gospel and the Acts of the Apostles, there is great significance placed on eating *and drinking*. Most Eastern Churches have always distributed communion under both kinds to all. In the United States and certain other English speaking countries, communion from the cup may ordinarily be given to everyone in the assembly at all masses, whether on weekdays or on Sundays.[25] Because communion from the cup was not permitted in the Roman rite for so many centuries, some communities still find it difficult to include it as standard practice at all liturgies.

The General Instruction of the Roman Missal encourages the practice and states that "holy communion has a more complete form as a sign when it is received under both kinds" and that "it is most desirable . . . that, in the instances when it is permitted, [the faithful] share in the chalice."[26] The American Directory, *This Holy and Living Sacrifice*, suggests that "Communion under both kinds is to be desired in all celebrations of the Mass."[27] Those communities that still restrict communion from the cup are not following the spirit of Roman and American hierarchical documents.

Although many parishes have made great strides in fostering a communal atmosphere during worship, it is still common that people imitate a pre-Vatican II practice immediately after partaking in the eucharistic bread and wine, shifting into a very personal and individualistic piety. Sharing the eucharistic bread and wine should be a high point of the mass, a moment that expresses the unity of the assembly as the Body of Christ. Yet it is commonplace to find some people kneeling in private prayer while others are standing, or to find decreased participation in singing the processional hymn or a soloist singing during this time that should resonate with a common expression of unity. In its comments on the communion song, the General Instruction of the Roman Missal emphasizes the expression of unity that should be evident while the sacramental elements are being shared. It states that the function of this song "is to express outwardly the communicants' union in spirit by means of the unity of their voices . . . and to make the procession to receive Christ's body more fully an act of community."[28]

Ideally, during the communion rite, all should be standing and participating in the singing as long as there are people in the assembly still in procession. One should not overlook the reality of sharing in the Lord's body and blood, but the appropriate time for personal prayer, reflection, and praise is after all have been nourished and the priest has returned to his chair. This communal period of prayer and silence may be concluded by a communal hymn, which in some places serves well as the final hymn by the assembly.[29]

Music: In most places, we have regained a sense of communal singing since the reemphasis on congregational singing. However, there still remains much that needs to happen.

One issue focuses on the style of music used in many parishes. Although the guitar remains a popular musical instrument at mass, it is less and less an instrument used at formal affairs, sacred or secular. For instance, one does not hear the national anthem at the beginning of a baseball game accompanied by a guitar. Yet, unfortunately, in some parishes keyboard instruments seem to have fallen into disrepute, while the guitar remains the instrument of choice. Some musical styles and choices of instruments for accompaniment have now become dated after their introduction immediately after the Council. They may even be "old fashioned" sounding and are somewhat incongruous given the style of music used at other formal, public gatherings in our culture.

A related question concerns the quality and dignity of music used and its appropriateness to the occasion and to the assembly. Music suitable for use at retreat for high school students is not necessarily fitting for an assembly of senior citizens. Hymns that were popular in the first decade after the Second Vatican Council need to be reexamined for the artistic quality and suitability in the 1990s. Unfortunately, in some parishes (and the numbers are diminishing) musical repertory remains fixated in styles popular immediately after the Council or on songs written by certain popular composers.

We need to take a more careful look at the centuries-old Catholic musical heritage and tradition rather than merely dismissing hymns composed before the Council. We need to look at the wealth of styles that comprise the experience of religious music and perhaps, at least occasionally, choose selections that expose people to this treasure. The chorale style hymn, in which everyone sings all the verses, is not the only option available. The ease with which people can join in singing canons and antiphons, such as those composed at the monastery of Taizé, France, may suggest reevaluating the style of hymns chosen. The use of chant and psalms that are part of our classical tradition has unfortunately disappeared from widespread use and should be recaptured. This disappearance has caused some musicians to focus on newly-composed hymns that are sometimes ill-suited for certain parts of the liturgy rather than on music that is integrated with the ritual and on using biblical and liturgical texts. [30]

Another question is the proper understanding of song at worship and the roles of the assembly, the cantor, and the choir. Too many quality choir directors are professional musicians who continue to make choices that seem to value musical performance over its "servant" role in the liturgy. Too many choirs continue to see themselves as the sole singers rather than as servants of the song of the entire assembly. Despite dramatic improvements in many parishes, in some places, for example, the singers use microphones to overwhelm the assembly. Similarly, some cantors act as if they imagine themselves performing at a night club or at a concert rather than assisting fellow-Christians in singing forth God's praise.

American Catholics do not have a long history of vernacular liturgical singing, especially compared to our religious cousins from Germany or Poland, for example, or compared to many English-speaking non-Catholic Christians. We are learning from them the potentials and the pitfalls involved in congregational singing. And we are also learning, slowly, what it means to sing our liturgy and not just to add some song to a spoken liturgy. All our efforts to improve the singing forth of God's praise joyfully by all present is an ideal that is truly worth the energy.

In Conclusion

The mystery of the eucharist is the central liturgical mystery of our faith since it is the mystery of God's love and of Christ's abiding presence. It is the mystery of a God who nourishes us and promises to be with us always. It is the paschal mystery of Christ's death and resurrection, for "each time you eat this bread and drink this cup, you proclaim the death of the Lord until he comes" (1 COR 11:26).

The mystery of the eucharist is the mystery of a chosen people thanking their God for benefits received, both personal and communal. It is the mystery of a body broken and blood that was shed. It is the mystery of what we are and what we receive. It is the mystery of Christ in us.

Chapter 7

THE GREAT MYSTERY
OF PENANCE

Jesus, however, not only exhorted people to repentance so that they would abandon their sins and turn wholeheartedly to the Lord, but welcoming sinners, he actually reconciled them with the Father. . . . In the sacrament of penance the faithful "obtain from God's mercy pardon for having offended him and at the same time reconciliation with the Church, which they have wounded by their sins and which by charity, example, and prayer seeks their conversion." *(Rite of Penance: Introduction, nn. 1, 4, quoting: Vatican Council II, Constitution on the Church, n. 11)*

I. From Principles . . .

HISTORICAL OVERVIEW

The gospels depict the Lord forgiving individuals with the authority of God (MK 2:7), sometimes joining the forgiveness of sins with physical healing (MT 9:1 ff). When one examines the gospels, forgiveness of sins, a spiritual "healing," is a regular part of Christ's public ministry.

According to John's gospel, after the resurrection Christ bestowed the Spirit on the disciples gathered in the upper room and commanded them to forgive the sins of others (JN 20:22–23). Forgiving others is given in the Lord's Prayer as a condition for requesting forgiveness from God—"forgive us our sins as we forgive those who sin against us" (MT 6:12).

As is widely known, in the first centuries of Christianity, the formal absolution of sin was pronounced only by the local bishop and only for those who committed grave sins, such as idolatry, murder, apostasy, or adultery. The mystery of penance, then often called the *reconciliation of penitents,* was a public service often celebrated on Holy Thursday in preparation for the Easter Triduum. Some referred to it as a *second baptism* and considered that it, like baptism, could only be celebrated once. The solemn pronouncement of the absolution, often accompanied by the imposition of hands on the head of the penitent, came after a penitent had completed the assigned penance. Penance sometimes took several years to accomplish and was considered a sign of the penitent's change of heart and his or her determination to avoid future sin. Lesser sins were considered forgiven by personal penance and devout sharing in the eucharist, because the Lord's blood was shed "so that sins may be forgiven" (MT 26:28).

As Christianity took root in the British Isles, monastic piety gave rise to a new form of the mystery of forgiveness—the ancestor of "private confession." This new form was repeatable and was a private ritual in that no one was present other than the priest and penitent. With this form there developed the practice of receiving the absolution from the priest *before* the performance of the assigned penance.[1]

Recent Past

In the decades immediately before the Second Vatican Council, the celebration of penance was a common part of Catholic life. Many individuals responded to the exhortation by the clergy to receive the sacrament at least monthly. It was assumed that people conscious of committing serious sins would refrain from receiving communion until they had confessed their sins and received absolution. In the extreme, some people would always receive the sacrament of penance before receiving communion.

This sacramental mystery was regularly celebrated in "confessionals," which, as many people know, were small rooms or, more accurately, large closets, in which a priest sat in a middle compartment and two penitents knelt in separate compartments on either side. Communication was through a grating between the compartments that allowed sound to pass between priest and penitent. Anonymity was preserved by screens placed over the gratings that prevented the priest from identifying the penitent.[2] Secrecy was preserved by solid slides over the gratings which, when closed, prevented one penitent from hearing what the other penitent and priest were saying. In most cases, the lighting in both penitents' compartments was poor, giving a gloomy impression that added to the fear with which many people approached this sacrament.

The former rite of penance consisted of a penitent reciting a standard formula, usually some version of "Bless me, Father, for I have sinned. It has been *two weeks* since my last confession. These are my sins. . . . I am sorry for these sins and all the sins of my past life *especially for the sin of . . . and I ask penance and absolution from you, Father.*"

The priest usually gave little or no advice but only prescribed a penance that ordinarily consisted of the penitent's private recitation of a few prayers, for instance, three Our Fathers and three Hail Marys. Then the priest pronounced the absolution in Latin while the penitent simultaneously recited an Act of Contrition quietly. The penitent left the confessional and then recited the prayers that constituted the assigned penance.

In standard practice, the interaction in this former rite was somewhat limited. Penitents spoke the formula and disclosed their sins, and priests imposed penances and spoke the absolution. The common image of the role of the priest was that of a judge who had to determine the penitent's contrition and assign a "punishment to fit the crime." It was with this image in mind that priests and penitents alike were advised of the necessity of confessing individual sins, particularly mortal sins, in both kind and number. If there was any confusion in the mind of the priest as to the seriousness of the sin, he was to question the penitent not so much as to offer counseling, as to determine the nature of the offense in order to assign a fitting penance.

THE REVISED RITE OF 1973

In 1973, the Holy See issued the *Rite of Penance*, containing revised rites for celebrating reconciliation. As a collection of several rites, this document is noteworthy in several ways.

- First, the communal dimension was restored to the celebration of penance, so that even individual reconciliation is seen within the context of the ministry of reconciliation that is part of the entire Church. The communal dimension is particularly evident in the inclusion of newly composed rites for reconciling many penitents at a common service. Also included are examples of non-sacramental services that prepare people for reconciliation. Such services, often overlooked, would be ideal, for example, during the early part of Lent as a way of focusing on the need for ongoing conversion and of preparing people for a celebration of sacramental reconciliation.

- Second, the word of God is given a formal place within the celebration of these rites, including the rite celebrated with a priest and a single penitent. As with all the revised sacramental liturgies, the celebration of the word of God is seen as integral to a full, authentic liturgical celebration in the Church.

- Third, the texts, including the standard formula for sacramental absolution, have been judiciously revised and supplemented with alternative texts. There is a greater biblical orientation in the texts—for example, in some alternatives to the act of contrition. There is a better balance of trinitarian theology in the formula of absolution, which now begins by speaking about Father, Son and Spirit. There is a greater sense that this mystery is about healing human imperfection than about condemnation. The texts in combination with accompanying gestures display a rite marked by care and human concern, that is focused on reconciling penitents more than merely forgiving their sins.

II . . . to Practice

COMMUNAL DIMENSION OF SIN

One of the major breakthroughs in the revised *Rite of Penance* is the restoration to public consciousness of the social dimension of sin. Reconciliation with God goes hand in hand with reconciliation with our sisters and brothers who form the Church. This reality is expressed in the pastoral remarks in the Introduction and also in the ritual patterns for communal celebration of the sacrament. In the Introduction of the *Rite of Penance* we read:

> Penance always entails reconciliation with our brothers and sisters who are always harmed by our sins. . . . It is . . . fitting that they should help each other in doing penance so that freed from sin by the grace of Christ they may work with all men and women of good will for justice and peace in the world. . . .
>
> The whole Church, as a priestly people, acts in different ways in the work of reconciliation which has been entrusted to it by the Lord.[3]

Especially when communal penance services are celebrated, the ritual proclaims in word and action that as a community we acknowledge that no one is free from sin, that we are all called to a continual change of heart, and that we are all in need of God's merciful and healing love. Although each person may acknowledge particular sinful actions, there is also a renewed sense that we all have a share in what might be called the sinfulness of society. When the structures and the values of a society support or even foster material evil such as oppression, homelessness, or racism, sin is present in the society as a whole. Certain societal sins exert their evil influence because of the sometimes unconscious cooperation of many people, such as the collaboration of a government in the oppression of certain citizens. Our cooperation with injustice may be active or passive or even unwitting, and it becomes the task of the members of the Church to uncover the sinfulness of which they may be unaware.

Communal celebrations of the mystery of penance and of God's forgiving love have reemphasized the ancient truth that no one should feel alone in his or her experience of sin; neither should anyone feel separated from the forgiving love that God offers to each one who contritely approaches Divine Mercy.

THE RITE FOR RECONCILIATION OF INDIVIDUAL PENITENTS

The sacrament of penance has been renewed so that it follows the standard liturgical plan of the sacramental rites, which are meant to have a certain personal and human warmth to them. The atmosphere for the ritual celebration can take its cue from the initial rubric: "When the penitent comes to confess his or her sins, the priest welcomes the penitent warmly and greets the penitent with kindness."[4] The celebration of reconciliation, though following a ritual structure with prescribed prayers, should also be marked by warmth, kindness, and trust in God by priest and penitent alike.

When an individual penitent approaches a priest for reconciliation, after the initial sign of the cross (made and spoken by the penitent), the priest greets the penitent and exhorts him or her to trust in God's healing mercy. Ideally, the scripture is then proclaimed. Either the priest or the penitent may read (or even recite from memory) some appropriate passage. There are still many people who are so familiar with the older rite that it can be awkward for the priest to interrupt the familiar pattern here to share a few words from scripture. Although the rubrics mention that the proclamation of scripture is optional and may even be done by the penitent as part of private preparation,[5] for the sake of the liturgical experience, scripture is more appropriate within the rite. It is in response to the words of the prophets, of John the Baptist and of the Lord Jesus—who exhort us to turn away from evil—that the penitent opens his or her soul.

In confessing sins, a penitent ideally provides information about his or her life and the context in which certain failures occurred. Many priests are more interested in the circumstances that led to actions than in the actions themselves, because the context can affect the significance of the action. For instance, "getting angry" can mean many things. Getting angry at someone who is abusing another person may be a natural and even healthy response. Getting angry at a hungry infant or an elderly parent may mean that the penitent needs better self-discipline as well as ways to relieve tension and pressure, and should focus energy into relieving those pressures.

The role of the priest is to proclaim God's forgiving love and to offer appropriate counsel to the penitent in response to what has been said. Sometimes a priest needs to gain more information in order to offer appropriate advice. The priest also needs to be assured that the penitent is willing to make changes in his or her life to avoid sinful situations.

In response to what the penitent has said, the priest is supposed to assign some action of "satisfaction" (what is commonly called the penance). In recent times, some priests assign certain activities of charity or self-discipline, or the reading of scripture and meditative prayer. Certain types of sins, such as theft or slander, may require restitution, if possible.

Following the assignment of penance, the penitent expresses sorrow before God by means of prayer, either a form of the Act of Contrition or one of the alternative prayers in the ritual, or some impromptu prayer similar in content to those given as samples. In conclusion the priest extends his hands over (or on) the penitent's head and pronounces the formula of absolution.

After the absolution, there may be a short proclamation of praise followed by a dismissal.

The revised rite for reconciliation is well-crafted for its task. Its flow is similar to other revised rites, adapted to the reality that priest and penitent are celebrating this liturgy apart from the community. The rite calls for a dialogue—through the official texts and through extemporaneous discussion and counseling.

For many people, the former rite was approached with a certain amount of fear. The rite centered around the penitent's recitation of a list of sins and the priest's formal absolution, *"Ego te absolvo in nomine Patris. . . . "* As far as a new rite is concerned, the revision has, with some success, transformed a moment that some felt distasteful into a prayer-filled experience of God's forgiving and healing love, mediated through a fellow human being.

Yet there remains some ambiguity. For some people, there was a certain comfort in the anonymity of the dark confessional. For others there is a certain dread about confessing sins to a priest face-to-face. Nonetheless, the revised rite does provide a liturgical structure in which God's mercy as an unconditional response to human failures can be remembered and celebrated appropriately.

THE IMPOSITION OF HANDS

As noted in Chapter 3, one of the most significant gestures of worship has been the imposition of hands.[6] At certain times in the history of the sacrament of penance, the rite was called "the imposition of hands for reconciling penitents." This heritage was acknowledged in the former rite, which required the priest to raise his right hand toward the penitent while proclaiming the absolution, but often in practice this gesture seemed to be a strange form of salute or the gesture used when taking a public oath. But few penitents saw it at all. The gesture was often hidden behind the confessional grating. This beautiful, ancient gesture was rarely seen or understood as a symbol of conferring God's healing love and the power of the Spirit.

The revised rite has highlighted this gesture: The directions state that the priest should extend his hands over the penitent while praying the formula of absolution. In practice, it is appropriate for the priest actually to place his hands on the penitent's head and then, after a moment of silence, to pray the absolution with reverence and dignity. In the rare situation that this might be impossible, a priest should at least extend his right hand.

THE CHAPEL OF RECONCILIATION

With a change in the texts and a change in the mindset for celebrating the reconciliation of individual penitents, what is considered an appropriate setting for celebrating the sacrament has also changed. No longer are the cramped quarters of an old-style confessional seen as the fitting location for human interaction. The space for the reconciliation of individual penitents is now envisioned as a small chapel, a place appropriate for prayer and for giving advice, with suitable lighting and decoration.

In many places, the arrangement of this room still makes possible the Western tradition of anonymity for the penitent by including some sort of partition or grating behind which the penitent kneels or sits. But the room arrangement also accommodates the option for a penitent to face the priest during the liturgy. Often such a room has a crucifix and perhaps an appropriate painting or sculpture, such as that of the prodigal son with his father, or the Good Shepherd carrying the lost sheep. A bible is usually available in the room, and the chairs are comfortable to facilitate discussion between priest and penitent.

The vesture of the priest should be appropriate to the renewed liturgy. The older type of "confessional stole," often hardly bigger than a ribbon, does not speak of the dignity of liturgical symbols in a renewed liturgy. It is appropriate for the priest to wear an alb and a full-size stole as he would wear at other sacramental mysteries.

RITES FOR RECONCILIATION OF SEVERAL PENITENTS

Although in the early centuries of Christianity the sacrament of penance seems to have been celebrated only in communal liturgies, in the last several centuries before Vatican II only a rite for individuals remained in the *Roman Ritual*. The revised *Rite of Penance* formalized various local experiments with communal penance services from the 1960s and 70s.

There are actually two different communal rites provided in the *Rite of Penance*, one including individual confession of sins and individual absolution, and the other including a general confession and general absolution. Both rites present some difficulty in practice. The former rite assumes that several priests will be present to assist during the period for confession and absolution. The latter rite has been restricted by canon law so that in most places it may not be celebrated.[7]

The Rite for Reconciliation of Several Penitents with Individual Confession and Absolution, found as Chapter 2 of the *Rite of Penance*, follows a pattern similar to that of many other liturgies. Following an opening rite that includes a song, greeting, and prayer, the liturgy of the word is celebrated, which also includes a homily. After the homily, the liturgy of the sacrament is celebrated.

First, a period of silence is prescribed, during which the assembly reflects on sin through a kind of examination of conscience. This examination may take the form of a litany guided by a deacon or other minister. This is followed by a communal statement of sinfulness (most often the "I confess" from the opening rites of mass), a litany or song that expresses acknowledgment of sins, and the common recitation of the Lord's Prayer.

Afterwards, those present can confess their sins individually to one of the priests and receive individual absolution and an appropriate penance. All remain together during this time until the last penitent is finished. Since this period for individual confession is usually lengthy, it can include moments of subdued readings, instrumental music, and perhaps even quiet singing, such as the ostinatos from Taizé. This may make the period seem less burdensome and more prayerful but does not shorten the time for individual confessions. After the confessions are ended, a concluding hymn and prayer of thanksgiving is offered. The assembly is blessed and dismissed.

As at other communal liturgies, singing should be considered as integral to a communal penance service and trained liturgical ministers should be present—cantors, musicians, readers. In addition to the standard moments for music during a liturgy, it is also appropriate to sing during the acknowledgment of sin and, after confessions, in thanksgiving. Since litanies are traditionally sung, it would be most appropriate to highlight through song any litany that is included either as part of the examination of conscience or elsewhere.

The format found in Chapter 2 of the *Rite of Penance* is an attempt to blend what is understood by many as the core aspect of sacramental reconciliation—the individual confession and reception of absolution—into a communal, public service. The ritual manages to emphasize the communal aspect of sin while allowing individuals to express their sins privately. One major drawback to this rite is the length of time that it takes to hear the confessions of those present. As a result, many may leave before the service is ended. Nevertheless, having this communal rite as one possible way to celebrate reconciliation is a significant improvement over the days when private confession was the sole option for Catholics.

CHALLENGES

The manner of celebrating sacramental reconciliation in the Church has undergone significant changes since the Second Vatican Council. Whereas in 1960 many Catholics frequented the sacrament monthly or more often, today there are a significant number of Catholics who rarely celebrate this sacrament. Those Catholics who do celebrate reconciliation on a regular basis often do so at a communal service.

The reasons why Catholics do not celebrate reconciliation more frequently are many and varied. They range from the dread associated with telling one's sins to a priest, to a loss of a sense of sin and evil, whether personal or societal. The reality is that there are fewer people requesting sacramental reconciliation. The challenges are twofold. We need to help people, through catechesis and preaching, to realize the actuality of evil and personal sin in our world and to acknowledge that no one is without sin. We also need to provide liturgies that can truly celebrate human *metanoia* and divine forgiveness.

Since the benefits of a communal service can be many, another challenge for the Church is to direct the evolution of a communal rite that is based on solid liturgical principles, yet pastorally practical. The pattern of the Rite for Reconciliation of Several Penitents with Individual Confession and Absolution provides the structure for most communal penance services. But critics have argued this pattern is unique among the revised liturgical rites in demanding the presence of several priests as a practical necessity as well as mixing communal dimensions with individual dimensions, in particular, with individual confession and absolution.[8]

Except for the eucharist, in other liturgies when there are a number of individuals requesting a sacrament, for instance, confirmation or the anointing of the sick, only a fraction of the assembly actually approach the sacramental minister. Thus one minister often suffices. In the case of reconciliation, however, the proportion is quite different. The vast majority of those present at communal services usually wish to experience forgiveness sacramentally. According to present regulations, they must individually approach a priest. In larger parishes in the United States, several hundred people may assemble at services before Christmas and Easter. Such a crowd necessitates a large number of priests, a long period of time, or both, and none of these options is particularly desirable. It is not unheard of that the number of penitents overwhelms even a large number of priests, and a service lasts an hour and a half or more.

The Rite for Reconciliation of Several Penitents with General Confession and Absolution, found in Chapter 3 of the *Rite of Penance,* cannot be celebrated according to canon law in view of the number of priests in the United States and in many other countries. But the pattern of this rite makes more sense as a communal service. There is no attempt to include individual activity within the complete service. Using this pattern of service, there are also no time delays nor need to gather numerous priests together. The liturgical principle of a single presider is not compromised since he alone pronounces the absolution over all present.

The dialogue over the structure of communal penance services and over appropriate use of general absolution will continue for the foreseeable future. In the meantime, communities should reflect on the services actually in use locally and see if improvements are called for either with the rite itself or with issues regarding scheduling.

For example, given the problems of safety in some cities, people are understandably hesitant to stay out too late. This concern might suggest scheduling a service in the afternoon. A large number of penitents at communal services and a shortage of available priests may suggest scheduling more than one service. To address some of these concerns, some communities rearrange the format of communal services so that the final blessing occurs before individual confessions and absolution. People can then leave immediately after receiving absolution. But this arrangement in some sense defeats the purpose of a communal service and confuses its structure.[9]

The practical difficulty that many communities experience when celebrating reconciliation communally and the uneasiness that many experience approaching this sacrament point to the necessity of future reflection on this sacramental mystery. The manner of celebrating this sacrament has evolved much since the first few centuries and even in recent decades. We can only trust that God will continue to guide the Church in developing sacramental rites that appropriately enable Catholics to acknowledge human failure, celebrate God's mercy, and receive assurances of forgiveness.

In Conclusion

One of the accusations leveled against Jesus was that he was a "friend of tax collectors and sinners" (LK 7:34). He reached out to those whom many shunned, such as lepers, Samaritans, and other individuals thought to be sinners. He reached out in love and mercy to heal and forgive through the power of God's mysterious love.

The mystery of iniquity is the mystery of Adam and Eve's fall, perpetuated in the human race through the centuries. The mystery of reconciliation and the sacrament through which the Church makes present forgiveness to

Christians is the mystery of Christ's death and resurrection, the mystery of the blood of Jesus shed for the forgiveness of sins. It is the mystery of the God who so loved the world that Jesus, the only Son of God, was sent so that those who believe might have life and avoid condemnation (cf. JN 3:16,18).

In the mystery of reconciliation, the Church, through the ministry of the priest, speaks to penitents as Jesus spoke to the woman at the house of Simon, "Your sins are forgiven" (LK 7:48). The Church challenges penitents as Jesus challenged the woman caught in adultery, "Go, but sin no more" (JN 8:11). Ultimately, through the mystery of reconciliation the Church stands with the father of the prodigal son to rejoice, "Your brother was dead, and has come back to life. He was lost, and is found" (LK 15:32).

Chapter 8

THE GREAT MYSTERY
OF ANOINTING

Suffering and illness have always been among the greatest problems that trouble the human spirit. Christians feel and experience pain as do all other people; yet their faith helps them to grasp more deeply the mystery of suffering and to bear their pain with greater courage. . . . Through the sacrament of anointing, Christ strengthens the faithful who are afflicted by illness, providing them with the strongest means of support. *(Pastoral Care of the Sick: Rites of Anointing and Viaticum: General Introduction, nn. 1, 5)*

I. From Principles . . .

HISTORICAL OVERVIEW

The sacramental mystery of the anointing of the sick finds its origin in the healing ministry of Jesus himself and of his disciples. It finds its scriptural mandate particularly in the letter of James, which so eloquently highlights the key elements of prayer for the sick person and anointing with oil by the elders of the Church (JAMES 5:13–16). Also included in the ritual is the laying on of hands, inspired by the gospel references to Jesus laying his hands on the sick.

The central ritual of the sacrament consists of several anointings of the sick person with oil blessed for this purpose. The traditional places for the anointings are the various senses. According to the 1614 *Roman Ritual* the sick person was anointed on the eyes, ears, nose, mouth, hands and feet. In Byzantine Catholic and Eastern Orthodox Churches, the anointings are performed on the forehead, nose, both cheeks, mouth, breast, and both sides of the hands.

Most people are well aware that until recently, the sacrament of the sick was practiced as a sacrament of the dying, and so was commonly called *extreme unction* and celebrated as part of the *last rites* that also included viaticum and penance. Because the letter of James mentions the forgiveness of sins in conjunction with the anointing, when celebrated with the dying the sacrament took on a tenor of being a sacrament of final reconciliation rather than a sacrament of healing. Documents of the Council of Trent suggest that the effects of the sacrament were the forgiveness of sin and the comfort of the sick. The sacramental formulas that were included in the 1614 *Roman Ritual* mentioned the forgiveness of sins and did not speak at all about healing. For instance, the formula used while anointing the eyes read: "May the Lord forgive you by this holy anointing and his most loving mercy whatever sins you have committed by the use of your sight." Only in the prayers said after the anointings were there any references to the healing of the sick person.

1972 REVISED RITE OF ANOINTING

In response to the reorientation called for by the Second Vatican Council,[1] in the fall of 1972 the *Rite of Anointing and Pastoral Care of the Sick* was published. A provisional English translation appeared in 1974 for interim use. In this revised form, the sacrament of the sick again focuses on the mystery of God's healing power and has again become a sacrament for all those who because of illness or infirmity can benefit from its prayer, gesture, and action. A concern for healing and for the Lord's power to save and to raise up has replaced the sacrament's emphasis on forgiveness of sin that predominated in the texts of the former rite.

Ultimately, the sacramental celebration of the anointing of the sick, this experience of the mystery of God's love, is about care and concern, prayer, natural medication through the anointing with oil, human contact in the laying on of hands, and God's healing presence experienced through these actions.

The rite for the sacramental mystery of the anointing of the sick is now placed in the broader context of the pastoral care of the sick. The liturgical book not only proves the rites for celebrating the sacrament of the anointing but also includes suggestions for visiting the sick and includes rites for communion of the sick. For those who are gravely ill, texts for viaticum are included, along with appropriate prayers for the commendation of the dying. Also included are rites for exceptional and emergency situations.

This collection of rites focuses the Church's attention on those who are ill and on their spiritual comfort. The various rites—whether it is a short, pastoral visit with a moment of prayer, a communion service, or the sacrament of the anointing—provide the opportunity for the Church to be present through the pastoral minister to someone who is sick. The gentle and hope-filled prayers, the scripture passages, and the rubrics regarding the ritual gestures all direct the minister to celebrate the rites with tenderness, sensitivity, and concern. Perhaps more than in any other liturgical book, the rubrics speak about adapting the services and prayers to the needs of the sick person and to the surroundings.[2]

1983 REVISED ENGLISH EDITION

A decade passed between the publication in 1974 of the provisional translation of the rites for the sick and the publication in 1983 of the definitive English edition, entitled *Pastoral Care of the Sick: Rites of Anointing and Viaticum.* In that period we learned much about the utility of the original edition and its translation. Comments were solicited from priests involved in ministering to the sick and the dying, and comments were also solicited from other pastoral caregivers and health-care workers. In addressing the issue of adaptations, the General Introduction permits conferences of bishops "to arrange the material . . . in a format that will be as suitable as possible for pastoral use," and to "add other texts of the same kind" whenever the Latin original provides several alternative texts.[3] In response to these suggestions, the 1983 edition adapted the provisional translation, rearranging texts, and augmenting some of the skeletal rites. However nothing of great moment was changed, and the revision is a substantially improved liturgical book, from the point of view of pastoral ministers, that not only addresses the celebration of the sacrament of the anointing of the sick, but also is a resource for other pastoral ministry toward those who are infirm.

Pastoral Care of the Sick was the first of the "second generation" English language liturgical books to appear, books that are not merely literal translations of the Latin original. One of the more notable features is the presence of what are called "pastoral notes," found at the beginning of each chapter. These brief commentaries can help ministers interpret the directions and suggestions offered in the General Introduction and in the various rubrics and have been provided to assist the minister to gain a fuller appreciation and understanding of the rite being celebrated. Similar notes have been included in other liturgical books subsequently revised.

There are numerous minor differences in the 1983 English edition when compared with the 1974 provisional text. For example, the former edition included sections that only contained rubrics and references. Some of these sections have been filled out with prayers and scriptural texts, such as in the section dealing with visits to the sick (nn. 57–61) or the section dealing with anointing during mass (nn. 136–148).

The present edition offers additional adapted rites with all texts in place for special situations, such as the abbreviated rite for use in hospitals and institutions, when the anointing of the sick is celebrated several times but in separate rooms (nn. 154–160) and the rite for emergencies (nn. 259–274). Other rites have been augmented appropriately, for instance, the Lord's Prayer has been inserted into the "short" rite of distributing communion (n. 94). New prayers have been composed, in particular, prayers for a Mass for Anointing the Sick, including a preface and intercessions for eucharistic prayers I, II and III (nn. 136–148).

Texts from other liturgical books have been arranged in separate sections or joined with the rite of anointing in appropriate places. For example, there is now a complete section for Christian Initiation for the Dying (nn. 275–296), a separate section with prayers for the dead (nn. 223–231) immediately following the texts for the commendation of the dying, and an appendix with texts for celebrating the sacrament of penance (nn. 299–305). All these additions and rearrangements have provided ministers with a liturgical book that is easier to use and contains better texts for consoling people in time of illness or death.

The Paschal Mystery and the Mystery of Those who are Sick

The rite of the anointing of the sick, as revised after the Council and adapted in the latest English version, provides the Church with a model for celebrating the mystery of God's healing power as it confronts human illness and the mystery of suffering. As such, this celebration mirrors the mystery of God's life-giving love that triumphs over human weakness, even over death. Ultimately the sacrament is a celebration of the paschal mystery of Christ's death and resurrection, of new life through suffering and death. This sacramental rite provides us with the structure to celebrate God's life-giving power, a celebration that is experienced during some of our weakest moments.

II . . . to Practice

Laying On of Hands

As previously mentioned, one core gesture associated with sacramental rites is laying hands on a person's head. This gesture is especially important in the sacrament of the sick because scriptural passages on which the ritual is based often speak about Jesus and his disciples laying hands on the sick (LUKE 4:40; MARK 16:18) and about the elders of the community praying over and anointing the sick (JAMES 5:14). Human touch is important to us, even if we may be unaware of its power. Sometimes we react negatively when others touch us and invade our "personal space." At other times, we crave and even require affectionate touch. Few experiences can relax a tense person as much as a few moments of gentle massage of the neck. Even when a person is unconscious or semi-conscious, often the person can still perceive the presence of others through their touch.

The imposition of hands involved in this sacrament is considered one of three integral aspects, along with the anointing with oil and the prayer of faith.[4] This biblical gesture is done in silence and should not be performed perfunctorily. Because the letter of James speaks about presbyters praying over the sick, the General Introduction to the rite permits all priests present to lay hands on those to be anointed.[5]

ANOINTING

The use of oil in this sacrament should reflect the generosity of God's love and mercy that is evident in scripture. In the past, the oil was wiped off moments after it was applied so the holy oil could not be touched by unconsecrated hands. Of course, removing the oil makes little sense, and it also makes little sense to apply the oil in a miserly fashion. For this reason, a pastoral note in the present edition reminds us:

> If the anointing is to be an effective sacramental symbol, there should be a generous use of oil so that it will be seen and felt by the sick person as a sign of the Spirit's healing and strengthening presence. For the same reason, it is not desirable to wipe off the oil after the anointing.[6]

The rubrics of the revised rite prescribe that a sick person be anointed on the forehead and on the hands while the two-part sacramental formula is being said.[7] The priest anoints the person's forehead while saying: "Through this holy anointing may the Lord in his love and mercy help you with the grace of the Holy Spirit." He anoints the person's hands while saying: "May the Lord who frees you from sin save you and raise you up." The sick person is to affirm the formula's sentiments by responding "Amen" to each part. In the older ritual, while the priest anointed the person on the senses the formula was repeated six times with only a slight change at the end to correspond to the sense being anointed. There was no provision for any response on the part of the sick person.

For a serious reason, the anointing on the hands can be omitted, in which case the complete formula is said while anointing the forehead or, if necessary, some other part of the body. If the local customs suggest it, the sick person may be anointed on other parts of the body, for example, the area of pain or injury, in which case no additional formula is said.[8]

Although it is common to anoint the person by tracing a cross with the blessed oil on the person's forehead and hands, a gesture that imitates the prescription in the rite of confirmation and the former rite of the anointing of the sick, no sign of the cross is prescribed by the rubrics of the present rite.[9] The rubrics do not specify whether the hands should be anointed on the back or on the palm. (According to the 1614 *Ritual*, priests were anointed on the backs of the hands, and other people were anointed on their palms.)

COMMUNAL ANOINTING SERVICES

In many places, following the suggestion of the Council,[10] the sick of a community are anointed as a group at a special mass. Some parishes regularly schedule such a mass of anointing several times a year, at which the infirm, the elderly, and those with long-term illnesses such as cancer or AIDS can be consoled and comforted by friends and members of the parish community. Such events should be encouraged and well-planned. At such celebrations, other priests can be invited to assist with anointing all the sick, and the special presidential prayers, including the preface and intercessions of the eucharistic prayer, can be used. When preparing for such a special liturgy, some effort might also be made to arrange pastoral visits, communion calls and private celebrations of the sacrament of the sick for members of the parish who are interested but unable to attend the communal mass and anointing. In this way, all are united, at least in spirit, in the single eucharistic celebration.

Care should be taken at such liturgies to ensure that liturgical principles are not overlooked. At communal celebrations when numbers are large, the parish may be tempted to simplify the rite, for example by omitting the individual imposition of hands. If there is a large number of sick to be anointed, it may not be advisable for every priest to lay hands on every sick person, but the sacramental experience should not be reduced to anointing the forehead. At the minimum, a priest in silence should lay hands on each sick person to be anointed and should recite the sacramental formula for each person who is anointed. Communal singing should be included, well trained readers should exercise their ministry, and those sick who can exercise some ministry might be invited to serve as they are able.

OIL CONTAINERS

Thought should be given as to how the oil of the sick is displayed and reverenced in the parish church. The oil has commonly been kept in stocks with cotton to avoid spillage when a priest takes the oil to the home of a sick person.[11] But the cotton often confuses people because it masks the oil itself. As long as oil stocks have tight-fitting lids, spilling the oil during transportation is not a problem and so cotton is not really necessary.

In church during a communal celebration of the sacrament, the oil can be put in a clear glass vessel or bowl. To highlight the oil during the celebration and maintain its distinctiveness, the oil can be placed on a pedestal or column—something that does not rival or imitate the altar—and be surrounded with candles to make it sparkle. After the prayer of thanksgiving over the oil or, in special circumstances, the prayer of blessing, the oil can be poured into smaller containers for the priests who will perform the anointings.

BLESSING FRESH OIL

If the sacrament is administered regularly and the oil is applied generously, then it may happen that the supply of oil of the sick, annually blessed by the bishop, may run out. It could also happen that, because of warm weather, the oil becomes rancid. A fresh supply of oil may be obtained from the diocesan reserve, but, in cases of necessity, the priest can bless the oil as part of the celebration of the sacrament.[12] Whenever a bishop presides at a communal celebration of the sacrament, he may and should bless fresh oil as part of the ritual authenticity.[13]

PROPER SUBJECTS

Pastoral Care of the Sick recalls that the intention of the Vatican Council in authorizing the revision of the anointing of the sick was to encourage those who could benefit from this sacrament to "seek it at the beginning of a serious illness" rather than when they are near death as was the prior practice. However, the rite cautions that "the intent of the conciliar reform . . . should not be used to anoint those who are not proper subjects for the sacrament. The sacrament of the anointing of the sick should be celebrated only when a Christian's health is seriously impaired by sickness or old age."[14] This caveat is reiterated elsewhere: "the practice of indiscriminately anointing numbers of people . . . simply because they are ill or have reached an advanced age is to be avoided. Only those whose health is seriously impaired by sickness or old age are proper subjects for the sacrament."[15]

Before the reforms of the Council, we did not make enough use of this sacrament because it was reserved for the dying. Perhaps nowadays we administer the sacrament too freely by celebrating it with people who are not seriously ill. As with any sacrament or ritual celebration, some misuse can occur because of a lack of appreciation of the depth of the ritual, or the misuse can occur by administering the sacrament indiscriminately.

In the General Introduction, we read: "the faithful whose health is seriously impaired by sickness or old age [should] receive this sacrament."[16] The footnote alongside the word *seriously* comments on its translation from the Latin *periculose*: "On the one hand, the sacrament may and should be given to anyone whose health is seriously impaired; on the other hand, it may not be given indiscriminately or to any person whose health is not seriously impaired."

It is inappropriate to administer this sacrament routinely as if it were the St. Blase blessing of throats, as a kind of preventive medicine. The person's activity should in some way be impaired by illness. It is precisely in this sort of weakness and disability that the sick person is an image of the sufferings of Christ. It is precisely through an illness that the sick person can experience God's healing presence. If genuine illness is not present, then the imagery of the sacrament is compromised. Father John M. Huels, a noted canonist, posed the problem in these words:

> More is at stake here than the observance of canon law. When healthy or slightly ill persons routinely receive the anointing, its symbolic value as a special sacrament reserved for the seriously ill is jeopardized. As liturgical theologian Jennifer Glen puts it: "Rites that attempt to include every meaning risk losing all meaning."[17]

Certainly, a condition or illness that requires hospitalization suggests that the mystery of the anointing of the sick should be celebrated. An incurable illness such as cancer or HIV would, of course, also be a reason to celebrate anointing. Old age, of itself, may not be an appropriate reason for anointing unless it is accompanied by debility (for instance, when a person needs a cane to walk). There are no blanket guidelines possible for whether or not to administer a sacrament. Common sense should be used. For example, certain illnesses are serious for the elderly and perhaps not serious for the young. One should not trivialize the sacrament nor should it be reserved for extreme cases. As the General Introduction to the rite states: "A prudent or reasonably sure judgment, without scruple, is sufficient for deciding on the seriousness of an illness."[18]

Praying for the Dead

The sacrament of the sick is no longer one of the "last rites." However, the Church continues to celebrate a sacrament that might be called the "last rite": viaticum.[19] The eucharist is the "food for the journey," which is what "viaticum" means.

All the sacraments, including viaticum, are meant for the living and are not to be celebrated with the dead. The publication of the 1983 *Code of*

Canon Law introduced emendations into the text of the rite of anointing omitting all references and rubrics concerning "conditional anointing," formerly administered when there was doubt whether or not the person was dead. The first printings of the *Pastoral Care of the Sick* had references to conditional anointing, but recent reprintings have omitted such references.[20] In line with canon 1005, the text should now read that if there is doubt whether the person is still alive, the sacrament is administered (as if the person is living) without any special "condition," such as "If life is in you . . ." If it is certain that the person is dead, the sacrament should not be administered. Instead, an adapted form of the rite of commendation of the dying or a prayer service for the dead would be celebrated.[21]

Celebrating one of these non-sacramental rites can be a powerful experience for all who are gathered in the presence of the dead, especially if the suggested gestures of the sign of the cross on the forehead of the dead person or the sprinkling of holy water are performed. Perhaps everyone present can be invited to make the sign of the cross on the forehead of the deceased or sprinkle the body with holy water.

In Conclusion

With the sacrament of the sick, as with others, the celebration demands more than the recitation of texts. We now realize how important it is that the minister speak in a friendly, human manner, and that the minister possess a basic sense of how the ritual components join to form a unified rite. If the minister fails to appreciate the ritual as a whole, the result can be an impoverished experience for the person who is ill and who desires comfort and consolation from the sacrament of the sick.

As already mentioned, there are three key moments to an integral celebration of this sacrament: the moments of prayer, the imposition of hands, and the anointing. To omit prayer or the imposition of hands is to impoverish the sacramental experience. To celebrate the sacrament quickly, rattling the words like a tobacco auctioneer, is to reduce a moment of gentle human interaction to a magic show. Keep in mind the presence of friends and family and of health care workers, many of whom may not be Catholics, may not be Christians, or may not be members of any religion. They, too, are witnesses if not participants in this mystery.

In celebrating this sacramental mystery there should be a great concern for conveying the truth that the sick person is united to the mystery of Christ's own sufferings. There is the need to convey the presence of the mystery of God's never-failing love and support, even in the midst of diseases we cannot cure, pain we cannot fathom, and the aging process we cannot stop.

Chapter 9

THE GREAT MYSTERY
OF MARRIAGE

The intimate partnership of life and the love which constitutes the married state has been established by the creator and endowed by him with its own proper laws. . . . Christ our Lord has abundantly blessed this love, which is rich in its various features, coming as it does from the spring of divine love and modeled on Christ's own union with the Church. . . . Spouses, therefore, are fortified and, as it were, consecrated for the duties and dignity of their state by a special sacrament. *(Vatican Council II, The Church in the Modern World, n. 48)*

I. From Principles . . .

BIBLICAL IMAGES OF MARRIAGE

Besides recording the marriages of specific individuals, scripture also uses images associated with marriages in other contexts. In particular, the relationship between God and the chosen people is often depicted in scripture using marital imagery. Thus, the marriage covenant becomes one image for describing the covenant of Sinai. In the prophet Isaiah, we read: "For he who has become your husband is your Maker; his name is the LORD of hosts. . . . The LORD calls you back like a wife forsaken and grieved in spirit" (IS 54:5–6). God speaks to Israel: "I remember the devotion of your youth, how you loved me as a bride" (JER 2:2). Continuing this image, unfaithfulness to God and to the covenant is often likened to adultery (cf. EZ 16:15 ff).

The marital imagery is found in the Christian scriptures as well. In the letter to the Ephesians, Paul speaks to husbands and wives using the image of the love between Christ and the Church and says that "this is a great mystery"

(EPH 5:21–32). In the second letter to the Corinthians, Paul writes: "I betrothed you to one husband to present you as a chaste virgin to Christ" (2 COR 11:3). The book of Revelation speaks about the "wedding banquet of the Lamb" (REV 19:9) and about the new Jerusalem prepared "as a bride adorned for her husband" (REV 21:2).

Marital imagery is also used in reference to Jesus, the "one flesh" in whom the divine is wedded to the human. In the letter to the Ephesians, Paul quotes Genesis in reference to marriage, "the two shall become one flesh" (EPH 5:31), but in the same letter he uses similar words to refer to Christ, "he might create in himself one new person in place of the two" (EPH 2:15).

The application of wedding imagery to Jesus is found in some of the ancient hymns and antiphons present in the *Liturgy of the Hours*. This imagery is quite evident in the texts associated with the feast of the Epiphany, which in fact commemorates three epiphanies: the manifestation of Christ to the Magi, the manifestation of the Trinity at Christ's baptism, and the manifestation of Christ's power at the wedding at Cana. The Cana imagery is brought into the other two manifestations as we see in the antiphon for the Canticle of Zechariah, the *Benedictus*, sung at morning prayer:

> Today the Bridegroom claims his bride, the Church, since Christ
> has washed her sins away in Jordan's waters; the Magi hasten with
> their gifts to the royal wedding; and the wedding guests rejoice, for
> Christ has changed water into wine.

The Judeo-Christian tradition has made use of the natural institution of marriage and of human love to understand and describe the relationship between God and the human race. God's fidelity to us and God's love for us is particularly evident in the life, death and resurrection of Jesus. Because of Jesus, love takes on a new dimension, and in the sacrament of matrimony, the love between husband and wife is seen as a reflection of this divine love.

HISTORICAL OVERVIEW

When considering the history of sacramental rites, one notices that the Western Church began to exercise oversight over weddings relatively late.[1] Nuptial blessings appear in various early sacramentaries, and references to such blessings date to the fourth century. But it was not until around the seventh and eighth centuries that reference is made to nuptial consent being exchanged by the couple in the presence of an official of the Church, and then it was done in some places at the door of the church. Before that time, the Western Church accepted marriages recognized by the state and offered a blessing for a Christian couple.

Because of the lateness of the Church's involvement in celebrating the sacrament of marriage, throughout Europe there developed a variety of ceremonies pertaining to weddings, each used only in a certain region or by people who spoke a particular language. A rite of marriage did not enter the general *Roman Ritual* until 1614, and because of the many different wedding rites that were already in use in various parts of Europe, the rite in the *Roman Ritual* was used only in those places that had no local tradition.

According to the 1614 *Ritual*, a model of typical Roman simplicity, the priest questioned the bride and groom, who were kneeling before him, whether each took the other as husband or wife "according to the rite of our holy mother, the Church." The bride and groom each expressed their consent by individually answering "I do." Then the couple joined right hands and the priest confirmed their consent and publicly stated that they were married: *Ego conjungo vos in matrimonium. In nomine Patris . . .* , "I join you together in matrimony. In the name of the Father . . ."[2] After this, the couple was sprinkled with holy water. The priest then blessed the ring (of the bride), which the groom put on the bride's finger in silence while the priest recited the sign of the cross.[3] Finally, the priest pronounced a blessing. If the wedding was joined to a mass, after this blessing the nuptial mass would begin, during which a special nuptial blessing was imparted to the bride after the Lord's Prayer.

Answering the interrogation by the priest was considered to be the exchange of consent, and no additional formula of consent or "vows" were included in the Latin ritual. In those countries that had the tradition of vows, the couple recited these vows after the questions by the priest and before the concluding statement of ratification. In many English-speaking countries, the marriage vows were derived from the old Sarum rite of England. However, the vows were considered supplementary to the consent expressed by the "I do" in answer to the priest's question.

The common Western theological position is that since the bride and groom offer each other the indispensable matrimonial consent, the couple therefore marry each other and the priest is the Church's witness. It is therefore commonly said that the bride and groom are the ministers of the sacrament.[4] Because the priestly formula of ratification seemed inconsistent with this emphasis, alternative formulas were used in some countries. In some places in the United States, the priest proclaimed this formula: "By the authority of the Church I ratify and bless the bond of marriage you have contracted. In the name of the Father . . ."

As commonly practiced before the reform of the Second Vatican Council, in the United States, the wedding ceremony often took the following form: The wedding party would enter the church with the women coming in a formal procession from the main entrance of the church and the men from a side door or the sacristy. Men and women met in pairs before the gate to the sanctuary. The bride was usually escorted by her father who "gave her away" to the groom at the edge of the sanctuary. The couple would then enter the sanctuary and kneel before the priest. In many places, the priest would then read a short admonition before celebrating the rite described above, which may or may not have included mass. The bridal couple then left the church down the main aisle followed by their attendants and others in the assembly.

The 1614 *Roman Ritual* assumed that Catholics would be marrying only Catholics, so it did not include any rite for a marriage between a Catholic and a non-Catholic. Many national rituals included texts for such a service and alternative rites could be authorized by the local bishop. In general, the rite for "mixed marriages" was stark. The ceremony normally was not permitted within the body of the church nor with a great number of family and friends present. As a result, it often took place in the church sacristy or rectory parlor, usually only in the presence of the witnesses and perhaps the parents. The texts for a "mixed marriage" found in the older *Ritual* for the United States do not contain any reference to the Church or to Christ nor is any Trinitarian formula included. This rite was also unusual in that no prayers or blessings were offered for the couple and only in certain dioceses was it permitted to bless the rings. Some rituals also prohibited the presiding priest from wearing any vestment.

Prior to recent reforms, both in law and in theological reflections on marriage, the stress was placed on juridical questions, such as the freedom to marry, lack of coercion, "rights" and "obligations" of the bride and groom toward each other, and proper delegation of the minister, who was required to receive legal authorization to officiate. Relatively little was said about human love or how marriage was meant to reflect the divine covenant between God and the chosen people and the love between Christ and the Church.

In 1963, the *Constitution on the Sacred Liturgy* authorized some tentative changes to the old marriage rites by directing that the rite ordinarily should take place within mass after the homily.[5] It also directed that the scripture readings from the nuptial mass be read even if a marriage should take place outside mass. Additional norms were issued in 1966 pertaining to mixed marriages. All these were preliminary and foundational to the promulgation of the revised rites for marriages authorized by the Second Vatican Council.

1969 RITE OF MARRIAGE

In 1969, a revised *Rite of Marriage* was published that incorporated some of the suggestions found in the *Constitution on the Sacred Liturgy*. The revised rite provided a basic structure, in particular, reordering the seventeenth-century rite so that, if celebrated with mass, the exchange of consent occurs after the homily rather than before the introductory rite. It also incorporated some of the standard customs found throughout the Western Church, but allowed countries to publish their own rites based on their traditional usages. One of the benefits of the 1969 rite was to provide the Western Church with a renewed theology of marriage expressed in the liturgical texts, particularly in the three sets of presidential prayers and prefaces for use in a nuptial mass, the three different nuptial blessings, and the numerous scriptural readings for marriage.

The renewed rite also employs a ritual structure that has become standard in other revised rites: the celebration of the sacrament is always preceded by a liturgy of the word, whether within or outside mass. Thus, unlike the earlier rite, the present rite for celebrating human love is set in the context of recalling God's love as recorded in sacred scripture.

The present ritual suggests that the priest greet the couple at the door of the church and then move with them in procession toward the altar. After the liturgy of the word and homily, the rite provides a brief address to the couple, and then the priest asks the couple three questions concerning their freedom of choice, their faithfulness to each other, and (when appropriate) their acceptance and upbringing of children. The priest next invites the couple to join their right hands and declare their consent. The formula for consent is now worded as an exchange of vows by the bride and groom, although it is permitted for the priest to elicit the consent by wording the formula as a question. The priest ratifies the expression of consent and the entire assembly confirms this statement with their Amen. After this the rings are blessed and exchanged while the bride and groom say a prescribed formula. The rite is concluded by the general intercessions.

If the rite is celebrated within mass, the liturgy of the eucharist follows with the nuptial blessing being given in place of the embolism of the Our Father. If the wedding takes places outside mass, the nuptial blessing concludes the general intercessions, and is followed by the Lord's Prayer and a blessing. The 1969 rite does not mention the use of holy water at any point. However, the 1984 *Ceremonial of Bishops* and the 1990 edition of the *Rite of Marriage* permit the use of holy water at the blessing of the rings but its use is at the discretion of the priest.

In significant contrast to the earlier *Ritual*, if a Catholic marries a baptized non-Catholic, the same rite is used as when two Catholics marry. When a marriage between a Catholic and an unbaptized person takes place, a special rite is provided.

1990 Revised Latin Edition

In 1990 a revised edition of the *Rite of Marriage* was published in a Latin version. This new edition is not so much a revision of the rite as an attempt to improve the earlier version with a rewritten introduction, some revised prayer texts, and a few alternatives supplementing the corpus of texts. Since many of the changes may not be noticed without close examination, a few of the important changes are listed here:

- The Introduction is now more than twice the length of the 1969 version (44 paragraphs as compared to 18). The Introduction and norms governing the use of the nuptial mass have been updated according to the 1983 *Code of Canon Law* and the liturgical books published since the 1969 edition.

- There are new sample texts for the presiding minister to greet the couple as the rite begins.

- The penitential rite is now omitted at a wedding mass. The prayer for peace ("Lord Jesus Christ, you said to your apostles . . .") after the Our Father is omitted. Immediately after the nuptial blessing, the celebrant greets everyone ("The peace of the Lord . . ."), and then invites all to share God's peace.[6]

- Textual revisions of various prayers express greater equality between husband and wife. The selection of scripture readings recommended for use has been augmented.

- There is an alternative formula by which the presiding cleric accepts the expression of consent by the couple.

- There are intercessions to use in eucharistic prayers I, II and III for the newly married couple.

- The original three nuptial blessings now include an epiclesis, a calling forth of the Holy Spirit upon the couple.

- Textual revisions in the rite for celebrating a marriage between a Catholic and a non-Christian express more clearly that one of the parties may not be Christian. For example, the invocation of the Trinity ("in the name of the Father . . .") in the formula used for exchanging rings may be omitted at such a rite.

- A new chapter includes texts to be used when a person who is not a deacon or priest is delegated to preside at the celebration of a marriage. Special nuptial blessings have been provided for use at such a celebration.

Revised English Language Editions

A thorough revision of marriage ritual for the United States may take a while to achieve. In the meantime, revised versions of the older editions will be published, which likely will contain the revised introduction and the revised and alternative prayers, as found in the 1990 Latin edition.

In addition, every national edition may also include locally approved alternative texts and ritual elements incorporating older traditions, as approved by the national conference of bishops. For instance, the 1970 American edition included an alternative text for expressing consent, that is, the wedding vows, that had been traditional in the United States, along with a special solemn blessing. The 1979 Canadian wedding ritual contained extensive pastoral notes not found in editions published in the United States, and also included formulas for expressing consent in numerous languages, including Chinese, Ukrainian, and Greek. The older ritual book for England incorporated the signing of the registry, required by civil law in Britain.

Countries that have been able to undertake an in-depth study of traditional marriage customs may include in their rituals other alternatives and adaptations. For instance, the revised British marriage ritual includes prayers found in the old Sarum ritual and allows the nuptial blessing to be prayed after the exchange of rings rather than after the Our Father. In Filipino and Hispanic parishes, the marriage rite, even when celebrated in English, usually includes an exchange of coins and the imposition of the lasso over the shoulders of the bridal couple after the exchange of rings.

II . . . to Practice

A Celebration of God's Love

A marriage between two baptized Christians is a sacrament, and as such it is a public liturgical celebration of the entire people of God. This is the foundation on which the planning of any wedding liturgy must be built. Because marriage is a sacrament, it is fundamentally a celebration of the mystery of God's faithful love, shown through the death and resurrection of Jesus. It is a celebration that beyond the sufferings of Good Friday, there is the glory of Easter. It is a celebration that life consists of good times and bad, of sickness and health. It is a celebration that the fidelity which God shows to us can be reflected in a couple's fidelity to each other.

Too often couples come to prepare their weddings more conscious of what they have seen at friends' celebrations rather than what they know of the Church's liturgical prayer. The requests some couples make are often at odds with good theology and good liturgical practice. The foundations for celebrating this sacramental mystery, as with celebrating any other mystery, include a number of principles: a sacrament is a celebration of the entire assembly gathered as part of Christ's Church; any such celebration includes active and conscious participation by all present (and that also includes congregational singing); remembering and giving thanks for God's covenant of love is the context in which we celebrate. Human love is an image of and a participation in the love of God.

MINISTERIAL ROLE OF THE BRIDE AND THE GROOM

The bridal couple are the focus of the celebration of the mystery of marriage. Yet, as the ones who have invited others to witness their expression of love before God, they also have a pastoral responsibility toward those who will be present at the liturgical ceremony. In its pastoral notes, the 1979 Canadian marriage ritual in several places speaks about the "ministerial role" of the couple. This role is not limited to the expression of consent, but affects various aspects of the wedding.

For instance, as "hosts" of the celebration, it is appropriate that the bride and groom exercise a ministry of hospitality and welcome their guests to the liturgy by greeting them at the church doors as they arrive. In choosing scripture and other texts for the wedding, the couple should have the interests of the assembled Church in mind. When speaking during the rite, they should speak distinctly and loudly enough to be heard. As a pastoral note in the Canadian ritual states: "Couples are to be reminded again of their ministerial role: they are marrying each other before the Church; the Church should know it."[7]

PASTORAL CHALLENGES

Needless to say, weddings are a time charged with high emotions for the couple being married and for their families and friends. Weddings demand sensitive response on the part of the Church's ministers who are being asked to join the couple on a journey of faith—a journey many couples have barely begun. Couples come to the Church with mixed motivations. Desire for a church wedding can be more their parents' than their own, and their notions of what constitutes a "correct wedding" may be colored by the movies, by brides' magazines, by fantasies impossible to fulfill. And yet there is also the desire to stand before God and God's people to declare their love and to ask for divine blessings on their lives.

In trying to respond both to the couple and to the Church's ideals, priests and deacons have been known to go to extremes. On the one hand, one can find a deacon or priest who has a set pattern and will not allow a couple to upset that pattern, for instance, by not permitting the couple to choose the readings. On the other hand, there are those who allow couples to improvise the rite and all its texts and to read anything they like from any source as "readings" at the wedding. Some of these weddings can barely be considered Christian and may even fail to fulfill the Church's minimal legal requirements.

A major challenge for those who will preside over weddings is to help a couple realize that this celebration, like the celebration of any sacrament, is a celebration of the Church for the sake of the Church, because it is a celebration of Christ's paschal mystery. For that reason, Christ and the assembled people of God are the ultimate focus of any celebration. The couple should be led to understand that they are hospitable hosts, facilitators of prayer, and ministers of the sacrament alongside the presiding priest or deacon. This understanding does not come easily and the responsibilities are significant, so it is no wonder that marriage is for adults.

A related challenge is to help a couple realize that liturgical celebrations, by their nature, demand active participation by all assembled. In particular, this means that weddings are not exempt from liturgical principles such as those that assume congregational singing during certain points of the service. Catholic liturgies should not be occasions for soloists to usurp the assembly's proper role. If anything, weddings provide opportunities for parishes to educate guests and visitors to understand Christian marriage in the context of worship of God. They provide occasions to allow all present—Catholics and non-Catholics, church-goers and those who are not regular participants in religious services—the chance to participate in liturgies that engage the assembly rather than relegate them to the role of an audience. A crucial ingredient in such liturgies is congregational singing. Although the guests present at wedding liturgies are often from different religious backgrounds, it is still possible to choose common hymns and acclamations set to simple, yet dignified, tones that encourage communal participation.

Since a wedding in a Catholic church is a public ceremony of the Church and of society, the Church certainly has the right to ensure that its traditions and laws are observed. Once a couple comes to appreciate these traditions, which is usually part of the reason they desire a church wedding, the priest has solid ground to assist the couple in selecting readings and in organizing the rituals.

WEDDING CUSTOMS

Many of us are acutely aware of the gaps in our lives between the ideal and the real. There can be chasms between what we say and what we do. But even these chasms are insufficient reasons to abandon our ideals.

Some deacons and priests, myself included, when working with engaged couples, dread having to plan the nitty gritty of the wedding ceremony. The dread is due to the difference between what a wedding should be like in the minds of most couples—at least as passed on to the couple from their mothers and from the authors of wedding guides—and the ideal described in the rubrics of the Church's rite and in the writings of church teachers. It can be like pulling teeth to suggest that certain so-called "traditional" wedding practices might be dropped. For Christians some of these "traditions" are not traditional at all and may in fact be hostile to the faith. But the Christian perspective can be foreign to many of us especially because of the barrage of advertising by the wedding industry. As a result, parish ministers can find themselves swimming upstream when they confront the wedding propaganda that have influenced couples preparing for marriage.

Certain wedding customs common in the United States are neither ancient nor universal. Priests visiting from other countries are often overwhelmed when asked to perform a wedding in the United States. For example, in parts of India, wedding rehearsals and subsequent dinners are almost unheard of. In place of this, the couple is given a few instructions before the ceremony begins and the priest directs them as necessary during the celebration of the rite. Families in some countries who try to imitate the American practices they see in movies or magazines can find themselves in debt for life.

Perhaps most striking is the discrepancy between the simplicity of the gospel message of Jesus and the extreme lavishness of many weddings. Jesus began his ministry at the wedding at Cana, but the festive abundance of Cana probably pales when compared with the extravagance of some contemporary weddings. Jesus spoke against the social mores of his times, especially when those social customs did harm to the simple, little ones. Jesus was content with eating with the social outcasts, since those who knew the proper things to do usually thought themselves too good for Jesus. Unfortunately, for many of us, what seems to be more important when planning a wedding is to make sure that the (supposedly) socially correct thing is done. Great amounts of time and money are spent in worrying about the white runner down the main aisle, when and where the grandmothers and mothers are seated, when the bride's veil should be removed and who should do it, the clothing, the flowers, the musicians, the photographers, the videotaping, the number of attendants, whom to invite, what goes on at the rehearsal dinner and the reception, and then all the details of the honeymoon.

If it is possible to judge from the letters written to Ann Landers and Miss Manners, weddings and showers have become the premier occasion in America for hurting other people's feelings and going into debt. It might leave us wondering if things could get much worse. Many of the social customs associated with weddings are accepted unreflectively, and this is unfortunate since too often these customs are non-Christian and even anti-Christian.

Nietzsche said: "Every tradition grows ever more venerable—the more remote is its origin, the more confused that origin is."[8] How true that statement is when applied to wedding customs!

- A Catholic wedding does not need several pairs of attendants. Only two witnesses are needed for the ritual, and they may even be of the same sex. They are the official witnesses in civil and church law, who can publicly testify that the wedding actually took place.

- The custom of identical attire for the attendants may have its origins in superstition:

    The custom of having the bridesmaids dress like the bride and the groomsmen like the groom was a way of protecting the bride and groom from evil spirits. If all the women were dressed similarly and all the men were dressed similarly, the evil spirits would not know who the real bride and groom were, and, thus, could not bother the couple.[9]

- Certain customs pertaining to the groom may also find their origin in superstition:

    The custom whereby the groom is not permitted to see the bride before the wedding dates from a time when most marriages were arranged by the groom and the bride's father. In return for his daughter, the father received money or some other commodity from the groom. Often, the groom did not even meet his bride until the wedding when he made payment to the father. If the groom did not like what he saw, he could call off the wedding, and the father would not receive his payment. To avoid the possibility of such "bad luck," the father did not permit the groom to see the bride until the time of the transaction.[10]

- This same history also has given rise to the custom of keeping the face of the bride veiled until after the exchange of vows. Recall the humorous story of Jacob being duped into marrying the wrong daughter of Laban (GEN 29:23–25).

- In an age of heightened consciousness of the equality of men and women, it is odd that many mothers do not want to play a role in the actual wedding ceremony of their children, for example by walking in the entrance procession. Similarly, it is odd that many brides still want to retain a kind of "fashion show" entrance where the women come down the main aisle of the church. The oddest of all is the notion that a father can give away his daughter.

In contrast, there are Christian traditions that can be observed and appropriately incorporated at weddings. For instance, there is an authentic tradition of preparation before participating in any sacrament, a preparation that often took the form of prayer and fasting. Such a tradition might be adapted to contemporary life. Certainly time for reflection, personal prayer, and being by oneself is appropriate for the bride and the groom during the days before the wedding. A moment of prayer and a blessing of the couple might be used to begin the rehearsal.

But instead of the bride secluding herself immediately before the ceremony, on the day of the wedding the bride and groom might observe a custom common in some European countries: They meet each other at one of the parents' houses and ask blessings from both sets of parents before leaving to the church together. They, along with the witnesses and the presiding priest or deacon, might also consider greeting arriving guests at the door of the church, showing the genuine hospitality of Christ to visitors.

The church ceremony requires individuals involved in specialized roles including cantors, musicians, readers, eucharistic ministers, greeters and ushers. Given the gospel concern for simplicity, it is more appropriate to have fewer attendants than to have many and, instead, to invite friends and relatives who are qualified to exercise one of these significant ministries.

Although certain authentic customs may not be widely practiced, they may be more consistent with the mystery of love and with liturgical principles than many we are familiar with.

Any couple contemplating marriage in the Catholic Church should confront the many so-called customs and expectations surrounding weddings in our society and ponder and pray over the ideal of the rite of marriage proposed by the Church. The signs and symbols of the wedding ceremony should speak of the gospel, and not of sexist practices or of lavish extravagance. The symbols of the modern Catholic wedding can speak of unity, hope, equality, faith, simplicity, love. With appropriate preparation, a modern Catholic wedding can be a splendid and traditional celebration in which guests are received as Christ among us and in which love and fidelity are declared in a setting of beauty and grace.

This is the challenge presented to every couple and to every Christian.

THE WEDDING ENTRANCE PROCESSION

The entrance procession commonly practiced until recent years in many places consists of the seating of the grandmothers and mothers, then the entrance of the flower girl and ring bearer, the bridesmaids, the maid of honor, and then, finally, the bride escorted by her father. Often this is accompanied by three different instrumental pieces on the organ, one for the mothers, one for the attendants, and one for the bride. While the attention of the assembly is focused on this procession, the priest, the groom, and the male attendants have discreetly entered the sanctuary from a sacristy door or a side door of the church. Each man in the sanctuary meets his respective partner as she reaches the front of the church.

The older style of procession has been challenged on several grounds. It is not ancient, nor widespread in the Church, and certainly not at all liturgical. And so it is not even a permitted option in the Roman Catholic rite. This style of entrance ignores the presiding minister, relegates the groom and his attendants to a secondary position, and has its origins in the days when women were the property of men.

In an earlier age, daughters were considered the legal property of their fathers and marriages were arranged by fathers. Love between the couple was not considered an important factor, and it was not unheard of that the bride or groom would not have met each other until they met at the altar. In exchange for his daughter, the father of the bride received some sort of payment from the groom and his family. It was not unknown that an unwilling bride was in fact dragged down the aisle by her father as an unwilling participant to her own marriage, particularly if the marriage was arranged for political reasons with a family from a distant city. Customs associated with attitudes toward women such as these should no longer be tolerated in any church.

The 1614 *Roman Ritual* did not make any mention about how the bridal couple and their witnesses entered the church. Lacking any official direction, local customs developed and then became canonized, and the directions found in the revised *Rite of Marriage* are, unfortunately, overlooked or ignored.

The *Rite of Marriage* now prescribes a ritual format common in several European countries: The wedding begins with a "liminal rite" at the door of the church. Here the priest greets the bride and groom.[11] Then, as in any liturgy, the entrance procession begins. At the entrance procession of a wedding, the priest is followed by the groom with his parents and the bride with her parents.[12] The official witnesses also take part and, in some places, other family members or friends are included, not as "attendants" but as companions and fellow witnesses to this mystery of marriage. This procession appropriately is led by incense, cross, candle bearers, and reader. During this procession, all in the assembly will be standing and singing an opening song, as is common at the beginning of any liturgical service. To enable everyone, including the bridal couple, to join in the singing it may occasionally be appropriate to accompany the procession with instrumental music and to begin the opening song when the procession reaches the sanctuary.

The Church's procession incarnates several significant points:

- There is an equality of the bride and groom. Both are part of the entrance procession.

- There is equality for the parents. The procession includes a place for the mother of the bride as well as the parents of the groom.

- There is appropriate symbolism. The full procession into the assembly of all of the principal ministers and witnesses—priest and ministers, bride and groom, witnesses and parents—is an image of the Church entering the mystery of Christ.

First impressions are lasting. How one starts an enterprise is symbolic of a vision for the rest of that enterprise. Married life officially begins with the wedding ceremony, and the wedding ceremony officially begins with the entrance procession. In subtle, unconscious ways and sometimes in not-so-subtle, obvious ways, this procession and the entire ceremony make a statement about our vision of marriage.

Couples planning weddings should not yield to anachronistic practices liturgically questionable at best and out of touch with contemporary sensibilities and values. All involved in preparing the ceremony—bride, groom, presiding minister, parish wedding coordinator, musicians, cantors, and others—should come to know the various options that are provided by the official rite. Even florists and photographers can be eager to participate appropriately in the Church's hospitable ways of celebrating marriage, once they become familiar with it.

THE WEDDING "VOWS"

There can be a tension between a couple who wants to write their own vows, and the minister who in conscience must verify before religious superiors and civil authorities that the formulas pronounced satisfied legal requirements. The wording of the vows is significant since these formulas are considered to be the core expression of consent.

People also sometimes overlook the civil requirements of a wedding. For example, in England the formula for the exchange of consent must be one that is recognized in civil law; the formula cannot be altered. The Roman Catholic ritual books for marriages published in England emphasize this.[13] Other places may have laws that are less well known but equally binding to ensure civil validity.[14]

Some parishes tolerate the couple writing their own vows, as long as the vows express what is contained in Catholic tradition. However, accepting a variation in the standard formula is one thing, and encouraging the practice at every wedding is another. There is wisdom in having one standard formula that all bridal couples use to proclaim publicly their consent and commitment. By repeating the same words used throughout the generations, a couple unites with other married couples in a kind of ageless mystery.

Some couples base their antagonism to prescribed vows on what they have heard on TV and in the movies, not on the Church's actual language. As a result, they may come to the parish with some unfounded prejudices. It may take some time to point out that the Church's formula does not say anything, for instance, about wives having to obey their husbands (a common sore spot). In fact, the vows for bride and groom are essentially the same.

For couples who insist on amending the text of the vows, the 1979 Canadian marriage ritual offers counsel on this matter:

> To be a proper sign, the form must express all that the Church normally expresses, and contain nothing contrary to the Church's faith or practice. Thus the form is to indicate that the other person is being accepted as husband or wife, that each will be faithful to the other, and that the marriage is lifelong. Each declares this separately to the other in the presence of the required witnesses and the community. The consent has to be unconditional: a proviso such as "as long as love shall last" invalidates the expression of consent in the eyes of the Catholic Church. . . . The form must be clear and concise: florid, sentimental, wordy and confusing formulations should be avoided. Again here, couples are to be reminded of their ministerial function toward the assembly.[15]

It should also be noted that in the *Constitution on the Sacred Liturgy*, the *Rite of Marriage*, and the *Code of Canon Law*[16] the validity of the rite also depends on the involvement of the minister who acts as the official witness. The minister must actively take part in the exchange of consent by *requesting* it and then *ratifying* it. This present legislation has its historical origin in a time when some couples would pronounce their consent before priests who were unwilling participants in the event. To prevent clandestine marriages and to ensure that the exchange of consent is an action recognized by the Church, the present practice, written into law, demands the active assent and guidance of the minister.

POSTURE AND PLACEMENT OF THE BRIDAL COUPLE

The 1614 *Ritual* specifically mentioned that the bridal couple should be *kneeling* before the altar during the marriage rite with the priest facing them. Since kneeling was the standard posture for those in the assembly at mass before the reforms of the Second Vatican Council and the altar was against the wall, in most parishes the couple knelt on kneelers in the sanctuary for the entire service. The assembly could only see the backs of the bridal couple throughout the liturgy.

In the 1969 *Rite of Marriage*, a rubric specifically states that after the homily all should stand for the exchange of consent and rings, "including the bride and bridgroom." This is a notable change from past practice and is sometimes overlooked in practice. In the present rite, the priest and the couple stand and face each other without anything between them (such as kneelers). Since everyone is standing, it is possible for the priest to have the couple face each other for the exchange of consent and the exchange of rings so that their faces can be seen by the assembly during these important moments.

The present rite gives no specifics as to the posture and placement of the bridal couple during the liturgy of the word and the liturgy of the eucharist. Nor is there any mention of a posture of the couple during the nuptial blessing. Thus, the wedding couple should sit, stand or kneel at the same times as the rest of the assembly. The couple would not be kneeling while the rest of the assembly is standing. The bridal couple needs comfortable chairs and kneelers (if the parish customarily kneels during the eucharistic prayer). Since the normal posture of the assembly during blessings is to stand, standing is the appropriate posture for the bridal couple during the solemn nuptial blessing.

The chairs for the bridal couple should be arranged "so that the faithful may have a complete view of the liturgical rites" (to borrow a principle from the ordination rites). This principle would preclude placing the bridal couple immediately before an altar. (If the couple were to stand, the priest would be hidden from the rest of the assembly.)

In some parishes it might be the custom that the bridal couple would sit in the first row of seats in the assembly and come forward only for the wedding rite. In most parishes, the couple usually are assigned a special place near the altar and ambo. It might be best if the couple were seated together, perhaps near or on the opposite side of the sanctuary as the presidential chair. But the chairs for the couple should not appear to compromise the presiding role of the priest. The couple should have an unimpeded view of the liturgy of the word and the liturgy of the eucharist. For the wedding rite the couple can stand in front of the altar or even in the main aisle. For the eucharistic prayer, the couple might either return to their seats, or, depending on the church, stand near the altar facing the priest, with their faces visible to the assembly. If it is the local custom to stand for the entire eucharistic prayer, there is no need to have kneelers for the couple. The guiding principle should be everyone's ability to see the liturgical action.

The placement and seating of the witnesses and other attendants should be appropriate to the liturgical space. Since witnesses perform their role during the exchange of consent, there is no liturgical necessity for them to be in the sanctuary at other times of the liturgy. By keeping the sanctuary free of anyone other than the bridal couple and the presiding minister (and deacon), the liturgical roles are kept clear and the role of the bride and groom is emphasized. Of course, all liturgical ministers (including the bride and groom, the witnesses and attendants, the servers and all members of the assembly) have their parts to play. If roles are unclear, or if someone is unfamiliar with basic liturgical participation including participation in song, then some instruction is needed and there may be much to rehearse.

WEDDINGS OUTSIDE OF THE EUCHARIST

As already noted, the *Constitution on the Sacred Liturgy* directed that the sacrament of marriage should normally be celebrated during mass. Yet there are circumstances surrounding marriages that might recommend that marriage be celebrated outside the context of the eucharist.

One of the most obvious situations occurs when one of the spouses is a non-Christian. The ritual itself does not permit the celebration of mass in this case. The eucharist is the major rite in which Christians express their faith and thus the presence of non-baptized during its celebration is anomalous, and, according to ancient tradition, even forbidden. It is becoming more and more commonplace in parishes to dismiss the catechumens before the liturgy of the eucharist. Catholics may be more and more familiar with the expectation that only the baptized participate in the eucharist. Although Christians join other Christians in praying to God through Christ, it is obviously more difficult for non-Christians to feel comfortable at Christian prayer. Since many in the assembly may be family and friends of the non-Christian spouse and may also be non-Christian, the eucharist would clearly be inappropriate.

When Catholics marry non-Catholic Christians, mass is permitted, but intercommunion is always a touchy point. By general law, the non-Catholic is not permitted to receive communion, although in some dioceses the local bishop may have approved norms permitting the non-Catholic spouse to receive communion if that spouse expresses Catholic faith in the eucharist. However, such permission is not usually given indiscriminately for other non-Catholics in the assembly. It would be misleading to invite all present to receive communion since this is contrary to general law and, in a sense, it trivializes the eucharist, allowing the external occasion to determine who communicates, rather than interior faith and spiritual dispositions. (One can also speculate as to how Catholics who do not consider themselves able to receive communion feel when witnessing non-Catholics being invited to communion.)

Reception of communion is a rich, multi-layered symbol: The communicant expresses union with the Church (presupposing forgiveness of grave sins), and the communicant expresses faith in the eucharistic mystery. To overlook the depth of meaning that participating in communion implies, even for the sake of extending hospitality to non-Catholics, may not be in the best interests of ecumenical relations. That is why it is probably best to forego the eucharist if it would be necessary to remind some members of the assembly that they are not welcome at communion. The eucharist, in this case, is turned into a "sacrament" of disunity. Admittedly there is an inconsistency present: people are permitted to participate in the praise of God through the central prayer of the mass, the eucharistic prayer, but then may not be allowed to partake in the eucharistic elements. The early tradition of the Church did not permit non-communicants to be present for the eucharist and perhaps the present inconsistency deserves further reflection.

Finally there is the situation in which both bride and groom are baptized Catholics, but one or both of them may not be active in the faith. It is not uncommon in our highly mobile society, to find young adults who never were confirmed or never celebrated their first communion. The parish's first task may be to determine why the couple want to celebrate their wedding in a Catholic ceremony if regular participation in the life of the Church is not a priority. If it seems that their faith can be nourished and that the wedding may be a significant step in helping them participate in the Church, especially in the life of the parish and its work in the community, then it likely is appropriate to celebrate the wedding. But we still are left with the questions, Will this couple and the assembly be able to participate in the wedding liturgy? Will they be able to participate in the eucharist and share in communion? If they are unable to do this, then it probably would be better to celebrate the wedding without the mass.

There are also some couples who are regular churchgoers but who may request that mass not be celebrated. The reasons might be trivial—to shorten the ceremony—or profound—because they feel the eucharist would be troubling to many of their guests. The Church encourages the celebration of marriage within the eucharist, itself a sacrament of love, but by no means requires it.

ADDITIONAL PRACTICES

The Wedding Candle: Recently it has become common at weddings for the couple to participate in a candle lighting ceremony, usually done after the exchange of rings, during which the bride and groom, each holding small candles, together light a larger one. On the surface, this ceremony speaks of unity, symbolizing how two become one. Although not in the official ritual, it is consistent with other symbols and explanatory ceremonies associated with weddings, such as the "lasso" common in Spanish-speaking countries. Couples may be encouraged to light the large candle on their wedding anniversaries, and thus to recall and nourish their love.

A version of this ceremony has been included for optional use in the revision of the British marriage ritual, but some have suggested that there be more reflection on this ceremony before including it in other national editions. A basic question is whether this novel use of candles is consistent with the traditional use of candles in the Roman rite, specifically, the Easter candle and baptismal candles lit from the Easter candle. Some suggest that the large "unity" candle sometimes may compete in significance with the Easter candle. Other questions are raised as well. If the bride and groom extinguish their individual candles after lighting the common candle, does this indicate a cessation of their individual personalities?

If done well, lighting a common candle can reinforce other images of unity that are part of marriage celebrations. Care should be taken, however, that this minor rite not overshadow the traditional symbols of unity at a wedding—the exchange of rings and eucharistic participation in one loaf and one cup.

Flowers for Mary: It is a common custom in many places that the bride leaves a rose or a bouquet of flowers at the church's shrine for Mary. The woman then prays privately for Our Lady's assistance to be a good wife and mother, often while a hymn in honor of Mary is sung. On the one hand, Catholics have had a long-standing tradition of love and affection for Mary, for Joseph, for the saints. It seems only right to include in weddings some mention of Mary, some sign of affection for her and for the Holy Family. But, on the other hand, is it appropriate to interrupt the wedding liturgy with a moment of the bride's "private" prayer? And does a bride's prayer to Mary not seem odd without a groom's prayer to Joseph?

Perhaps some liturgical creativity is needed here in reminding us of the intercession of the saints and of their presence in our lives and, in particular, of their presence within the sacrament of marriage. Without some fresh approach, it seems difficult to try to incorporate this custom, as it is, into the rite, and it would probably be better were the couple to express any such devotion at some other time or in some other way.

Common Prayer by the Couple: Some planning books suggest that a couple may wish to pray publicly for each other after the exchange of rings or, alternatively, after communion. In one sense, this provides the opportunity for personal creativity, which may be what some couples desire when they ask if they can compose their own vows. As with other ceremonies not included in the official ritual, such a ceremony has both merits and drawbacks. It provides an opportunity for the bride and groom to express personal sentiments for the other before God and the assembly. Yet, often, for those untrained in religious writing, such statements and prayers can become sentimental or florid to the point of being humorous and even un-Christian. More significantly, there is no other occasion in liturgical rites in which a single participant prays as an individual for another individual. The nature of liturgical prayer is communal.

It would be better if the sentiments of the couple could be molded into a coherent intercession by others more experienced (and such individuals are rare) and then used as part of the general intercessions. In the intercessions, the entire assembly prays for the bride and groom, and it may be possible to craft the sentiments and phrases of certain of the intercessions to reflect the hopes and concerns of the couple.

Non-Scriptural Readings: For a couple of decades now, it has occasionally happened that people read excerpts from *The Prophet* by Kahlil Gibran or from some other non-scriptural source at a Catholic wedding. A couple may still request that a poem or other passage that speaks of love or of some other personal concern might somehow be incorporated into their wedding ceremony. All sorts of pop lyrics have also been used by couples at weddings, an astounding phenomenon of "church weddings" in which readings and music had nothing to do with the Church. Interestingly, this phenomenon is relatively rare in many Protestant denominations. This "secularization" of religious weddings has been going on for so long that some couples come to prepare their wedding with the expectation that they are supposed to select such secular texts.

The tradition of the Church has set the reading of the word of God apart from non-scriptural readings, with the exception of the Office of Readings, where the non-scriptural reading is usually a commentary or homily on the preceding scripture. In sacred scripture the Christian community has found unsettling challenges as well as uplifting words of comfort. In biblical texts, the Church has found a perennial message that endures.

The scriptures are the Church's heritage, proclaimed in the assembly of believers, its pride and treasure. Couples have ample opportunity to share non-scriptural texts they consider significant with their guests, for instance, at the rehearsal dinner, or the reception, or when then open their gifts. In church, however, the Church proclaims God's word, which, ultimately, is more than enough.

In Conclusion

The authentic celebration of a Christian marriage poses a particularly difficult challenge to the bridal couple and the minister as well. Much in Western society seems to go against the stability of a marriage and against virtues traditionally associated with family life. Divorce is an accepted reality in our contemporary society, yet couples promise to marry "until death."

Often what certain couples think important about married life and the wedding ceremony is far from the virtues reverenced in scripture and by the Christian tradition.

Yet in the face of the many different voices and values present in the world, the Christian community is called to celebrate God's love and God's commitment as embodied in a couple who marry. The readings and symbols that are part of the marriage rite symbolize a couple's personal hopes and the faith of the Christian Church. The wedding celebration should be supportive of them as they begin their new life together. But the wedding rite only marks the beginning of a mystical journey that points toward a life of love and joy.

The mystery that is the sacrament of marriage reveals itself only as the years unfold. It is the mystery of discovering the depths of God's love present in another human being. It is the mystery of finding joy through pain, of the giving up of self to find another, of renouncing individuality to find companionship, of giving love to others only to receive it back in unexpected ways.

Chapter 10

THE GREAT MYSTERY
OF ORDER

Those of the faithful who are consecrated by holy orders are appointed to feed the Church in Christ's name with the word and grace of God. . . . Christ, whom the Father has sanctified and sent into the world, through his apostles has made their successors, the bishops, sharers in his consecration and mission. . . . In virtue of the sacrament of orders, in the image of Christ the eternal High Priest, [presbyters] are consecrated to preach the Gospel, to shepherd the faithful, and to celebrate divine worship as true priests of the New Testament. . . . Strengthened by sacramental grace [deacons] have as their service for the people of God, in communion with the bishop and his college of presbyters, the *diakonia* of liturgy, word, and charity. *(Constitution on the Church, nn. 11, 28, 29)*

I. From Principles . . .

HISTORICAL OVERVIEW

Every human organization has individuals in leadership roles, whether a family or a multinational corporation. It is not surprising that Christian communities from the time of Jesus have had people in such roles. What is different, at least in the ideal, about leadership within Christianity is its imitation of Christ as servant. Those who are called to the mystery of leadership in the Christian community are also called to conform to the Lord's words, "whoever would be great among you must be your servant" (MT 20:26).

The reason for being a servant is imitation of Christ, since "the Son of Man came not to be served but to serve" (MT 20:28). Those who would imitate Christ's care for others, like the Good Shepherd, are invited to imitate the shepherd's goodness by being willing to lay down their lives for the flock (JN 10:11). The servant dimension of Christian leadership is given dramatic expression by the Lord himself who on the night before he died took on the role of a slave and washed the feet of the disciples (cf. JN 13:4–17).

An analysis of the Acts of the Apostles, the letters of Paul and other New Testament writings suggests that leadership in early Christianity often was based on God-given gifts, on charisms. Different titles sometimes were given the different individuals who used their gifts for the sake of the community. Preachers, prophets, teachers, healers, speakers in tongues, interpreters, all coexisted in the community (cf. 1 COR 12:28–30).

By the beginning of the second century the leadership structure stabilized. One sometimes disputed theory is that the Christian community adopted structures of leadership from two different sources and eventually blended them together. In certain Jewish communities, the leadership format consisted of a council of elders, which is *presbuteroi* in Greek. A Greek leadership format consisted of a single overseer with several assistants. The title of the "overseer" was *episkopos* in Greek. The English word "supervisor," based on Latin, means the same as *episkopos*. The assistants to the *episkopos* were called servants, *diakonoi* in Greek. The contemporary English terms for these leadership roles are bishop (derived from *episkopos*), presbyter or priest (derived from *presbuteros*), and deacon (derived from *diakonos*).

In Acts 20:17, Paul summons the elders of the Church at Miletus to Ephesus where he addresses them. In the course of this address, he speaks about these elders taking care of the flock over which the Holy Spirit made them *episkopoi* (overseers) (ACTS 20:28). Here the "supervision" of the flock was one of the ministries that elders exercised.[1]

The ministry of "supervision" becoming limited to one person per town may not have occurred until the second century. It is only in the letters of Ignatius of Antioch (who died around the year 107) that we begin to see a standardized structure for leadership in communities to which he wrote. This structure consisted of three offices: a single bishop, a group of presbyters, and a group of deacons.[2] It is Ignatius' position that one of the prime duties of the bishop is to lead the eucharistic celebration. For example in his letter to the Smyrnaeans, Ignatius writes: "Only that eucharist is valid which is celebrated by the bishop or by his delegate" (Chapter 8). Although his letters to various Christian communities repeatedly mention reverencing the bishop of the town and respecting the presbyters and deacons, such references are oddly lacking in the letter to the Romans.

PRIESTS AND PRESBYTERS

We have often used the English word "priest" as a translation of the Latin *presbyter* or the Greek *presbuteros* as well as a translation of the Latin *sacerdos* or the Greek *hiereus.* The *presbuteros* was an elder who exercised leadership as part of a group. In contrast, when the letter to the Hebrews speaks about the priesthood of Christ or when St. Peter speaks about the Christian community being a priestly people, a form of the word *hiereus* is used. The *hiereus* offers sacrifice to God, and the way that Christians, including presbyters and bishops, offer sacrifice is by sharing in the hieratic priesthood of Christ.

In contemporary ecclesiastical texts, *presbyter* is a word used specifically for the second of the three orders of deacon, presbyter (priest), and bishop. Because of the centuries-old tradition of interpreting the presidency at the eucharist as the office of offering sacrifice in the person of Christ, *sacerdos* is applied to those ministers (bishops and presbyters) who preside at the eucharist. [3]

Those unaccustomed to using two different English words to refer to two different biblical concepts may be mystified by the recent attempt to regain an ancient distinction. However, such a distinction in fact can help clarify the role of presbyters who also with all the baptized share in the holy and royal priesthood of Christ (1 PET 2:5, 9).

EARLY INSTITUTION CEREMONIES

One early reference to appointing individuals to a particular role occurs early in the Acts of the Apostles (ACTS 6:1–6), in which seven individuals are chosen "to serve table" (in Greek, *diakonein trapezais*). Their institution in this office in the community was accomplished by prayer and the laying on of hands (ACTS 6:6). Although this incident is popularly understood as the ordination of the first deacons, scripture scholars caution us not to apply later ecclesiastical designations to this event.

A kind of institution rite initiating someone into the office of overseer is mentioned in Paul's letter to Timothy (1 TIM 4:14), where Paul refers to the action of the community's elders laying hands on Timothy and the gift he received as a result of this ritual activity. The laying on of hands is again referred to later in the same letter (1 TIM 5:22). Earlier in this letter, Paul describes the qualifications of overseers and of servants (3:1–13) and later he speaks about elders (5:17–19).

The *Apostolic Tradition* of Hippolytus describes the ordination rite of a bishop (Chapters 2–4) as well as those of presbyters and deacons (Chapters 7, 8). Each of these orders is conferred by the laying on of hands of at least the presiding bishop and by prayer. The picture given by this document is of a church leadership structure that includes three major ministries: that of a deacon, a presbyter, and a bishop. Besides these ranks or orders, there are other ministries in the church. Subsequent chapters (9–14) describe the offices of confessor, widow, subdeacon, virgin, reader, and healer. The *Apostolic Tradition* specifically mentions that those who become members of these other ranks do not receive the laying on of hands.

As the centuries progressed, it became an established custom that those to be ordained bishops must first have been ordained presbyters, and those to be ordained presbyters must first have been ordained deacons. In contrast, the *Apostolic Tradition* states: "if a confessor has been in prison for the name of the Lord, you do not lay hands on him for the offices of presbyter or deacon. He has the office of the presbyter by his confession. If he is made bishop, however, hands are to be laid on him" (Chapter 9).

MEDIEVAL WESTERN ORDINATION RITES

The laying on of hands is a foundational element in the history of Christian liturgy and finds its origin in scripture. Both the New Testament and early Christian documents speak about commissioning individuals in ministry through the laying on of hands and prayer. Although this tradition was never lost from ordination rites, as the centuries progressed additional ritual elements were introduced into the ordination ceremonies. Eventually these new and secondary ritual elements became so prominent that in practice and in explanations they overshadowed what was historically the central moment of the ordination rite—prayer and the laying on of hands. Thus in the ordination of deacons, a ritual for the handing over of the book of the gospels came to be seen as the central moment of the rite. In the ordination of priests the most important rite came to be seen as the handing over of the paten and chalice immediately after the anointing and binding of the candidate's hands.

When describing the Roman Church's understanding of the sacraments as a basis for union with the Armenian Church, the decree of the Council of Florence, *Exultate Deo* (November 22, 1439), stated that the core elements (the matter and form) of the sacrament of ordination are the *traditiones* (the handing-over ceremonies). This decree makes no reference to prayer and laying on of hands. At this time, the Western Church considered central certain elements not found in the rituals of the Eastern Churches or even in the ancient rituals of the West. Inspired by the impetus of the early leaders of the Liturgical Movement, Pope Pius XII in 1947 issued the Apostolic Constitution *Sacramentum Ordinis* in which he addressed the central rites of ordination and determined what was to be considered the core ritual, that is, the matter and form of the sacrament. His determination restored the centrality of the action of the laying on of hands with the accompanying prayer that corresponds to the order being conferred.

Aside from the question of which of the many ritual elements were to be considered central, there were other problems associated with the sacrament of orders as understood in the Western Church. One major problem dealt with which three ministries were considered part of this sacrament.

For centuries, the Western Church had an order of subdeacon, which was considered to be a "major order," along with that of deacon and priest. The "minor orders" in the West were the four ranks of doorkeeper (porter), exorcist, reader, and acolyte. It was sometimes taught that the three ranks that comprised the sacrament of orders were, in fact, the major orders of subdeacon, deacon, and priest. Even the Council of Florence explicitly mentions the subdiaconate when speaking about the sacrament of orders. A related question that the Church in the West debated was whether the order of bishop was truly distinct from that of presbyter. Some held that the episcopal institution ceremony conferred additional jurisdiction to a bishop but no additional sacramental "character," other than the "character" of the priesthood. For this reason, the liturgical books spoke about the "consecration" of a bishop, rather than his ordination.

Other problems dealt with the ceremonies themselves. For instance, one aspect that led to a lack of clarity was the placement of ritual elements throughout the mass. The central ordination rites occurred at various points during the introductory rites and the liturgy of the word. For example, presbyteral ordination occurred immediately prior to the Alleluia before the gospel. However, after communion the newly ordained presbyters recited the Apostles' Creed and received the command to forgive sins. Since during the ordination ceremony itself, the newly ordained was vested in a chasuble in which the back part was folded up, the chasuble was now completely unfolded. Finally, the newly ordained made a promise of obedience to the bishop and received from him a kiss of peace.

There were other archaic ritual features in the rites. For instance, a presbyteral ordination included a final admonition that the newly ordained should "learn diligently from experienced priests the whole order of mass, particularly the consecration and breaking of the host, and the communion, before you proceed to celebrate mass," as if they had not attended a seminary. There was the practice of binding the hands of a newly ordained priest together with a cloth (called the *manutergium*) after the bishop had anointed the hands with the oil of the catechumens. The priest gave this cloth to his mother who, upon her death, was buried with the *manutergium* wrapped around her own hands.

Although the newly ordained priest concelebrated the mass with the bishop, the rite gave the impression of simultaneous masses rather than concelebration. Each priest in unison with the bishop recited all the prayers from the offertory onward until communion. At communion, each newly ordained knelt and received the host on his tongue from the hand of the bishop. They then drank from a chalice of unconsecrated wine held by an assisting priest.

When compared with other liturgical practices of the period, the ordination rites seem to have totally overshadowed the significance of other rites. When present at mass, few laity participated in eucharistic communion, and the liturgical rites for celebrating marriage and confirmation were austere to an extreme. Meanwhile, the rites for ordaining bishops, presbyters, and deacons become more and more complicated, in some ways imitating the ancient rites of initiation that had fallen into disuse.

The various features in the old ordination rites obscured what was central in tradition and the resulting confusion was felt by the clergy as well as by the laity.

REVISED ORDINATION RITES

In 1968, Pope Paul VI approved the text of the ordination rites revised by the post-conciliar liturgical Consilium. As with other sacramental rites revised after the Second Vatican Council, these rites now occur during mass after the word is proclaimed. The revision has attempted to highlight what is primary, to deemphasize what is secondary, and to eliminate archaic gestures or formulas.

A similar structure is followed for the ordination of bishops, presbyters, and deacons, which is basically as follows:

After the gospel, those to be ordained are called by name and are presented to the ordaining bishop. For someone who is to be ordained a bishop, an apostolic mandate is read, to which the assembly gives its consent. Those to be ordained priests or deacons are "elected" by the bishop, to which the assembly gives its consent. After this the homily follows.

After the homily, the candidates are examined as a group through a series of questions asked by the bishop. As part of these questions, those to be ordained deacons make a promise of celibacy unless they are married. Then those to be ordained deacons or priests individually make a promise of obedience received by the bishop. The core ritual elements—prayer and the laying on of hands—occur next.

All present join in prayer for those to be ordained. The litany of the saints is sung, during which the candidates lie prostrate.

After the litany, the bishop imposes hands on the candidates. When a bishop is ordained, all bishops present do the same. When priests are ordained, all priests present may also impose hands. When deacons are ordained, only the bishop imposes hands.

After the imposition of hands, a solemn prayer of consecration is proclaimed by the presiding bishop. For each order a separate prayer is used, which is considered to be essential for the conferral of the sacrament.[4] When a bishop is ordained, during the consecratory prayer two deacons hold an open *Book of Gospels* over the bishop-elect's head.

With the completion of the consecratory prayer after the imposition of hands, the candidates are considered ordained. The rites that follow are "explanatory rites" that help emphasize particular aspects of each order.

Bishops are anointed on the head with chrism and then are presented with the *Book of Gospels*, receive the mitre, ring, and pastoral staff, and are formally seated on the bishop's chair.

Deacons and priests are first vested in the vestments of their order by fellow deacons and priests (rather than by the ordaining bishop, as happened in the former rite). The formulas that formerly accompanied putting on each vestment have been omitted. After the vesting, deacons are presented with the *Book of Gospels* and priests are anointed on their hands with chrism (rather than the oil of the catechumens) and then are presented with the bread and wine for the eucharist on a plate and in the cup.[5]

Each ordination rite ends with the kiss of peace exchanged as a sign of welcome into the new order. The ordaining bishop first greets each of the newly ordained and then others in the same order may also exchange the peace (for instance, if deacons were ordained, they now are greeted by their fellow deacons). After this exchange, the liturgy continues with the preparation of the altar, and the newly ordained participate fully according to their new order among the other ordained ministers.

In 1989, a second edition of the rites of ordination was published. This rite now includes an Introduction similar to those found for other sacramental rites. More importantly, however, certain prayers were amended to correct what some suggested were deficiencies in the earlier texts. In particular, the consecratory prayer for presbyteral ordination has been enriched by new references to the Holy Spirit and to sacramental ministry.

II . . . to Practice

CELEBRATION OF THE CHURCH

In origin and ideal, ordained ministry in the Christian community is for service to the community. This community is already united in the common and foundational sacramental mystery of baptism, which has united them to Christ and thus to one another. The sacrament of orders is meant to serve the ordered life of the community. Through this sacramental mystery, certain Christians are officially constituted as special servants for the community.

These servants often have greater visiblity than other members of the

Church. This heightened visibility may even suggest that they are the Church and not servants of the Church. Leaders of any organization are not the totality of what they lead. It may even be necessary to remind ourselves that, within the Church, the ordained ministers—bishops, presbyters, deacons— are not the Church, but are servants of the Church in their exercise of leadership.

It is unfortunate that theological reflection and the social climate led to an interpretation of the mystery of orders as a "setting apart" of the ordained from the baptized. Excessive emphasis was put on the jurisdiction and the power of the ordained to perform certain sacred rites. The focus shifted from service to power, from the community to the minister over and above the community, from the person's *acting* as a minister to *being* a minister. The spirit of humble service, emphasized in Matthew's gospel, was overlooked as the Church seemed to become engulfed in legalism and in power struggles.

Leadership in human society is an ambiguous institution. It is rare to find political or religious figures who do not receive more than their share of criticism, some of which is justified. Jesus himself criticized the religious authorities of his day who did not "practice what they preached" (MT 23:4). Although power sometimes corrupts (as the proverb says), more often it seems that prestige breeds complacency. In addition, tasks that once energized leaders can, because of sheer magnitude, easily turn into burdens that sap a person's strength.

Problems associated with leadership, even within the Church, are not new. In a sixth century homily, St. Gregory the Great wrote:

> Look about you and see how full the world is of priests, yet in God's harvest a laborer is rarely to be found; for although we have accepted the priestly office, we do not fulfill its demands. . . . [We] are called bishops to our detriment, for we retain the honorable office but fail to practice the virtues proper to it.[6]

In spite of the renewal experienced by the Church after the Second Vatican Council, some of the piety of earlier centuries continues to influence the way ordained ministers exercise their roles of service in the Church and the ways that ordinations are celebrated (despite the revision of these rites).

The link between an ordained minister and a community served by that minister was perceived to be so strong and so necessary that the Council of Chalcedon (451) condemned any "absolute consecration," that is, ordination outside of the context of a particular community. Canon 6 of that Council suggests that the ordination of anyone not called by a particular community is null and void. In other words, deacons, priests, and bishops are not ordained merely to *be* ministers but to *act* as ministerial servants for the sake of a particular community.[7]

ORDER AND THE CHURCH

Liturgical and canonical tradition, past and present, officially refers to the mystery of ministry as the "sacrament of order" (in the singular, *sacramentum ordinis*, as in canon 1008). The use of the singular is deliberate. If the sacrament was called holy orders, one cannot but be conscious of the several ranks of ministry and of the individuals who are ordained to each rank. On the other hand, if the sacrament is called holy order, we may be led to think of the Church as a whole, and how order is necessary in the Church through leadership. The focus of *order* is the Church, but the focus of *orders* may seem to be the individuals who have been ordained.

CELEBRATING ORDINATION RITES

During liturgical celebrations, sensitivity is demanded toward various groups in the Church, especially groups that have been largely overlooked or excluded in the past. An ordination liturgy sometimes can be a time of heightened tension since it highlights the existing reality that the Catholic Church does not ordain women and is therefore dominated by males in leadership positions. In addition, ordination rites often tend to emphasize the prerogatives of the ordained ministers over and above the ministries exercised by the non-ordained.

The revised ordination rites were approved in 1968, one of the first sacramental rites to be revised. As a result, the revision suffers from a lack of the insights that have been gained in the past two decades. Although some textual changes were incorporated into the second edition published in 1989, other practices remain unchanged. The rites are often perceived by many as being too self-congratulatory especially for those called to service in the Church. Unfortunately, certain additional elements occasionally included exacerbate this situation.

For example, in order to provide public testimony as a response to the bishop's question, "Do you know if they are worthy?" in some places individuals are invited to testify to the ministerial qualifications of those to be ordained. These statements often sound as if they were meant for canonization rites or retirement parties rather than for someone embarking on a new ministry. Another result of these "eulogies" is that they tend to distance the ordained ministers further from the people they serve.

In some places, the vesting of the newly ordained is done by family members or the kiss of peace that concludes the rites is immediately extended to everyone. Such adaptations are minor but are sometimes included without an appreciation for the values that are part of the official rite. At these two moments in the rite, the older members of an order assist or greet those newly ordained in the same order. Although these moments may seem exclusive or cliquish, they can be moments of poignancy if the representatives are judiciously chosen. For example, it can be a very moving experience to see a newly ordained priest being vested by an older priest well-respected for his ministry, or to witness a newly ordained exchanging peace with a venerated retired priest. Such moments can be symbols of hope for the community— hope that God's grace will enable the new priests to follow in the footsteps of the beloved servants of previous generations. Similar rituals exist in popular traditions at weddings, where the bride and groom are assisted by the married women and married men. Among certain nationalities, for instance, it is customary for the older married women to gather at some point during the reception and ritually remove the bride's veil.

It is undeniable that all Christians are made equal in Christ through their baptism (cf. GAL 3:27–28), yet it is also true that the tradition of the Church has given rise to a leadership structure that is hierarchical. The challenge at an ordination, as at every sacramental celebration, is to balance the tradition of the Church with the pastoral needs and sensitivities of the assembly. Since certain ritual elements may be more counter-productive than they seem at first glance, a related challenge is to scrutinize both established practices and customs as well as any possible adaptations to identify what will truly speak of service in the Church today.

In Conclusion

Through their ordination, bishops, presbyters, and deacons have expressed their willingness to imitate Christ as servant and shepherd. One of the most common images of the ordained has been that of an *alter Christus*, "another Christ." The Second Vatican Council reiterated the tradition that presbyters take on the image of Christ and share in the office of Christ as mediator.[8] But even as early as the second century, St. Ignatius of Antioch advised the Trallians that they should obey the bishop as if he were Jesus as well as respect the deacons as they do Christ.[9]

Each in their own way, bishops, presbyters, and deacons, have accepted the task to preach the gospel, to teach the faithful, and to care for the less fortunate. Though the ministry of each order has evolved over the centuries, what remains the same is service of the Church both in society and at worship. The specific demands and challenges of each order were well summarized in the Second Vatican Council's *Constitution on the Church, Decree on the Pastoral Office of Bishops in the Church,* and *Decree on the Ministry and Life of Priests.*

In continuing the biblical tradition of "supervision," a bishop presides over a local Church. In particular, the bishop is the one who moderates the sacramental life of his Church, leading fellow Christians to a deeper appreciation of the mystery of Christ's death and resurrection. In particular he does this by presiding at the eucharist, initiating people into the Christian community, and ordaining priests and deacons to serve the local flock. Following ancient tradition,

> it is very fitting that when the bishop . . . is present at a liturgical celebration in which a congregation takes part, he personally preside. The reason for this is not to give added outward solemnity to the rite, but to make the celebration a more striking sign of the mystery of the Church. . . .
>
> The preeminent manifestation of the local Church is present when the bishop, as high priest of his flock, celebrates the eucharist and particularly when he celebrates in the cathedral, surrounded by his college of presbyters and by his ministers, and with the full, active participation of all God's holy people.[10]

As co-workers with bishops, presbyters exercise their ministry most visibly when they preside at the eucharist in local communities and when they lead other sacramental celebrations, commonly those of baptism, penance, anointing of the sick, and marriage. With bishops, presbyters also imitate Christ as teacher and sanctifier. In the sample homily included in the rite of presbyteral ordination, those to be ordained are told to "teach what you believe, and put into practice what you teach." One of the most common titles of Christ found in the gospels is "Teacher," and by their sharing of God-given wisdom with others, presbyters become an icon of Christ the Teacher and continue a hallowed Judeo-Christian tradition. As the prophet Malachi said: "Instruction is to be sought from the mouth of the priest, because he is the messenger of the LORD of hosts" (MAL 2:7).[11]

Deacons assist the bishop and his presbyters in serving the people of God in the *diakonia* of liturgy, word, and charity.[12] In the Roman and Byzantine liturgies, the deacon is the minister who proclaims the gospel and who leads the assembly in prayer by proclaiming the intentions of litanies. A deacon also assists at the altar by caring for the chalice and ministering the Lord's blood during communion. According to current Roman law, when necessary, deacons may preside at baptisms and marriages. The deacon's role of servant at the liturgy is mirrored in the deacon's ministry of charity in the community as well.

The mystery of the Church is the mystery of Christ, the head, and Christians, the body. The mystery of the Church is the mystery of different gifts given to different individuals. The mystery of the Church is the mystery of unity through diversity, of differences without divisions. The mystery of the Church is the mystery of leadership that is based on serving rather than on being served.

Chapter 11

THE MYSTERY OF DEATH
AND THE RITES FOR THE DEAD

At the funerals of its children the Church confidently celebrates Christ's paschal mystery. Its intention is that those who by baptism were made one body with the dead and risen Christ may with him pass from death to life. In soul they are to be cleansed and taken up into heaven with the saints and elect; in body they await the blessed hope of Christ's coming and the resurrection of the dead. *(Introduction, 1969 Ordo Exsequiarum, n. 1)*

I. *From Principles . . .*

HISTORICAL OVERVIEW

The celebration of the mystery of a death of a faithful Christian is ultimately the celebration of that person's *dies natalis* or "birthday" into paradise. Most feast days of saints that are celebrated during the year are, in fact, observed on the day of their death. For Christians, the paradigm of a faith-filled death is Christ's own death, a passage from a life in this world, a life in time, to a life in paradise, a life in eternity. Since Christ's paschal mystery is one event with several moments, we cannot separate Christ's death from his resurrection. And so also, for every Christian, the mystery of death is bound up with the mystery of Christ's victory over death.

St. Paul reminds us that through baptism each Christian is united to Christ in his death, a union that becomes the promise of the resurrection (ROM 6:3–5). Thus, the entire life of a Christian is, in some sense, ordered toward a death that is transfigured into a share in the new life of the resurrection. Paul continues his theme when he proclaims: "I tell you a mystery: we shall not all sleep, but we shall all be changed. . . . 'Where, O Death, is your victory?

138

Where, O Death, is your sting?' . . . Thanks be to God who has given us the victory through our Lord Jesus Christ" (1 COR 15:51–57).

The Christian rites associated with honoring the dead, praying for them, and committing their mortal remains to the earth were initially derived from Jewish customs and adapted to Christian beliefs, especially belief in a personal afterlife. From the gospel accounts of the death of Lazarus and of Jesus, we know that at that time, the dead were wrapped with a shroud into which spices and perfumes were placed, and the body was either buried in the earth or entombed in a cave.

Christian funeral rites and customs throughout the centuries have been influenced by various situations in which the Church has found itself and by the various cultures in which Christians have lived. In the days of persecution and martyrdom, customs surrounding the dead were necessarily minimal and often consisted of obtaining the remains and with some haste interring them in a shelf in subterranean catacombs with reverence and prayer. Customs and superstitions meant that the dead would often be buried within a day after expiring, if not within hours. Up until recent times, family members took care of preparing the body for burial or entombment and even in building the coffin.[1]

One of the earliest rituals associated with funerals was the public procession with the body to the place of burial, a procession that, for some, became an image of the pilgrimage to the new Jerusalem. During such a procession, it was common to sing appropriate psalms, litanies, and short hymns. By the medieval period, funerals commonly included some sort of services in conjunction with the procession. A service took place at three locations: the place of death (or the home), the church, and the place of burial. There are, now, two processions motivated by the practical necessity of first moving the body of the deceased from the place of death or from the deceased's home to the church, and then moving the body from the church to the place of burial. As the emphasis shifted more and more toward the services in the church and at the grave, the processions became merely pragmatic and secondary.

THE PRE-VATICAN II RITUAL

Those Catholics who remember the rites of the dead that predate the reforms of Vatican II often comment on the dreary atmosphere that the black vestments, mournful chants, and dread-filled prayers conveyed to the mourners. The rites were consistent with a theological perspective that emphasized human failure and divine justice, rather than human goodness and divine mercy, and emphasized the sacrificial death of Christ, rather than Christ's victory over sin and death. There was often the fear in the minds of the faithful that those who had died were not worthy of being with God in heaven, and that even if they were worthy, they likely would suffer the pains of purgatory for quite a while, or if they had committed a mortal sin and had not confessed it, they would be condemned to the fires of hell for eternity.

Before the reforms of Vatican II, the religious aspect of a funeral of an American Catholic often followed this pattern: The body of the deceased would be prepared for burial and the coffin placed in an appropriate room at a funeral parlor or in the home of the deceased. Relatives and friends would gather at the ordinarily open coffin so that people could pay their respects and offer condolences to family members. Sometimes the visitation of the deceased and the family was extended over several days. If there was some sort of service during this period of the wake, especially among some ethnic groups it often consisted merely of the recitation of the rosary. On the day of the funeral mass, the family gathered around the coffin, bid farewell, and then the coffin was closed, after which the procession to the church took place. In small towns, this could be a public affair, with a priest and assisting ministers leading the procession and family and friends all walking behind the coffin.

After entering the church, the coffin was placed before the altar, draped with a black pall, and surrounded with six large candlesticks containing unbleached wax candles. The ritual book prescribed that the coffin of a lay person should be oriented so that the feet were closest to the altar, and the coffin of an ordained cleric should be oriented so that the head was closest to the altar (imitating the orientation of the individual during the celebration of mass).

The funeral mass was celebrated with black vestments and often sung by a small choir of school children or by an individual singer who sometimes was the organist as well. The sung parts of the liturgy consisted of the prescribed antiphons found in the *Roman Missal* including the lengthy sequence before the gospel, *Dies Irae*:

> Day of wrath, that dreadful day,
> when heav'n and earth shall in ashes lay,
> as David and the Sybil say.
>
> What horror shall invade the mind
> when the approaching judge shall sift and find
> and judge the deeds of humankind.
>   . . .

Sometimes the priest gave a eulogy in which some of the good deeds of the deceased were extolled, but often without reference to Christian beliefs or the resurrection of the Lord.

In the Tridentine missal, there were certain rubrical distinctions associated with masses for the dead, for example, omitting Psalm 43 during the prayers at the foot of the altar, omitting the prayer for peace and the exchange of peace among the ordained ministers, changing the "have mercy on us" of the *Agnus Dei* to "grant them rest," and omitting the final blessing. These distinctions added to the impression that the funeral mass was meant to be very somber and austere.

The ritual celebrated in the church immediately following the funeral mass consisted of two prayers that begged God's forgiveness, and in effect constituted a final request to grant absolution to the deceased for his or her sins. After the first prayer, the responsory *Libera me, Domine* was sung in which the choir prayed, "Deliver me, O Lord, from everlasting death on that day of terror: When the heavens and the earth will be shaken. . . . I am in fear and trembling at the judgment and the wrath that is to come. . . . That day will be a day of wrath, of misery, and of ruin: a day of grandeur and great horror. . . ." From our contemporary perspective, it was fortunate that the prayers and responsory were in Latin and that very few in the congregation knew what the words meant.

After the responsory, the silent recitation of the Lord's Prayer was accompanied by sprinkling the coffin with holy water and by incensing it, actions associated in the earlier ritual books with purification or blessing rites. After the second prayer, the body was then taken in procession to the cemetery and buried with prayers that spoke more about human sinfulness and about keeping the departed from eternal damnation than about any hope in sharing the resurrection of Christ. In the United States it was common to offer several additional prayers in English, including prayers for the bystanders. It was also not uncommon, among certain nationalities, to have testimonials at the graveside in honor of the deceased after the Church's rites were finished.

It was forbidden to celebrate the funeral mass for Catholics who had not been married in the Church or were public sinners. If someone wished to be buried with non-Catholic relatives in a non-Catholic cemetery, a priest could not officiate at the graveside service. Cremation was forbidden by Church law because of its association with cults that denied the resurrection of the body.

The Gregorian chant and the liturgical symbols that were part of Catholic funerals in the decades before Vatican II often gave solace to the mourners and supported their faith. But, in general, the customs and prayers in the liturgical books did not give much witness to the Christian belief of sharing in the promise of the resurrection of Christ.

The Order of Christian Funerals

The *Constitution on the Sacred Liturgy*[2] mandated a reform of the rites of burial to bring out their paschal character, and specifically mentioned that this might affect the color of vestments used. As a result, one of the first set of rites revised after the Council was the collection of rites pertaining to Catholic funerals. First published in Latin in 1969 as the *Ordo Exsequiarum*, the English version of these revised rites is now titled the *Order of Christian Funerals*. Recognizing a diversity of local customs and situations, this revised ritual gave some general plans but permits regional developments consistent with the general outlook and thrust of the rites.[3]

The norms of the rites and the texts strike a balance between acknowledging human grief, begging forgiveness for sin and imperfections, and proclaiming faith in God's mercy and Christ's victory over death in his own resurrection. As a general norm, violet vestments may be used in place of black,[4] but countries may also determine other alternatives, and many places (including the United States) permit the use of white as consistent with the paschal nature of Christian funerals.[5]

The rites, as the norm, continue the ancient tradition of marking the death of a Christian with three services separated by two processions. The first service may take one of several forms. One option is a brief service, similar to what was found in the 1614 *Ritual*, in which the mourners are greeted, a psalm (or other passage of scripture) is read, and a prayer offered. The procession to the church then takes place. Other forms provide a more formal, liturgical wake at the funeral home or at the home of the deceased. This service is flexible, but should normally include scripture reading and prayers. Noted by its absence in the *Order of Christian Funerals* is any reference to the former custom of saying the rosary. (The rosary is understood not as public ritual prayer but as the private devotion of individuals.) After the wake, there is a procession from the home of the deceased or the funeral parlor to the church.

In English speaking countries, it is now customary to greet the body at the entrance of the church with holy water as a baptismal reminder and then clothe the coffin with a white pall, a reminder of the white baptismal garment,[6] after which the body is brought before the altar. The liturgy of the word takes place during which a sung Alleluia may be used. The sequence *Dies Irae* is no longer included among the texts for use at a funeral mass. There are numerous options for scripture readings at services for the dead and most speak of God's mercy and comfort, Christ's victory over death, or the beauties of heaven. There is relatively little emphasis on sin. The prayers do continue to speak about human sin and failure, but also about God's mercy toward someone who shared in the eucharist. There are also prayers for the mourners, a happy addition to what was available in the former ritual.

The service with which the funeral mass concludes is recast as a farewell rite, called the final commendation rather than the "absolution."[7] As the Introduction to the 1969 *Ordo Exsequiarum* states: "The meaning of the rite does not signify a kind of purification of the deceased; that is what the eucharistic sacrifice accomplishes."[8] The center of this rite is the song of farewell, which is sung by all present and should be "the high point of the entire rite."[9] The priest introduces the song with a brief address to the assembly, and then concludes with a prayer. As part of the introduction, a friend or relative of the deceased may briefly address the assembly. During the song, the coffin may be incensed and sprinkled with holy water. After the concluding prayer, the body of the deceased is carried out of the church, followed by the mourners, and a procession to the cemetery takes place.

Since the most important moments of the entire sequence of rites have already taken place, that is, the eucharist and the final commendation, the graveside service is deliberately austere. It should be seen as a conclusion to the liturgical service that normally immediately precedes it, rather than as a separate service. The function of this service as a concluding rite is most evident in situations such as in small towns where the cemetery is located next to the church, and all go in procession from the church to the graveside. Ideally, this final service begins with blessing the grave or giving thanks to God (if the grave was already blessed). Then the coffin is lowered into the grave while the statement of committal is proclaimed. Finally those present join in general intercessions, the Lord's Prayer, and a final prayer for the dead (and for the mourners).

An interim English translation of the 1969 *Ordo Exsequiarum* was used for over a decade. In the early 1980s English-speaking countries were presented with the *Order of Christian Funerals*, prepared by the International Commission on English in the Liturgy (ICEL). In this new edition, all the texts were presented in a revised translation, included were abundant pastoral notes that expanded on the Latin rubrics, and the texts were arranged in sections that facilitated their use by ministers. The ICEL version was further adapted by those English-speaking episcopal conferences that accepted it as their standard text to reflect national practices and circumstances.

II . . . to Practice

FUNERAL SYMBOLS

The pastoral notes in the *Order of Christian Funerals* comment on traditional symbols used in the liturgical rites for the dead, symbols sometimes taken for granted.[10]

The Easter candle recalls Christ's light shining in the darkness and his victory over death. It may stand near the coffin during the liturgy in church. The coffin may also be surrounded by other candles, as was the custom in the

1614 *Ritual,* and this practice may be appropriate in places where the Easter candle cannot easily be moved.

Holy water is a special reminder of baptism and is normally used when the body is greeted at the door of the church.

Although not found in the *Ordo Exsequiarum,* the *Order of Christian Funerals* permits the use of a funeral pall. The pall is a reminder of the white garment of baptism and serves the purpose of covering the coffin during the liturgy, signifying that all are equal in death before God.

Pastoral notes of the *Order of Christian Funerals* highlight the fact that draping a national flag over a coffin during mass as a substitute for the pall is not an acceptable practice.[11] This later admonition has met with opposition by some groups, but the liturgical principle stands—flags are emblems that can separate one Christian from another, but the liturgy is a place for unity.

Incense is used to honor what is holy and its use during the final commendation reminds us that the human body is a temple of the Holy Spirit. In addition, Psalm 141 associates the rising of incense smoke with prayers offered to God.

The *Book of Gospels* or a bible may be placed on the coffin as a reminder that God's word is the source of Christian living.

Aside from these traditional symbols, restraint is appropriate during the liturgical rites. It would be preferable to display any special personal mementos of the deceased at receptions before or after the funeral rites rather than try to incorporate them into the liturgy.

NATIONAL VARIATIONS

Because of regional funeral customs, there are currently more variations in national editions of the *Order of Christian Funerals* than in some of the other ritual books. Because of these differences, visiting priests who preside at funerals in other English-speaking countries should carefully examine the local edition, instead of assuming that all the rites are the same as at home. The following provide a sample of the variations.

- The Canadian edition includes two introductions to be used at the greeting of the body at the door of the church that are rather different from the formulas printed in the British, Irish, and American versions. They are statements welcoming the body of the deceased as the person was once welcomed on the day of baptism.

- The Irish edition does not include the rite of reception at the beginning of the mass since it is common custom that the body is brought to a parish church earlier.

- The British edition contains a separate section for the burial or entombment of remains after cremation. This section includes prayers that are found in appendices in the American edition. This is an acknowledgment of the situation in Great Britain, in which cremation is chosen by over 70% of the population.

- The Canadian edition omits any reference to the practice of a member of the family or a friend speaking about the deceased during the funeral mass (usually immediately before the final commendation). The General Introduction in the Canadian edition notes that it would be appropriate to include such a speech at the vigil service rather than during the eucharistic liturgy. A rubric permitting this practice is included in the American and British editions, although it is placed before the final commendation rather than after the priest's introduction, as in the *Ordo Exsequiarum*.

- The Canadian edition includes optional brief explanatory statements before the use of water and incense at the final commendation.

- In the British edition, the pall is placed on the coffin *after* the entrance procession and the positioning of the coffin before the altar. The ritual mentions the custom of carrying Christian symbols, such as the *Book of Gospels*, a bible, or a cross, in the entrance procession and then placing them on the coffin after the pall has been draped over it. Appropriate texts are given in place, rather than in an appendix, as in the U.S. edition.

- The Canadian edition is emphatic that only the pall should be draped over the coffin at the funeral mass. Both in the introduction, and in the introductory rubric to the texts of the funeral mass, the ritual says that national flags and flags or insignia of associations are to be removed at the door of the church. The ritual adds the words "even Christian associations" and even includes the phrase "or symbols of ministry." These specifications in the Canadian edition try to emphasize that those things that distinguish people during life—military service, membership in Catholic fraternal organizations, even ordained ministries within the Church—must not distinguish the dead, who are equal before God.

The variations found in the rituals point out the necessity of being careful when reading commentaries on the different national versions of the *Order of Christian Funerals*. On the one hand, although the general structure of the rite and most of the texts are identical, some detailed suggestions valid for one English-speaking country may not be recommended elsewhere. On the other hand, certain details in a particular version may express wise principles that may be applicable to our own situations.

VIGIL

The vigil service provides a religious focal point for the "wake" period before the funeral. It has long been customary for individuals, both acquaintances and strangers, to visit the funeral parlor and offer condolences to family members of the deceased, and to gaze prayerfully at the face of the deceased for one last time.

Since the former *Ritual* came from an era in which the dead often were buried within hours after expiring, it only included the optional brief rite of greeting the body immediately before the solemn procession to the church for the funeral mass. Nowadays, in most English-speaking countries, several days may pass between death and burial, allowing relatives and friends the opportunity to travel to the funeral services and allowing them some time to come to grips with the reality of death. During this period there is ample time to schedule a vigil before the funeral mass. An evening vigil also provides the opportunity for individuals to worship who might otherwise be unable to participate in worship during the day. It is a special time during which priests and deacons can lead others in praying for the dead and can minister to those grieving. When ordained ministers are not available, a qualified lay person should lead a vigil liturgy using texts provided in the *Order of Christian Funerals*.

The sample service follows what has become the standard pattern for a liturgy of the word, namely, a greeting, opening prayer, scripture reading and psalm singing, followed by a brief homily. The homily is followed by intercessions, the Lord's Prayer, and a concluding rite that includes the blessing of those present.

Appropriate hymns are encouraged, and the *Order of Christian Funerals* presupposes music at least during the vigil, the funeral mass, and at the graveside. It is difficult to imagine a more pastoral role for a music minister than at a vigil service for the dead.

The vigil provides a fitting time and surroundings for friends or relatives to offer some reflections and reminiscences about the deceased, a far more appropriate setting rather than at the end of the funeral mass.

Any such address should be brief, not duplicating or overshadowing a homily either in content, length, or oratorical style. It should not be a eulogy, either. Often, a long-time friend of the deceased may be asked to "say a few words," but if the text is not written out, or if the person is not accustomed to speaking in public, the "few words" can easily expand into a major speech.

The basic structure of the vigil is flexible, and prayer and readings should be chosen to fit the situation of the deceased and the mourners. For such services, when those present are from various religious backgrounds, the General Instruction of the Roman Missal offers wise counsel:

> Pastors should, moreover, take into special account those who are present at a liturgical celebration or hear the Gospel only because of the funeral. These may be non-Catholics or Catholics who never or rarely share in the eucharist or who have apparently lost the faith. Priests are, after all, ministers of Christ's Gospel for all people.[12]

OTHER MOMENTS FOR COMMUNAL PRAYING

The *Order of Christian Funerals* also provides texts for other short services before the funeral mass that can appropriately be used according to various circumstances.[13] In many cases, the one who may lead the service may be a priest, deacon, or member of a parish support group. But in some situations it would be fitting for a medical staff person, a funeral director, or a family member to lead these rites of the Church.

"Prayers after Death" might be used in a hospital room or a home to comfort the family when a person has just died. It might also be used if a pastoral minister visits family members after hearing about the death.

"Gathering in the Presence of the Body" might be led by someone who is with the family when they first view the body in the coffin and before friends and relatives come to pay respects. This moment can be traumatic and at the same time the right moment for prayer.

In many places, on the day of the burial the family gathers at the coffin to take the deceased to the church. "Transfer of the Body to the Church or to the Place of Committal" is the Church's prayer ritual for the closing of the coffin in preparation for this procession. After the coffin is closed, the first funeral procession begins, in which family members accompany the body of the deceased from the home or funeral parlor to the church. In neighborhoods in which a funeral parlor is near the church, such a procession can be public, being led by a crossbearer and involving singing. Meanwhile, at the church other mourners gather to await the arrival of the deceased and the family.

FUNERAL MASS

At the door of the church, the priest greets those present. He then may sprinkle holy water on the coffin while proclaiming a formula that relates this action to baptism. If the baptismal font is near the main entrance of the church, it would be appropriate for the priest to dip his hand in the font and sprinkle the coffin with his wet hand rather than using a separate bucket and sprinkler. Even if the font is some distance away, it would be appropriate as part of the rite to fill a container with water from the font, thus emphasizing the relationship of the sprinkling to the waters of baptism.

The coffin may then be covered with a pall, symbolic of the white baptismal garment. Following this, the procession to the altar takes place during which an appropriate song is sung. In such situations, it may be preferable to use a hymn that has a simple refrain or a litany. When the coffin is in place (and the old custom of orienting the body differently for the ordained and non-ordained may still be observed), Christian symbols, such as the *Book of Gospels*, a bible, or a cross, may be placed on the coffin. Appropriate formulas can be found in the *Order of Christian Funerals*[14] but are not necessary if the symbols are self-evident.

The penitential rite is omitted and the opening prayer follows after the priest venerates the altar and goes to the chair. The liturgy of the word uses appropriate readings from the large selection offered in the *Lectionary*. The homily follows but, as the General Instruction of the Roman Missal states, is "never a eulogy of any kind"[15] since the focus should be on Christian faith and hope in the victory of Christ over death.

The rest of the mass takes place as usual until after communion. It should be emphasized that as much as possible every effort should be made to celebrate the funeral mass as one would celebrate a typical Sunday liturgy. This can be difficult, given the grief that many will feel and the number of non-Catholics present, but these obstacles are no reason for ignoring the basics of good liturgy. For example, throughout the liturgy, congregational singing is essential. Singing by the entire assembly, and not just a soloist, should be encouraged during the entrance procession, the psalm, the gospel acclamation, the acclamations to the eucharistic prayer, and during the communion procession. Communion would be given under both kinds even if this is not the Sunday practice yet, a practice specifically approved for the U.S. in 1970. Appropriate people should exercise their ministry as readers of scripture and of intercessions, or as eucharistic ministers as needed.

Final Commendation

After communion and after the prayer after communion, the usual concluding blessing and dismissal are omitted and the final commendation takes place. This rite is interpreted as a way of commending the deceased to God and bidding farewell through song and prayer.

Immediately before the introduction of the final commendation (that is, *after* the prayer after communion), a friend or relative of the deceased may speak in remembrance of the deceased. Yet, as noted in the Canadian edition, such an address is more appropriate during a vigil.

During the final commendation, the presiding priest normally stands between the altar and the coffin, facing the people, and invites the assembly to participate in this rite through song and prayer. He may use one of the texts in the ritual or his own words.

After a few moments of silence, all should join in singing a song of farewell. The hymn selected should be possible to be sung by all present. During this hymn, the coffin may be incensed and sprinkled with holy water, although if holy water was used during the opening rites, it is better to omit its use here to avoid repeating the use of a symbol.

Following the song of farewell, the priest offers a prayer of commendation, after which the pall and any symbols are removed from the coffin and the procession from the church takes place. The ministers lead with incense and cross, followed by the priest. After the priest come the pallbearers with the coffin, followed by the mourners. During this procession out of the church, the traditional *In paradisum* ("May the angels lead you into paradise") may be sung, or some other song expressing Christian hope in the resurrection.

The abundant use of incense during the final commendation brings to mind the cloud of God's presence, the clouds of heaven. The procession, through poetic imagery, escorts the dead into eternity.

It is appropriate that the ministers and priest lead the coffin and the mourners directly out of the church to the hearse. It was formerly a common custom, though not prescribed by the old *Ritual*, to sprinkle the coffin with holy water as it left the church, but this practice duplicates the previous action and should be discouraged. It was also customary for the priest and ministers to remain in the vestibule of the church rather than to go to the hearse. That custom also should be discouraged.

If burial is to take place immediately after the funeral mass, it would be appropriate for the family and friends to avoid greeting one another at the entrance of the church to preserve a sense of continuity. In this way, the procession to the cemetery might be seen as part of communal prayer, a continuation of the liturgy.

GRAVESIDE SERVICE

As in the former rite, the graveside service is rather brief. The graveside service is necessary, yet it should not overshadow the eucharistic sacrifice and the final commendation.

In typical situations, the hearse with the coffin parks on a roadway near the gravesite and there is a procession to the grave. When possible, it is good to emphasize continuity between what occurred earlier at the church and what is occurring at the cemetery. This might be done by the priest reciting one of the suggested psalms (Psalms 118, 42, 93) while he leads the procession from the road to the grave. If it is possible for everyone to sing a psalm, a hymn, or a litany, that would be even better. (The litany of the saints is a splendid choice for this procession.)

When all have gathered at the grave, the priest invites those present to pray for the deceased and then a brief verse from scripture is read. Next comes the blessing of the grave, a prayer of thanksgiving, or another prayer in those situations when this final service does not take place at the graveside. Following this prayer, the priest says the statement of committal. Ideally, it would be during this statement that the coffin is lowered into the grave or placed in the mausoleum vault.

It is unfortunate that in some places the coffin is not lowered until after the mourners leave, and in some places the cemetery rite does not even take place at the graveside. This may happen not because the family requests it but because the funeral directors or cemetery staff presume the family would prefer it. Although cemetery personnel are rightfully apprehensive about liabilities because of injuries near open graves, our seeing a coffin descend into the ground is something that should not be dispensed with. Burying the dead is a corporal work of mercy that the mourners have come to perform and, among some ethnic groups, it is the duty of children to put the first shovel-full of earth into the grave of a parent. The deceased should not be left to be buried by strangers. Whenever possible, the actual lowering of the coffin should not be delayed until after the mourners leave, but should be integrated into the liturgical rite. Appropriate safeguards can be taken to avoid mishaps.

It would be appropriate to sing during the committal as well as after the concluding dismissal. Following the committal, the mourners are led in intercessions and then pray the Lord's Prayer together. The priest concludes with a final prayer and then blesses and dismisses those present.

In many places, a cross, which earlier was placed in the coffin, is given to the relatives. It would be appropriate for the priest to bless and present this cross before the blessing so that the dismissal by the priest marks the conclusion of the rite. Similarly, any announcements or statements of remembrance by acquaintances should be integrated into the rite to avoid the incongruity of continuing on after being dismissed.

The rubrics of the *Order of Christian Funerals* no longer mention the use of holy water at the cemetery. Holy water sprinklers can seem like odd devices that magically contain the water inside the handle. For those unfamiliar with the device, it can seem as if the priest were waving a small scepter at the coffin rather than sprinkling baptismal water onto the grave. If the use of holy water is deemed desirable, the water should be contained in a bucket and the priest might sprinkle the grave using his hand or an evergreen branch.

It is customary among some people to include some gesture of leave-taking performed by each person as he or she leaves the graveside. In some places, flowers or petals are provided that are strewn into the grave. Other places preserve a custom of placing a shovel-full or handful of earth on the coffin. These practices can remind us of what we have come to do—to bury the dead, to return our beloved to the earth from which we were made. They also help the grieving process, bringing some sense of peace and finality to those present.

CREMATION

Cremation is now permitted as an option for Catholics and is a common practice in some countries. Yet the tradition of the Church has been that it is the body that is honored during the funeral rites and liturgy. As a result, the ideal is that cremation would take place only *after* the funeral mass with final commendation, at which the body of the deceased is present in a coffin. After the mass, the rite of committal can be celebrated at the crematory before cremation of the body,[16] or the committal can be delayed until after the cremation when the urn is buried or placed in a vault. Most dioceses prescribe that ashes should be buried in a cemetery or entombed in a columbarium and not scattered. When ashes are buried or entombed the rite of committal continues as usual with a special text being used at the actual committal.[17]

The *Order of Christian Funerals* does provide for cases when the body is not present for the funeral mass.[18] In some cases, it might be necessary to cremate the remains before mourners have had time to arrive. In cases such as these, a mass for the dead may be scheduled to allow time for travel and would be celebrated without the body or ashes present. In some cases, a picture of the deceased may be prominently displayed and provide a focal point for prayer before or after the liturgy. The mourners would gather at another time for the burial or entombment of the ashes, either before or after the mass.

By virtue of a 1984 indult, the funeral mass in the presence of the ashes is permitted in Canada under certain conditions.[19] When this is done, the ashes are not to be placed where the coffin normally would go and the Easter candle is not used. The final commendation may be celebrated but holy water and incense are not used.

"BLESSED ARE THEY WHO MOURN"

There is the old tradition of liturgically celebrating the anniversary of someone's death, a custom that has given rise to the observance of saints' feasts on the dates of their deaths. The General Instruction of the Roman missal still refers to this practice[20] and provides numerous prayers for use in this and other types of masses for the dead. It has also been a custom to remember the dead at a "month's mind" mass because of the prayers found in the Tridentine missal for use on the third, seventh and thirtieth day after death. (Eastern Christians, Jews and Muslims share a common tradition in remembering the dead especially on the fortieth day after death, a number with rich scriptural allusions.) Although such prayers are no longer found in the present *Roman Missal*, there is no reason why an adapted version of these customs might not be pastorally beneficial and of spiritual comfort in certain cases to the immediate family and close friends.

Sometimes, with all the details associated with mortuaries and cemeteries and numerous guests, the immediate relatives cannot find quiet time to mourn. A special mass or the liturgy of the hours celebrated in a small chapel or even at the home of the deceased for the immediate family within a few days or weeks after the funeral can help the grieving process take place.

This grieving and healing process can also be aided by those in the parish who are part of a bereavement ministry team. Such individuals, often widows and widowers themselves, can help with details and provide support for family members. In some parishes, they may even volunteer to provide food or companionship during the initial, difficult days after death. It seems fitting to provide special outreach and welcome to the grieving on certain days and seasons of the year.

Those who mourn may in fact have a special role in the parish as witnesses to death, and so deserve a special invitation to participate in worship on days such as All Souls' Day, the Assumption, Good Friday, or during November. They follow in the tradition of the early Christian order of widows who are "sacraments" of Christian faith in the face of death. Both the dead and the grieving deserve mention in the intercessions and, if the community keeps a memorial book, their names should be entered therein.

"Eternal rest grant to them, O Lord"

Without experiential knowledge of what lies beyond death, human beings must rely on tradition, revelation, and insight to guide our faith. Throughout the ages, theological perspectives and emphases have affected the tenor of Christian prayers and hymns associated with the rites of the dead as well as affecting reflection and preaching about the mystery of death. What we believe about death influences how we celebrate the death of a Christian, including what we say about death.

Responding to the Gnostics who believed that a person's soul passed immediately to heaven after death, St. Irenaeus in the late second century wrote that the dead went to a *place of rest* somewhere between earth and heaven and there awaited the final resurrection.[21] St. Hippolytus in the early third century used the image of the Church as a ship piloted by Christ, in which all, the living and the dead, travel until all come together to rest in the kingdom.[22] These images are consistent with New Testament statements that suggest that only after a final judgment, on the "last day," will all be raised up into glory. For instance, in John's gospel Jesus says: "Those who feed on my flesh and drink my blood have life eternal and I will raise them up on the last day" (JN 6:54). St. Paul writes that the Lord himself "with the voice of an archangel and with the trumpet of God will come down from heaven, and the dead in Christ will rise first. Then we who are alive, who are left, will be caught up together with them in the clouds to meet the Lord in the air" (1 THES 4:16–17).

This tradition emphasizes what may be called a corporate and future eschatology—all Christians, living and dead, await "our blessed hope, the appearing of our great God and Savior, Jesus Christ" (TIT 2:13). The dead dwell in a paradise of rest (but not in heaven), the living work on earth, both are united in prayer for each other. On the last day, the entire Christian community, as whole human beings—bodies with spirits—will enter the new heaven and the new earth (cf. REV 21:1).

Medieval concerns and liturgical practices led to a personal approach to sin and judgment. Liturgical texts frequently concerned themselves with the gloom of sin and the dread of eternal condemnation. It was in this context that in 1336, Pope Benedict XII declared the existence of a particular judgment of each Christian at the time of death. Piety began to focus on praying for souls in purgatory, who were undergoing purification for their sins.

This tradition emphasizes what may be called an individualistic and immediate eschatology—each Christian, at the moment of his or her death, is judged by God. If found worthy, the Christian is welcomed into God's presence, after atoning for sins through the pain of purgatory. There is no distinction between heaven and the paradise of rest, no waiting to enter the kingdom until the last day, no bond of solidarity with fellow Christians.

This tradition also betrays a dualism not present in the earlier tradition: the human body perishes while the human soul lives immortally. At the final judgment the dead are reunited with their bodies and, at that moment, fully reflect the risen Christ. Somehow the dead in heaven are even made happier when they are reunited with their bodies.[23] Meanwhile, their bodies return to dust while their souls live with God, in a sense suggesting that the dead are never really dead.

The present collection of liturgical texts in a sense reflects both eschatologies—immediate and personal as well as future and corporate. Ancient images are used with medieval concepts giving mixed messages. For example, how should we interpret "paradise"—as a place of rest where the dead await the "last day," or as a synonym for heaven?

Certain prayers speak holistically about the deceased awaiting the last day with all who have died in Christ. Other prayers speak about the deceased already enjoying fulfillment with God, but separate soul from body. The dualism of a separated body and soul is evident even in the opening paragraph of the Introduction of the *Ordo Exsequiarum* quoted at the beginning of this chapter. Some have suggested that this confusion and ambiguity can lead to pastoral problems if a proper balance is not struck. In the extreme, focusing only on immediate glory risks making Christ's victory over death irrelevant. The portrayal that individual resurrection is an accomplished fact may merely be a new disguise for the continued denial of death.

Happily, the revised rites for the dead have helped us focus on the death and resurrection of Christ as the image for understanding the death of any Christian. But, in practice, we often proclaim the victory of Easter without acknowledging the pain of Good Friday or the emptiness of Holy Saturday. As practiced, the prayers for the dead and the funeral rites often refuse to face human sorrow, horror, and grief and the awfulness of pain, separation, and death. It is one thing to commend a friend to God's care, in the "sure and certain hope" that someone we love will rise "on the last day."[24] It is quite another to proclaim without doubt that the deceased "is now in heaven."[25]

In an attempt to leave behind the negativity associated with the pre-Vatican II funeral rites, we may have gone to extremes in denying human pain and in overlooking the ambiguity found in traditional Christian faith concerning death. A balanced approach to celebrating the rites for the dead may suggest a reevaluation of various practices now common. For instance, although white is the color of Easter and is common at many funerals, red and violet are also paschal colors in that they are used during Lent and the Easter Triduum. Although Alleluia is appropriate for Easter Sunday, it may sound shallow if sung triumphalistically at some funerals.

In both old and revised funeral rites, the antiphon indicated for the final procession from the church begins: "May the angels lead you into paradise, may the martyrs come to welcome you." While expressing faith and hope in God's mercy, these traditional words also suggest that the pilgrimage has not yet been completed. Such is the reality and ambiguity that we celebrate.

In Conclusion

Death is the great unknown, yet for a Christian, the death of Jesus is the source of our hope, since it was through death that Jesus gained eternal life. The mystery of death is one of the greatest mysteries that a Christian can participate in, for it completes his or her union with Christ that was begun in baptism, a baptism into Christ's death, as St. Paul proclaims. Death is the ultimate liminal experience—passing over the threshold from this life to a new one. As the primordial chaos preceded God's creation, so the uncertainty of death precedes God's new creation. As Christ lay in the tomb on the sabbath day, the day of rest, each of us enters the mystery of the dark tomb awaiting the dawn of the new first day, the day of resurrection.

Christians celebrate the death of a fellow Christian with faith in the resurrection and a "sure and certain hope" that we will be united again when we shall see God face-to-face on the last day. While bidding farewell to those who have died and while praying for them and their loved ones, the rites associated with Christian funerals are also meant to be a great source of hope and comfort for all who participate, as all prepare to experience the mystery of death themselves. Through the liturgical rites for the dead, we enter the mystery of death and the mystery of Christ's victory over death.

The paschal mystery of Christ's death and resurrection is the cornerstone on which our faith is founded. Through the celebration of Christian funerals, we enter more fully into this mystery as we realize our own mortality and come closer and closer to the mystery of death ourselves.

Chapter 12

THE MYSTERY
OF BLESSINGS

Blessings are signs that have God's word as their basis and that are celebrated from motives of faith. They are therefore meant to declare and to manifest the newness of life in Christ that has its origin and growth in the sacraments of the New Covenant established by the Lord. In addition, since they have been established as a kind of imitation of the sacraments, blessings are signs above all of spiritual effects that are achieved through the Church's intercession. *(Book of Blessings, General Introduction, n. 10)*

I. From Principles . . .

HISTORICAL OVERVIEW

The mystery of blessings is the mystery of recognizing and acknowledging God's presence in all of creation. The Hebrew Scriptures record at least three different activities that may be broadly considered "blessings." First of all, there is the blessing of God, the offering of praise, as is found in Psalm 103, "Bless the LORD, O my soul, and all my being bless God's holy name." Sometimes such a blessing includes thanksgiving for the wonders of creation or of some event associated with salvation. Then, there is the blessing of human beings, a calling upon God to show favor to an individual, as in the blessing of Aaron, "The LORD bless you and keep you" (NUM 6:24). And finally, there is the blessing of objects, a ritual dedication and setting apart, as in the blessing of the temple in Jerusalem (cf. 1 KINGS 8:22 ff; 2 CHRON 6:12 ff).

That certain types of blessings were expected as a birthright can be deduced from the feud of Esau and Jacob over receiving the blessing proper to a firstborn (GEN 27). Blessings were requested in other instances, as when

Jacob wrestled with God and demanded a blessing before letting the stranger go (GEN 32:27).

Blessings are considered to be "good words" (from the Greek for blessing, *eulogia*) spoken to God over a person, place, or object. The blessing of persons is commonly construed as requesting God's special help for someone in a certain role in society or ministry in the Church, for instance, for civil rulers or abbots or mothers. In contrast, the blessing of some objects or places sets these things apart for religious use, as in the blessing of palms, oils, churches, cemeteries, chalices, statues, religious medals, or rosaries. At other times, the blessing of objects requests God's protection for those who will use the objects, as in the blessing of homes, automobiles, or food.

CHRISTIAN TRADITION

In the Christian tradition, references to blessing oil, cheese, olives, and firstfruits appear in the *Apostolic Tradition* of Hippolytus.[1] St. Augustine (mid-fourth to early fifth century) referred to the practice of blessing baptismal waters when he expressed his concerns about the orthodoxy of certain prayers of blessing.[2]

In the Middle Ages, the importance of blessings grew in popular piety. In many places blessings took on a quasi-magical status. Participation in sacramental celebrations was slowly replaced by possession of blessed articles. Almost every religious activity is susceptible to corruption, and even in recent years, in practice some blessings border on the superstitious. Certain blessed objects, such as medals worn as jewelry or blessed water or oil, are considered by many to have magical powers.

This exaggerated status of blessings is not merely due to the ignorance of some of the faithful. Church customs seem to encourage such a perception, for instance, by requiring the blessing of a church building or of baptismal water before use. At the same time, there is often a lack of education and guidance given by Church leadership about appropriate reverence for blessed objects. It is rare to hear about the subject of superstition in homilies and, perhaps, many of us feel we are beyond that. Yet in many places catechesis is sorely needed. There are many Catholics among those who make use of "psychic hot lines," "magic crystals," and similar contemporary nonsense. Such reliance on objects or practices is, in effect, a form of idolatry and of slavery to ignorance. But Christ has freed us from such servitude and has revealed to us the goodness of God who alone provides salvation.

One can reasonably wonder what religious significance or meaning should be associated with the blessing of mountain climbing equipment or of electric generators, which were once found in the complete *Roman Ritual*. We might chuckle at the blessing of mechanical devices, but would it be wise to dismiss the concept of blessing altogether? Surely we all need to become more and more aware of God's presence, to see day-to-day objects and events as gifts from God. Surely it is appropriate to render thanks to the source of all we are and have.

In blessings we take the objects and events that we otherwise might take for granted, and even in their ordinariness come to acknowledge what is divine and holy. The ordinary things of our lives, the tools of our trades, the objects in our homes, the foods we eat all can provide occasions to give praise and thanks to God. A renewed piety of blessings would understand the ritual not as a quasi-magical "setting apart" of certain things, but as an opportunity to appreciate them as gifts of God that evoke our praise.

LITURGICAL CEREMONY

In the 1614 *Roman Ritual*, the rite for blessing people or objects was usually brief and quasi-private. The blessing required only a priest and one other person (to give the relatively few responses). In practice, priests sometimes blessed objects without anyone else present. The rite consisted of an opening dialogue, *Adjutorium nostrum in nomine Domini. Ṝ . Qui fecit cælum et terram* ("Our help is in the name of the Lord. Ṝ . Who made heaven and earth"), followed by one or more prayers of blessing. Over the objects or persons, signs of the cross were made and holy water was sprinkled. No scripture was proclaimed nor were there any intercessory prayers offered.

The objects for which blessings existed in the old *Ritual* were many and varied. Certain blessings were associated with feasts, such as the blessing of gold, frankincense, myrrh, Jordan water and chalk on Epiphany (January 6), of throats on the feast of St. Blase (February 3), of food on Easter, of a bonfire on the vigil of the birth of St. John the Baptist (June 24), of herbs and flowers on the Assumption (August 15), of wine on the feast of St. John the Evangelist (December 27). Other blessings were associated with certain saints, especially the blessings of water, breads, oils, or scapulars. Still others were associated with the occupations of certain peoples, such as the blessing of beer or seeds. Still others were blessings of objects of devotion such as crosses, statues, medals, rosaries.

THE REVISED BOOK OF BLESSINGS

One of the last sections of the 1614 *Roman Ritual* that was revised after the Second Vatican Council was the collection of blessings. The Latin text of the *Book of Blessings* was published in 1984 and the English version appeared in 1989. The General Introduction is particularly valuable in its discussion of the role of blessings in the life of the Church. Many blessings found in the previous *Ritual* have been omitted and newer blessings included which reflect the contemporary situation. National conferences of bishops may include other blessings, at their discretion.[3]

The ritual structure of blessings has been revised, so that, in the full rite, the proclamation of the word of God plays a key role, and intercessions are normally offered. Although alternative shorter rites are sometimes included, these are envisioned for use only in rare situations, as emphasized in the General Introduction:

> To ensure active participation in the celebration and to guard against any danger of superstition, it is ordinarily not permissible to impart the blessing of any article or place merely through a sign of blessing and without either the word of God or any sort of prayer being spoken.[4]

II . . . to Practice

A CHANGE IN STYLE

In some sense, the *Book of Blessings* reflects the norm that blessings are a communal, liturgical rite rather than a private rite that a priest accomplishes to make something or someone "holy." As a result, it assumes a public blessing of people, places, or objects and allows the integration of certain blessings into the celebration of mass.[5] The ordinary format includes the proclamation of scripture, the offering of intercessory prayers, and the use of song. The prayer of blessing over objects usually speaks more of the people who will make use of the object than of the object itself.

The *Book of Blessings* has restored an old custom, that of lay men and women offering many blessings. Sometimes this may occur when an ordained minister is not available. But more often, this may occur because of a particular relationship, such as the blessing of children by their parents. At other times, such as before meals, the assumption is that any Christian will say some prayer of blessing at mealtimes. To encourage prayer and blessings at various moments of our lives, the American bishops issued *Catholic Household Blessings and Prayers* in 1988. This is a resource book intended for family use, which includes common Catholic prayers in addition to appropriate texts from the *Book of Blessings*.

THE ROLE OF BLESSINGS

Blessings provide the opportunity to acknowledge the religious significance of moments and things, the special and the ordinary, that are too often overlooked. Certain occasions are religious by nature—entering religious life, dedicating a church building, thanking God for the birth of a child—and so it is appropriate to mark these and other events with appropriate celebrations and prayers, and with formal, solemn blessings. At other times, the public and solemn celebration of a blessing, with presider, readers and ministers of music and song, is a way to give proper attention to certain events and individuals whose religious dimension may not be regularly acknowledged.

In many ways, the celebration of blessings can help to call attention to God's presence in all aspects of human life. By singling out specific occasions, objects, or individuals, and by associating them with a prayer of blessing, we call attention to God's constant care in our lives. We acknowledge the need to see God's presence in the day-to-day and the ordinary as well as in once-in-a-lifetime events in our lives.

In Conclusion

Blessings are part of a "balanced liturgical diet" of Catholic Christians. They are no less wonderful mysteries than the "major mysteries," the sacraments of the Church. The daily blessing of meals calls attention to God's nourishment. This daily attention in turn can help us appreciate the special nourishment that is ours in the great mystery of the eucharist. The blessings of throats on St. Blase's Day can help us give thanks for the healing presence of God that we experience throughout our lives and particularly in the great mystery of the anointing of the sick. The blessing of children by parents can help us appreciate one dimension of human love that the Church celebrates in the great mystery of marriage.

The *Book of Blessings* reminds us: "At all times and in every situation, then, the faithful have an occasion for praising God through Christ in the Holy Spirit, for calling on divine help, and for giving thanks in all things."[6] There are many reasons why we need to praise and bless God, and there are many concerns for which we ask God's help and protection.

Ultimately, celebrating blessings is celebrating the mystery of God's presence, protection, care, and love, the mystery of the gift of God's love, visibly seen in Jesus, and the mystery of God's gift of the Spirit inspiring us to offer thanks and praise.

Chapter 13

OBFUSCATING THE MYSTERY

Celebrating the mystery of Christ's death, burial, and resurrection is a right, a privilege, and a challenge that we as Christians are blessed to be able to participate in. The mystery of Christ's life in us is something we reach toward to experience more fully in the assembly of Christians.

The Church's tradition has provided us with structures and texts to help us celebrate and experience the divine mystery. These liturgical rites are meant to be times of ritual interaction by Christians eager to celebrate Christ. Christians come together to be nourished by the Lord in order to live in this confusing and contradictory world. The contemporary liturgical rites have been sculptured over the centuries, recently pruned of many unnecessary accretions, and reformed to more accurately reflect the Church's authentic tradition. We are faced with the ongoing process of understanding and reforming the rites more thoroughly without imposing preconceptions on the reforms, including any too hasty adaptation to local culture. We are ultimately faced with the challenge of becoming at home with these rites with their gestures, texts, and objects. In this familiarity, the liturgy nourishes and supports us on our pilgrimage toward God.

Unfortunately, the reality of human nature is that limitations and imperfections are part of who we are. Oftentimes even good intentions and innocent misunderstandings can and do impede the power of the liturgical rites from having an effect on the lives of those present. Even in those parishes that try to make sacramental celebrations "come alive," sometimes misunderstanding or incomplete knowledge of the rites or of liturgical tradition, or a particular agenda, or even our innate human weakness will all combine to cloud rather than to clarify the mystery we celebrate.

Father Aidan Kavanagh, OSB, suggests that some contemporary American attitudes negatively influence the liturgical experience. This influence is pervasive. The cultural attitudes are shared not only by the members of a pastoral staff or by a liturgy committee but by parishioners in general. In commenting on the results of an 1987 study of fifteen U.S. parishes, Kavanagh writes:

> The expressions . . . in the study are consistently genial and benign, but all betray not so much a theological or liturgical rationale as a certain American middle-class attitude, which is more-or-less continually distrustful of expertise, experience, authority, and tradition. Clerical abdication of liturgical and doctrinal responsibility abets this, often receiving in return expressions of support, moral respect, personal affirmation, and a sense of purpose from the groups themselves. Some of this is remarkably arrogant. As a first-year student at Yale recently told a faculty lecturer, "I will let you know when you say something I do not understand."[1]

We should not expect to have a "peak experience" or some epiphany at every Sunday eucharist. Yet we have all been at liturgical celebrations that have lacked the power we have the right to expect to be associated with worship. In some cases, fundamental principles are hopelessly diluted and emptied of any strength. In some cases, services display the worst emphases of an older theology that seemed to value ritualism over public participation, at which ministers go through the motions with little regard for the assembly's roles.

When we, as Christians, gather together, we can be on fire with God's love given us through our union with Christ. This is possible and attainable by everyone in the assembly and by those who lead and serve it. In the interest of stoking the Spirit's fire, we should be eager to identify those influences that inhibit our enthusiasm and that knock the wind out of the sails of our communal energy.

In this chapter, I attempt to identify some liturgical pitfalls that may dampen rather than enliven the celebration of the sacramental mysteries. By becoming conscious of obstacles that often arise, we may prepare for our celebrations accordingly. In the end, it is God alone who gives the gift of immersion into mystery. But appropriate preparation and quality celebrations help make us into a field of good soil, receptive to the seed and rain of God's gentle presence.

THE SIN OF CONVENIENCE

One of the most frequent sins committed by a great number of ministers and others involved in coordinating and preparing liturgies might be called "convenience." When committing this sin, people often are attempting to respond to human needs, either their own or what they understand to be the "needs" of others.[2]

Take as an example all the excuses we make for not celebrating infant baptism in the context of the Church's full form of this rite, within the parish community at the Sunday mass. Perhaps instead the baptism is celebrated on Sunday afternoons with just the family, without music, without participation. Or perhaps the baptism takes place in the family's home, a practice contrary to the Church's norms.

It may be inconvenient for a family to gather all the friends and relatives at a parish church on a Sunday and travel plans may need to be adjusted. Yet the communal form of the baptismal rite, especially when celebrated during a Sunday mass, highlights the fundamental reality that baptism is incorporation into a community of faith, a church community far wider than just friends and relatives. Baptism is incorporation into the life of Christ and the body of Christ, a belief brought out when several individuals are baptized at once. The mystery of baptism is ultimately the mystery of the Church. When the broader community is excluded, as necessarily occurs when baptism is performed in a family home, the ecclesial context of the sacrament is omitted and the fuller meaning of baptism is clouded. What unconsciously seems to be highlighted in a "private" baptism is an aspect of the older theology that saw baptism primarily as a way of saving a child from "limbo" and from being perpetually separated from God.

Other examples of succumbing to the sin of convenience are numerous. For example, some priests who are not associated with a parish may habitually celebrate mass without anyone else present. This practice may be a convenience for them but is far from the ideal envisioned in Church documents, an ideal that portrays the mass as a communal celebration of unity. Solitary celebrations of the mass separate the priest from other members of Christ's body, and too often this is done without reflecting on the symbolic implications or considering other alternatives. For example, those who live in religious communities might consider participating in a community mass or celebrating with several others present.

Some liturgical coordinators find it inconvenient to prepare an appropriate amount of altar bread for mass. As a result, eucharistic bread is distributed from the tabernacle as a rule, rather than as an exception. Such a practice violates liturgical principles (as well as liturgical law), thereby obfuscating the mystery of the unity of the assembly partaking in the one bread and the one cup.

Sometimes laziness or sloppy habits have solidified unchallenged practices into set patterns. As a result, "convenience" becomes "making the exception the rule."

When individuals succumb to the temptation of convenience, they sometimes do so with the intention of avoiding the perceived and experienced rigidity of rules and rituals, and of accommodating the tastes and time constraints of the contemporary world. Yet, this can at the same time undermine the foundational mysteries upon which liturgical celebrations are built. The intent of the revised liturgical rite may be diluted to the point of loosing the impact it was meant to have. As Gabe Huck writes, "convenience triumphs over beauty and, even more, over meaning."[3] Without insisting on certain fundamental realities associated with our revised vision of liturgy and worship, our liturgical celebrations may again be infected with the mechanistic and minimalistic approaches associated with worship in the days before the Second Vatican Council.

An appeal to convenience can easily result in a poorer celebration of one of the many mysteries of God's love. Yet it is easy to be swayed by such an appeal. It is not always convenient to celebrate liturgy in its fullness, for example, with baptism by immersion, with altar bread that is recognizable as food, with well-trained readers and singers. In fact, authentic liturgy is hard work that of necessity involves many ministries. If convenience were a guideline in the evaluation of liturgy, a good liturgy might be one that could be seen in video format! But for liturgy to be real and live, it must be a product of effort, not of expedience. The reality is that our liturgical rites can be moments of joyous celebration by Christians eager to experience more deeply the mystery of the risen Christ.

THE SNARE OF PASTORAL SOLUTIONS

The snare of so-called "pastoral" solutions is a first-cousin to the "sin" of convenience. Those who are seduced by this snare are well-meaning individuals who sometimes bend liturgical law until it is meaningless. In this way, they unconsciously subvert the underlying spirit of the revised liturgy all in the name of pastoral privilege.

For example, when celebrating the anointing of the sick in a hospital room, a priest might use the abbreviated rite even though the presence of family and friends would suggest that the standard rite would be preferable. Some parishes may truncate the processions of Passion Sunday and of the Easter Triduum resulting in something that bears little resemblance to the people of God on pilgrimage. Some adult converts may be allowed, without sufficient reason, to skip the communal rites of the catechumenate and be received into the Church in a private celebration of initiation. These and other shortcuts are often justified in the name of "pastoral" solutions to local needs.

Of its nature, liturgy is "pastoral" because liturgy is concerned with the good shepherding of the people of God. The rites are in the language of the people. They have been formulated to reflect the insights of many different bishops and other "practitioners" of the pastoral arts—in our own generation and throughout the generations. They include various options for use at the discretion of the presiding minister.

Yet, a point that sometimes gets lost is that liturgy is for the people of God and not for private individuals. Liturgy is a celebration of the entire Church incarnated in the local Christian community, which often is a geographically determined parish. Because of this broader reality, liturgy is not the personal property of a family who wants a special ceremony for their newborn child, or of a couple looking toward their marriage, or of an individual priest, who perhaps more than others should appreciate the communal nature of public worship, including the sacraments. Individuals are not free to adapt liturgy to their personal needs. The purpose of any permitted adaptations is to serve the community, the people who will gather for the celebration of the sacramental mystery.

Certainly there are situations that were never envisioned by the framers of the rubrics. In these cases, the presiding minister must adapt as best as possible. After all, it was Jesus who said "the sabbath was made for human beings and not human beings for the sabbath" (MK 2:27). A "pastoral approach" takes each situation as it comes and does not apply blanket solutions to common problems.

The noted French liturgical center is called the *Centre de Pastorale Liturgique de Paris*. *Pastorale* is the noun and *Liturgique* is the adjective. In English we speak of *pastoral liturgy*. But the French term implies *liturgical pastoral practice*. The liturgy (and its spirit, its history, etc.) forms and informs pastoral practice. We tend to think the other way around. We think pastoral concerns are reasons for changing liturgy. The French phrase suggests that liturgy can affect the ways we minister, that the spirit of the liturgy can direct our work. A person should never have to choose between being pastoral or being liturgical, since good liturgy is ultimately pastoral.

Our cultural concern with efficiency has colored the way we evaluate what is important and what is not. This is true in business and it is true in our thinking about liturgy, as well. We say things like, "too much music will lengthen the service so the people won't come," or, "we can't determine exactly how many people will go to communion so we need to store plenty of extra hosts in the tabernacle," or, "we can't have silence because of the babies crying in our churches." These thoughts betray the fact that the liturgical spirit is still not the driving force in how we evaluate what is important in our communal Christian life.

Robert McClory reminds us of the distance we have to travel in having the spirit of the liturgy form our pastoral actions. He writes:

Near the end of their peace pastoral, the U.S. bishops in 1982 urged the faithful to pray and fast for nuclear disarmament because of the danger the arms race poses. If they were truly formed in the liturgy, several liturgists have argued, they would have *begun* the pastoral with the argument, "Because we are a people who pray and fast, we cannot condone the nuclear arms race," and proceeded from there. In such poignant subtleties lies the genius and elusiveness of liturgical literacy.[4]

ABANDONING RITUAL IN SEARCH OF GRACIOUSNESS

Those who omit the formal liturgical greeting and replace it with "Good morning, everyone" suggest that it is difficult to convey graciousness and genuine human warmth through the words of a ritual. To affect a loose informality in a situation where everything else denotes ritual is to present a flood of mixed signals.[5] We are in a special place and the presiding minister is wearing special clothes. All this is saying that something different is about to happen.

When anyone departs from the formal atmosphere of a situation, that person suggests to others that ritual behavior is incompatible with gracious human interaction or profound human emotion. In the interactive liturgical setting, informality and spontaneity by the presiding minister can send unintended (and even negative) signals to others in the assembly, since their texts are always scripted and formal. But it is the experience of many that it is possible to convey the deepest of emotions through formal speech or ritual behavior. Many formal addresses do leave hearers deeply moved. Simple ritual gestures such as touching a name on a monument or throwing earth on a coffin can bring tears to people's eyes.

Even when the presiding minister does not use the all-too-common, "Good morning, everyone," there is a tendency for some priests to be "schizophrenic" during liturgy. They can be informal during certain points and formal when reading the official prayer texts. For example, a priest may greet the assembly with the official "The Lord be with you," but then as part of the introduction, he may ramble on informally, telling a joke or two, giving what seems like the first of several homilies. In this situation, the priest has abdicated his function as president of a liturgical assembly and taken on the role of a talk show host, *à la* Oprah Winfrey or Phil Donahue. In this mindset, it becomes the burden of the presider to inspire and to entertain, and his success can either make or break a liturgy as far as the assembly is concerned.[6]

This "talk show host syndrome" puts the burden of success or failure on the priest's personality. The other ministers—deacon, readers, musicians, eucharistic ministers, servers—become Ed McMahons and Doc Severinsons to the priest's Johnny Carson.

When a presiding priest takes the model of a TV talk show as his guide for celebrational style, he places the assembly in a passive role of responding to the "show." The assembly becomes an audience. But the presider should be a leader of prayer, rather than the factotum, and a good leader knows the cues that will elicit active participation and responses by those present. When expected liturgical cues are given by the priest, an eager assembly will respond, and the experience of prayer will actually be enhanced even though the text is well-known and formal. In our liturgical rites, everyone present has been called together by God to form one assembly, and it is the united body of the assembly that offers praise and thanksgiving to a loving God through Jesus, empowered by the Spirit.

In an attempt to convey informality, a priest may sometimes feel compelled to amend some text. (This practice becomes a problem when cues are altered or when these emendations create confusion.) Changing liturgical texts is an art few of us possess. It can happen that the resulting text is grammatically incorrect and literally inferior to the official text. Additions of words or phrases can lengthen the text so that it becomes too much to grasp. Often the result is that the common received text becomes no longer common because it has become the individual prayer of the presider.

There are occasions when the official texts of prayers may and should be changed according to circumstances. This is explicitly mentioned in reference to masses of the dead and masses with children.[7] But often it is more important to grasp and prayerfully convey the content of a text rather than attempt to adapt it on the fly.

Sometimes adaptations are unconscious and subtle, and the minister may not realize what is occurring. For example, take the presider who has developed the bad habit of inserting "and" at the beginning of every presidential text. The results can be deadly. "*And* we begin in the name of the Father. . . . *And* the Lord be with you. . . . *And* may almighty God have mercy on us. . . . *And* let us pray. . . . *And* we ask this through. . . ." Enough! It is difficult to see how such emendations can be considered to be any improvement over the official, though often stark, words found in the approved liturgical books.

Does this mean that presiders should never try to exhibit graciousness during liturgies? Far from it! Everyone in the assembly must feel at home in the house of God, and a true home is marked by graciousness, warmth, and concern. Does this mean that prayers should be proclaimed coldly or without emotion? Not at all! The more we ponder the words of our common prayers, the more those words will demand feeling when spoken aloud.

In our Western cultures, we tend to forget that ritual and graciousness, warmth and formality can co-exist. In Christian liturgy, we are challenged to foster a climate in which together they open us up to the mystery of God with us.

Inadequate Preparation and Inappropriate Choices

The revised liturgical books present communities and liturgical ministers with a healthy tension and challenge: balancing fidelity to the spirit and vision of the liturgy with the ability to accommodate the details to specific situations. The Lord himself criticized those who were rigid in the application of the Mosaic law or used the law as a reason to avoid compassion and concern for others (cf. MK 7:9 ff).

The revised liturgical rites in many places suggest a flexibility and freedom that was not present in the Tridentine books. At numerous points the rubrics state that the presiding minister says something "in these or similar words." In the different rites, those planning services have numerous options from which to choose, especially among the scripture texts. In certain rites, the priest is directed to greet individuals in a warm and friendly manner without any specific text being provided.

The Lord told us to put new wine into fresh wineskins (MT 9:17). In other words, new ways of doing things demand new attitudes and outlooks. The revised liturgy is not merely a different script for a play or a different score for a symphony with the same old approach to the performance. The revised liturgy is primarily a renewed vision of the Church. In a real sense, the revised *texts* are secondary to this renewed *outlook*.

Occasionally, one encounters someone who is uncomfortable with the freedom and vision of the revised rites and prefers the security found in the Tridentine missal. Such a person may also prefer that the celebration be a "one-man show," and be uneasy in coordinating the roles of several different ministers. Such rigidity can inhibit communal prayer rather than enhance it.

Sometimes inflexibility is justified by citing, apart from their context, the words of the *Constitution on the Sacred Liturgy* that "no other person, not even a priest, may . . . change anything in the liturgy."[8] But interpreting liturgical law is not an easy task, since canonical tradition itself suggests that law must be interpreted according to the text as well as the context.[9] Different liturgical books may offer different insights into the same liturgical practice. To interpret a law properly, a person needs to be conversant with more than merely one liturgical rite. Thus interpretation of some liturgical laws may be considered as more of an art than a science.

In a concern for correctness, certain individuals overlook the freedom found in the rites themselves and eliminate much of the warmth and good human interaction upon which liturgy can build. Ritual and fidelity are not incompatible with freedom and graciousness. Although some priests may be uplifted by their own celebrational style, whether informal or rigid, they also may be oblivious to the negative effect they have on some in the assembly. In some cases, rather than enhancing the worship experience, the people of God may, in fact, become distanced from the mystery being celebrated.

NON-INTEGRATION OF VARIOUS MINISTRIES

The proper celebration of liturgical rites assumes the presence of several ministers in addition to the one presiding. At the minimum, a typical celebration includes a reader, a cantor and a server. This is in stark contrast to the Tridentine missal and the 1614 *Ritual*, which presumed the presence only of a server and which also required the priest to repeat quietly texts sung by the choir or proclaimed by the deacon and subdeacon.

The *Constitution on the Sacred Liturgy* encourages the distribution of tasks during liturgical services and cautions that ministers "should carry out all and only those parts" that pertain to their ministry. Such advice is repeated in the liturgical books themselves, for example, when the General Instruction of the Roman Missal states that the presiding priest should not proclaim the gospel if a deacon or another priest is present.[10]

Integration and coordination of ministries presupposes several things. It presupposes the existence of qualified ministers. It presumes that all ministers know what is proper to their own ministry and what is proper to other ministers. It also assumes that the presiding minister actually permits and encourages other ministers to do all that their ministry requires.

It may be difficult to recruit and train enough ministers to fill all the liturgical needs of a community. But such difficulty is no excuse for certain ministers regularly to usurp the roles of others. God has given the members of the assembly various gifts and talents, and they should not be overlooked. Gifted individuals need to be identified and their talents cultivated for the benefit of the community.

We should no more consider certain ministries optional than we should consider vesture or vessels optional. A reader at mass, for example, whether on Sunday or during the week, is not a nice addition when one is present. In most cases, the participation of a reader should be considered a necessity if the celebration is to be considered authentic. Without bread and wine, we cannot celebrate the mystery of the eucharist. We should also think twice about the advisability of celebrating any liturgical mystery without the assistance of appropriate ministers.

Considering Music as Auxiliary Rather Than as Essential

The persecution of Catholics in Ireland and England was one factor that led them to celebrate liturgical rites devoid of anything that could draw attention. In particular, it led to the practice of celebrating mass without singing. English-speaking Catholics who immigrated to the United States brought with them the customs they had known and, to some extent, considered normal. Some even disdained singing in churches since it reminded them of their Anglican overlords. But one result of that unfortunate history is the notion that song and music is auxiliary to the mass and to sacramental rites rather than being an integral and standard aspect of every liturgical celebration.[11]

This notion is not universally held, however. Often parishes whose members came from German or Polish heritages had significantly different traditions. And many Eastern Catholics to this day do not celebrate any liturgical mystery without song, no matter how few may be present.

Great strides have been made in integrating music and song into the celebration of Sunday mass. American Catholics are learning what it means to sing the liturgy rather than sing a few songs during the liturgy. They have taken to heart the words of *Music in Catholic Worship,* "Good celebrations foster and nourish faith. Poor celebrations may weaken and destroy it. . . . Among the many signs and symbols used by the Church to celebrate its faith, music is of preeminent importance."[12] Yet there is still work to be done.

Some communities may need to focus their efforts on integrating song into non-eucharistic celebrations, such as the celebration of infant baptism or of a vigil for the dead. Other communities may want to examine the quality of participation at weddings and funerals. Still others may need to evaluate their musical priorities. There may be ritual texts that should be sung, for instance the psalm, the general intercessions, or the preface, and which are not regularly being sung.

The General Instruction of the Roman Missal quotes St. Paul who encouraged the faithful to sing psalms, hymns and inspired songs (cf. COL 3:16). It also reminds us of St. Augustine's words, "To sing belongs to lovers."[13] Expressing our faith and our love through song must be seen ever more as integral to our common worship.

Words Hiding the Word

The Latin text by which the deacon invites the assembly to share God's peace consists of three words: *Offerte vobis pacem* (Offer yourselves peace). This invitation is short, direct, and devoid of frills. How often do our adaptations of this text and other texts in the *Sacramentary* convey the same directness? An English translation of one alternative invitation to the sign of peace in the Italian sacramentary consists of twenty-one words: "In Christ, who through his cross has made us all brothers and sisters, exchange now a sign of reconciliation and peace." A simple directive of three words has become seven times as long!

We tend to misuse words in our liturgy. Sometimes we attempt to be more personal, and sometimes we misunderstand the text. The priest or deacon who expands the simple greeting and says: "The Lord be with each and every one of you," can be accused of fragmenting the assembly rather than uniting them. The priest who interpolates his own few words into a text, for instance: "Pray, my dear friends, that our sacrifice—these gifts of bread and wine—will be found acceptable to God our loving Father," runs the risk of altering the theology behind the original language. In this case, the added words localize the sacrifice to the earthly elements of the eucharist and neglect that greater sacrifice, the *sacrificium laudis* (sacrifice of praise), of the entire eucharistic celebration. The most annoying misuse of words is when we speak the obvious, as does the cantor who announces, "Please stand," instead of using a gentle hand gesture, or the minister who tells us what will happen next, "And now we will have the washing of the feet," "and now the gift-bearers will bring up the bread and wine." Explanations have a way of disenfranchising us from the liturgy because they sound as if we do not know what is going on. (Although some in the assembly may be unaware, explanations only emphasize the fact.)

Father Robert Hovda gave special "thanks to presiders and other specialized ministers serving the ministering assembly who refuse to say more than is absolutely necessary."[14] The underlying principle can be summarized by the maxim: "More is less and less is more." In an article about words, Gabe Huck suggests, "It is not enough at liturgy that there be words. The words must be right." Huck later quotes the poet Anne Sexton: "Be careful of words, even the miraculous ones. . . . Once broken they are impossible things to repair."[15]

The liturgical rites incorporate several different types of texts: presidential prayers and scripture readings associated with the day, hymns chosen from a wide variety of options, common texts for the presiding minister and the assembly (for instance, the *Confiteor* or Nicene Creed), prayers chosen from a limited number of options (such as the eucharistic prayers). The day-to-day variation of many texts coupled with the sheer number of words can overpower many in the assembly leading them to "tune out." Some feel as if they are being buried in an avalanche, so much so that some of the important words, for instance, the words of the eucharistic prayer, are lost. There is wisdom in the practice found in other liturgical traditions, such as among Byzantine Churches, in which variety is limited and words are always joined to music.

The way words are spoken can affect what is heard. Some priests have a tendency to speed up when proclaiming a prescribed text, such as the prayers or greetings. The tendency to race through a printed text is a common trait, but it can be avoided. Winston Churchill had to force himself to speak slowly and deliberately.[16] Haste can give undesirable messages to those listening. For example, the speed may suggest to some that the texts are not really important or that they do not have to be proclaimed clearly and distinctly because it does not matter whether or not we hear them. In effect it says that it doesn't matter that the assembly is present. Others may think that the priest is unfriendly, uninterested, shy, or afraid. Whatever the cause, the reality is that rapid speech detracts from the reverence appropriate for the mystery being celebrated by those assembled, and should be avoided whenever possible.

We must be careful of the words we use and how we speak them, lest we distort the message of God's unique Word, or so bury that message in such an avalanche of words that the Word can never be found.

Volunteerism in Lieu of Ministry

There are many generous souls in every parish, but not every individual has been given the same gifts and talents by God to be able to serve as any minister among the people of God. We need people to serve, and we need individuals who respond to Christ's admonition to "freely give of what you have freely received" (MT 10:8). However, we must be aware that true ministry in the Church requires talents and competency that cannot always be supplied by an abundance of good will or generosity of heart. True ministry involves an attitude of service toward others, the root meaning of the Latin word "minister." True ministry also involves making use of the various God-given gifts that have been discovered and developed.

It is obvious that someone who cannot sing well should not be appointed as a cantor no matter how generous a spirit the person might have. Some individuals may possess talents appropriate for certain ministries. But they may not realize the selfless dedication that is necessary when someone ministers to, rather than merely performs a job for, the community. Think of the music directors who are more worried about the quality of the choir than whether or not the assembly is included in any of the music. Think of the many devoted, volunteer organists who are always present when needed but who overwhelm rather than accompany and engender the singing. Some talented and enthusiastic ministers may need gentle education to be able to serve even better.

For many ministries in the contemporary church, we are only beginning to understand the talents needed for their proper exercise. This process will take time. After all, we have only identified some of these ministries since

1965. As we make use of various ministers in the local communities, we will become more and more aware of which gifts are needed.

We will also realize that certain ministers need talents that our society considers of "professional" quality, talents which require a lifetime to develop and to hone. These individuals should be given proper remuneration for their professionalism. Some of these ministries are now recognized to include parochial administrators, musicians, cantors, liturgical coordinators, and educators. In the future, more paid ministers likely will be found necessary in parishes. For example, the liturgical ministry of sacristan is being rediscovered as a skilled and essential role.

It may be difficult to change established patterns in some places. It may be difficult to find talented and disciplined individuals to serve in various ministries. It may be difficult to suggest to people who have exercised a ministry faithfully, yet not up to standards, that they should consider participating in training workshops or even trying another ministry. We must strive to identify our strengths and our weaknesses, and encourage ourselves and others to use our strengths to build up the body of Christ.

RE-ENACTMENT REPLACING REMEMBRANCE

Both the past and the future shape and focus our liturgical celebrations. As Thomas Talley writes:

> We always live . . . between memory and hope, between [Christ's] coming and his coming; and the present which is the threshold between these, between memory and hope, between past and future, this present is the locus of the presence of him who is at once Lord of History and its consummation. [17]

In our Judeo-Christian tradition, we acknowledge that God has intervened in human history, particularly in the exodus from Egypt and in the passion of Jesus. Our *anamnesis*, our active remembering, of these events gives us strength for the present and hope for the future. An ancient piety sees certain historical events as prefigurements of God's ongoing interaction with us. The Jewish seder proclaims: "In every generation, each of us should regard ourselves as though we came out of Egypt. . . . It was not only our ancestors whom the Holy One, forever blessed, redeemed from slavery, but we too were redeemed with them." [18]

As Christians, we not only remember the past but we also look forward and "eagerly await the coming of our Savior, the Lord Jesus Christ" (PHIL 3:20). In joyous expectation, the Church repeats the early Christian prayer, "Maranatha—Come, Lord Jesus;" (1 COR 16:22, REV 22:20).

It is not easy to balance being inspired by the past and being eager for the future. One aspect seems to dominate, sometimes to the detriment of the other, and often to the detriment of our lives in the present. In the fifth century, Pope Leo the Great was able quite vividly to link the past to the present. Leo wrote: "The body that lay lifeless in the tomb is ours. The body that rose again on the third day is ours."[19] In a similar way, an authentic liturgical piety will continue to assist us to see our own city streets as those of Jerusalem, our own sufferings as the passion of our Savior, our own tombs as the tomb of Christ.

In attempting to reflect on the development of specialized celebrations and of religious practices that recall biblical events in dramatic ways, authors have used the word "historicism." Historicism describes the phenomenon that focuses on the events of Christ's life as a sequence of distinct occurrences that are remembered more as past history than as present reality.[20] Some authors, such as Anglican scholar Gregory Dix, sees the development of historicism as detrimental to authentic Christian liturgy, being opposed to a forward-looking, eschatological attitude. Others, such as Thomas Talley and Father Robert Taft, SJ, are more nuanced in their evaluation of the phenomenon. Taft notes that an appreciation of and a respect for *history* is not the same as *historicism.*[21]

When discussing historicism, scholars often focus on the celebrations of Holy Week. In these liturgical rites one often finds a concern for details that develops into a mimicry of historical events. In his study on Holy Week, Anglican liturgist Kenneth Stevenson identifies three types of piety related to liturgy, which he calls: *unitive, rememorative,* and *representational.*[22]

For Stevenson, unitive piety views the paschal mystery of Christ's death and resurrection as one event and does not separate the celebration of Christ's death from the celebration of his resurrection. This piety is often associated with an eschatological thrust in worship. Conscious of being renewed through the paschal mystery, Christians at prayer look toward the future, eagerly awaiting the *eschaton,* the end of the world and the fulfillment of all things in Christ.

Stevenson associates rememorative piety with remembering specific occurrences in the life of Christ. Liturgical rites based on this piety focus on one aspect of the mystery of Christ and commemorate historical events through the symbols of the liturgy in a vaguely historical fashion, without any sort of play-acting. This piety may have been promoted by pilgrims visiting shrines in the Holy Land identified with certain events in the life of Jesus.

Representational piety is linked with imitating historical events. Examples include dramatic re-enactments of scenes from the passion of Christ, or the washing of the feet of the twelve disciples.

Unitive piety enables us to remember the resurrection on Good Friday as well as remembering the cross on Easter. For many people this piety is at the foundation of liturgy. Through word and action, each person in the assembly becomes the presence that we together celebrate. Representational piety, on the other hand, appeals to our emotions and senses, and often emphasizes what is secondary in liturgy. It delights in using donkeys on Passion Sunday and tempts priests to break the altar bread during the eucharistic prayer, mimicking the gestures of Christ.

Stevenson's categories may not be nuanced enough and they may not be helpful when someone needs to make choices in preparing a liturgical celebration. Yet they provide one way to analyze the different influences that shape liturgical attitudes. He and others have made us aware that different religious pieties need to be acknowledged since they may be competing for prominence in our celebrations rather than coexisting and complementing each other.[23]

In liturgy, we are faced with remembering the past, yet challenged to avoid the temptation to relive it. A holistic liturgical piety balances remembering historical events with celebrating their meaning in our lives. A liturgical celebration that is dominated by vivid, representational rites can be counterproductive. Thomas Ryan cautions: "Liturgy is a symbolic way for a church to act out its identity. It is not a drama to be watched. The incursion of drama into the liturgy threatens to burn the sacrament with its heat."[24]

We are not accustomed to subtlety or symbol. We crave the obvious, and at times replace memory with mimicry. It is easier to watch the re-enactment of an historical event than to discuss how historical forces are present in our day-to-day lives. It is easier to be attentive to things that we see or hear than to the underlying reality conveyed by symbol. It is this mystery that shapes and motivates our hearts. How often do we spend hours writing prayer intercessions yet ignore using eucharistic bread that is recognizable as food? How often do we dramatize the gospel words yet overlook the gospel message in the lives of those assembled?

There may be times and places for a more dramatic type of piety. One should not lightly dismiss the power of well-celebrated stations of the cross. Pilgrimages to religious shrines can be occasions of intense spiritual experiences for individuals. Seeing the Passion Play at Oberammergau can be a once in a lifetime experience. Visiting Jerusalem and the sites of Christ's passion can provide spiritual nourishment for the heart for years to come.

Yet often in these situations, individuals usually remain individuals experiencing a very personal spiritual consolation. Many consider that what we do in liturgy is distinctively different, for in liturgy we continue Christ's presence in those assembled as we give praise to the God of all.

Our liturgical tradition has developed over 2,000 years and it is difficult to separate different types of piety in our lives. Yet an awareness of various pieties should also warn us to evaluate carefully liturgical embellishments.

Secondary elements can overwhelm what is primary, and a nostalgic longing for being with the historical Jesus may blind us to seeing the Lord present to us in the people and events of each day.

BECOMING COMFORTABLE WITH MEDIOCRITY

There are numerous factors in Western culture that lead to a spirit of mediocrity. We are surrounded by items that become obsolete in a few years, and so there is little drive to produce things that will endure. We extol the virtue of equality of every person, but that can sometimes lead to public entertainment that is based on the least common denominator. We value functionality over beauty, and ease of use over quality.

These societal influences affect our worship. There was a certain majesty in religious art of ages past. Much of that grandeur is not obvious in contemporary art. Whether it is the decorations, images, vesture, vessels, or music, one gets the impression that the composer or artisan was not concerned about permanence, and might unconsciously be fostering shoddy worship.

Some have suggested that the story of Cain and Abel can be seen as an image of authentic versus inauthentic worship. It is often said that God was not pleased with Cain's sacrifice because he did not offer the best of his crops. How often are we comfortable with second best in our worship, and do not use it as an opportunity to improve?

Music in Catholic Worship acknowledges that perfection is never achieved overnight. To this end, it quotes the words of St. Augustine: "Do not allow yourselves to be offended by the imperfect while you strive for the perfect."[25] But this document also emphasizes that improvement is a never-ending process and that music used in the liturgy should be of appropriate quality.

> Is the music technically, aesthetically, and expressively good? . . .
> Only artistically sound music will be effective in the long run. To admit the cheap, the trite, the musical cliché . . . is to cheapen the liturgy, to expose it to ridicule, and to invite failure.[26]

Environment and Art in Catholic Worship expresses similar sentiments when it speaks about quality, dignity, and beauty. It wisely suggests that all "implements used in liturgical celebration should be of such quality and design that they speak of the importance of the ritual action."[27] The same wisdom also applies to other areas of worship as well. These and similar statements prod us to move beyond mediocrity, wherever it appears, and ever strive to improve our liturgical life.

INADEQUATE WORSHIP SPACE

The statement, "We shape our buildings; thereafter they shape us," is attributed to Sir Winston Churchill.[28] The place in which we worship is itself a symbol of the action that occurs there. The space should be appropriate for the assembly to praise God and celebrate the mystery of the body of Christ. It should be a *domus ecclesiae,* "a house of the Church," more than a temple of God.[29]

Certain floorplans for worship spaces are more in keeping with the vision of the Church and of liturgy enunciated by Vatican II than other models. It is not hard to see why buildings that resemble auditoriums may inhibit celebration, since such floorplans are associated with people passively listening to a performance. Everything associated with the worship space should serve the assembly gathered for liturgy and promote active participation, rather than inhibit common prayer.

It is easy to see how a Byzantine Catholic church, with an iconostasis and lacking an ambo and musical instruments, might not lend itself to a proper celebration of the Roman mass. However, it is more difficult to realize that older Roman churches may also not be ideal for celebrating the revised Roman mass.

The arrangement of seating can help as well as hinder participation. The placement of the altar, the ambo, the tabernacle, the font, and the presidential chair makes a statement about what is important and what is not. For this reason, some unremodeled, older churches can cloud the mysteries that are celebrated within them. Older designs often instill an audience mentality among those assembled. Newer churches, unfortunately, can sometimes present a different set of problems. In an attempt to facilitate visibility, architects occasionally arrange seating that inhibits processions, or provide carpeted aisles that deaden the acoustics.[30]

The beauty of the visual arts should enhance the worship environment and not distract from the actions that take place. The placement of altar and tabernacle should indicate different aspects of the same reality rather than setting up foci that compete for the attention of the assembly. Everything in the worship space—from seating for the assembly to the table of God's word to the table of Christ's body and blood—must be arranged to be of service to the Christians who will gather to praise their God.

FORGETTING THAT LITURGY IS WORK

"Liturgy" is derived from a Greek word that means "the work of the people." Liturgy is work and should not be taken for granted. Introductions, intercessions, homilies cannot be prepared in a merely a few seconds. Preparing and coordinating the celebration of our sacramental mysteries takes time and energy.

But liturgy is also a "work of God" as the celebration of the Liturgy of the Hours is often called in the monastic tradition. We should never think that the right music, the right architecture, the right ministers, the right choices, the right style, or the right words will ever capture our God, who is beyond our human ability to comprehend and sequester.

Nevertheless, liturgy that is celebrated according to the best of Christian traditions can help open ourselves up to the mystery of God and of Christ's body, the Church. This is a goal well worth all our efforts.

POSTSCRIPT

This book began with a consideration of the phrase *liturgia semper reformanda* and it concludes on the same note. The liturgy will continue to evolve as the world changes. But through it all, the reality the Church celebrates will remain the same. As Christians, we celebrate God's love made visible through the mystery of the birth and life, but especially the death and resurrection of Christ.

There have been many changes in the world and in the Catholic Church in the last several decades and other changes continue to occur. One can pity instructors of contemporary politics or history who must read the morning paper to decide what to teach later during the day. As we continue to change with our world, our evolution as individuals, as communities, and as a Church will affect how we celebrate the mystery of Christ. Yet, the constant is that God's love will remain, and Christ's life will continue to be a paradigm for us to imitate. The mysteries that are part of our liturgical life are there to nourish and support us as we continue our struggle to respond to Christ's constant invitation to take up our crosses each day and to follow in his steps (cf. LK 9:23).

St. Paul reminds us that we are the body of Christ (1 COR 12:27). A body is an organism that lives, grows, and changes. There is continuity, yet there is adaptation and growth. So it is with the Church. As time passes, the Church and its members continue to grow toward maturity, and in the process the Church comes to a fuller understanding of the mystery of God's love, the mystery of Christ. The process is never really completed, but continues.

As we look toward the future, toward the mystery of Christ's coming in glory and the fulfillment of all things in Christ, our prayer should be that the sacramental mysteries we celebrate in our Christian assemblies draw us closer to the mystery of Christ's life in us. As we share in the mystery of Christ's life, may we also share the mystery of God's love with our world.

NOTES

Bibliographical references to books in the following notes are given in abbreviated form, by author and title only. The full reference can be found by consulting the Bibliography.

PREFACE

1. Ware, *The Orthodox Church*, p. 281. The fourth-century bishop Athanasius seems to have been first to use the term *mystery* in relationship to liturgical rites. Cf. Neunheuser, *Baptism and Confirmation*, p. 96. In this century, the Benedictine monk Odo Casel renewed the use of the term *mystery*. Cf. Casel, *The Mystery of Christian Worship*.

2. Hopko, *The Orthodox Faith: Vol. II—Worship*, p. 25.

3. Romano Guardini (1885–1968), an early leader of the contemporary liturgical movement, used a similar distinction when he wrote about the differences between *contemplating* and *analyzing* concepts. Cf. *The Church and the Catholic and the Spirit of the Liturgy*, p. 29.

4. Mark Searle, in Finn and Schellman, *Shaping English Liturgy*, p. 91.

5. See *Notitiae*, v. 25 (1989) p. 266, p. 506 and v. 28 (1992) pp. 9 ff, for notes on the *Liturgy of the Hours*. See *Notitiae*, v. 27 (1991), pp. 38 ff, for a report on the discussion on the planned third edition of the *Roman Missal*.

6. *Constitution on the Sacred Liturgy*, art. 11. Cf. art. 14.

CHAPTER 1—*LITURGIA SEMPER REFORMANDA*

1. *Decree on Ecumenism*, Chapter II, n. 6.

2. The immutability of doctrine has been the Catholic tradition but was called into question during the Reformation. In fact, the longer phrase, *Ecclesia reformata sed semper reformanda*, "the Church reformed but always needing to be reformed," seems to have originated in the reformed churches

of the sixteenth century, in particular among the Huguenots. (Meagher, *et al.*, *Encyclopedic Dictionary of Religion*, p. 1148.) Nevertheless, the abbreviated phrase is an appropriate expression of classical Catholic belief, especially in the context of conciliar decrees that include it in paraphrased form.

3. E.g., *Constitution on the Sacred Liturgy*, art. 2, 7, 8, 9.

4. *Ibid.*, art. 11.

5. *Ibid.*, art. 21.

6. Quoted in *The Making of the New Revised Standard Version of the Bible* by Metzger, *et al.*, p. 49. The authors note that Jerome's *Epistula ad Damasum* is included in Latin editions of the Vulgate as a preface.

7. *Ibid.*, p. 50.

8. *Constitution on the Sacred Liturgy*, art. 38 and 40.

9. The revision of translations was envisioned by the 1969 *Instruction on Translation of Liturgical Texts*, n. 1: "After sufficient experiment and passage of time, all translations will need review." After a revised translation along with any rubrical and ritual accommodations or textual rearrangements have been been approved by a national conference of bishops, usually any previous version may no longer be used. See, for example, the decree by the U.S. National Conference of Catholic Bishops contained in the revised *Pastoral Care of the Sick: Rites of Anointing and Viaticum*: "From that day forward no other vernacular versions of these rites may be used."

10. Cf. Chupungco, *Cultural Adaptation in the Liturgy*, especially pp. 81–86, for a discussion of the distinction between *acculturation* and *inculturation*. Also cf. Chupungco, *Liturgies of the Future*, pp. 25–33. Vatican support of inculturation is evidenced by *The Fourth Instruction for the Right Application of the Conciliar Constitution on the Liturgy: The Roman Liturgy and Inculturation*, January 25, 1994, and issued March 29, 1994 by the Congregation for Divine Worship and the Discipline of the Sacraments.

11. Mark Searle, "Renewing the Liturgy—Again: 'A' For the Council, 'C' for the Church," *Commonweal*, 18 November 1988, p. 620.

12. *Ibid.*, p. 618.

13. Talley, *Worship: Reforming Tradition*, p. 49.

CHAPTER 2—FROM PRINCIPLES TO PRACTICE

1. *Constitution on the Sacred Liturgy*, art. 14–20.

2. *Ibid.*, art. 7.

3. Thomas Kuhn, in his book, *The Structure of Scientific Revolutions*, used the phrase "paradigm shift" to describe a major shift in understanding that has taken place in human history, particularly due to scientific discoveries. The terminology has since been applied to significant changes in other human disciplines.

4. Steven R. Janco criticizes liberties sometimes taken in "Youth Masses." "Planners and presiders must be careful not to 'create' liturgies which are so unique that they bear little resemblance to Sunday worship in the Roman Rite. In abandoning the ritual in favor of something more 'relevant,' we run the risk of isolating teens from the Sunday assembly and from the larger church." Cf. "What About a Youth Mass?" *Modern Liturgy*, v. 19, n. 3 (April 1992), pp. 15–17. Also, cf. Smolarski, *How Not To Say Mass*, pp. 10, 26.

5. Theresa F. Koernke, "Toward an Ethics of Liturgical Behavior," *Worship*, v. 66, n. 1 (January 1992), pp. 25–38.

6. Mark Searle, "Renewing the Liturgy—Again: 'A' For the Council, 'C' for the Church," *Commonweal*, 18 November 1988, p. 621.

7. Kathleen Hughes, RSCJ, "Speaking in the Future Tense," p. 139 in Madden, *The Awakening Church: 25 Years of Liturgical Renewal*.

8. Bugnini, *The Reform of the Liturgy 1948–1975*. Botte, *From Silence to Participation*. Also see Finn and Schellman, *Shaping English Liturgy*.

Chapter 3—The Foundational Mysteries in the Church's Worship

1. Diekmann, "The Laying On of Hands: The Basic Sacramental Rite," *Liturgy*, v. 21, n. 1 (Jan. 1976), p. 22.

2. Referred to in Diekmann, *loc. cit.*, p. 27.

3. Hippolytus, *Apostolic Tradition*, Chapter 21.

4. *Rite of Christian Initiation of Adults*, n. 220, cf. Provisional English Text, 1974. Unfortunately in the present translation the introductory phrase, "Touching the candidate," no longer appears (cf. n. 226 of the U.S. edition).

5. Cf. *Rite of Penance*, nn. 19, 46. The rubrics allow the extension of the right hand only in those cases where it is impossible to extend both hands, for example, when a wall and grill make it physically impossible to hold both hands over the head of the penitent. Whenever there is no grill, the priest should hold both hands over the penitent's head while pronouncing the absolution, and, if it seems appropriate, lay his hands on the penitent's head during the absolution. The gentle gesture should be seen as a symbol that conveys God's healing, forgiving grace. A significant number of priests seem not to understand the importance of the laying on of hands. Perhaps they do not realize that the rubrics regarding the gesture were changed in the revision of the rite. As a result, even in face-to-face situations, some still follow the pre-1973 rubrics and raise only their right hands in an awkward gesture that resembles the taking of an oath.

6. Latin text, n. 45, *Pastoral Care of the Sick*, n. 61.

7. Krosnicki, in Finn and Schellman, *Shaping English Liturgy*, p. 104.

8. *Ibid.*

9. Thomas Day even suggests that "Good morning" is often associated with distancing someone from another, and that most such secular greetings call attention to the greeter, thereby expressing a "blatant display of the ego" when used by the presiding priest during a liturgical service. Cf. Day, *Why Catholics Can't Sing*, p. 54.

10. Hovda, "The Amen Corner: Cautionary Tales About Liturgy's Verbal Parts," *Worship*, v. 61, n. 3 (May 1987), p. 247.

11. E.g., Keifer, *To Give Thanks and Praise*, p. 109; Kavanagh, *The Elements of Rite*, p. 77; Challancin, *The Assembly Celebrates*, p. 27.

12. Keifer, *op. cit.*, p. 109; Walsh, *From Rubrics to Ritual: Celebrating the Difference!*, p. 26.

13. Hovda, *loc. cit.*, p. 247.

14. Hovda in Kay (ed.) *It Is Your Own Mystery*, pp. 31–33.

15. Hovda, *Strong, Loving and Wise*, pp. 70–72.

16. E.g., Victor W. Turner, *The Ritual Process: Structure and Anti-Structure*, "Passages, Margins, and Poverty: Religious Symbols of Communitas."

17. *Rite of Baptism for Children*, nn. 35, 74, 103.

18. *Rite of Marriage* (1969 edition), nn. 19, 39.

19. *Order of Christian Funerals* (1989 U.S. edition), n. 159.

20. Congregation for Divine Worship, *Circular Letter on Preparing and Celebrating the Paschal Feasts*, January 16, 1988, n. 23. Cf. *Ceremonial of Bishops*, n. 261.

21. General Instruction of the Liturgy of the Hours, n. 213.

22. Psalm 141:2. Also see 1 Tim 2:8.

23. For excerpts from the General Introduction to the adaptations for masses in Zaire, see *Notitiae*, v. 24, n. 7 (1988), pp. 454–72.

24. Tertullian, *On the Resurrection of the Flesh*, 8.

25. Baker, *A Stress Analysis of a Strapless Evening Gown: Essays for a Scientific Age*, Chapter 2: "Body Ritual Among the Nacirema" by Horace Miner, p. 6.

26. Collins, *Worship: Renewal to Practice*, p. 294.

27. Cf. "Ritual," in Fink, *The New Dictionary of Sacramental Worship*, pp. 1101–1106.

28. Talley, *Worship: Reforming Tradition*, pp. 151–53.

29. Quoted in *The National Bulletin on the Liturgy*, v. 25, n. 129 (Summer 1992), p. 99.

Chapter 4—The Great Mystery of Baptism

1. *Didache*, Chapter 7.

2. Hippolytus, *Apostolic Tradition*, Chapter 21.

3. Neunheuser, *Baptism and Confirmation*, p. 241.

4. Ware, *The Orthodox Church*, p. 282.

5. Fisher, *Confirmation: Then and Now*, p. 79.

6. *Christian Initiation*, General Introduction, nn. 3, 4, 5, 6.

7. General Instruction of the Liturgy of the Hours, nn. 7, 8.

8. *Christian Initiation*, General Introduction, n. 22.

9. Second Vatican Council, *Decree on the Missionary Activity of the Church*, nn. 13, 14; *Constitution on the Sacred Liturgy*, art. 64–69. Father Aidan Kavanagh, OSB writes: "The conciliar emphasis is clearly on the adult nature of the norm of Christian initiation. . . . In this, the normal as defined by tradition is differentiated from the usual as defined by convention. . . . But [infant baptism's] abnormality does not require one to conclude that it is illegitimate." *The Shape of Baptism*, p. 109.

10. *Constitution on the Sacred Liturgy*, art. 64–66.

11. *Rite of Christian Initiation of Adults*, n. 215. Cf. *Code of Canon Law*, canon 885 §2. This canon is cited in the United States National Statues for the Catechumenate (11 November 1986), n. 13, included as Appendix III in the United States editions of the RCIA.

12. *Rite of Baptism for Children*, Introduction, n. 14. Cf. Rite of Baptism for Several Children, n. 43.

13. *Rite of Baptism for Children*, n. 51.

14. Since many Latin rite Catholic priests are unfamiliar with baptizing infants by immersion, an initial attempt at using this option may require some careful practice and consultation with those more experienced. Here are three points to consider.

- If the infant is slowly lowered into a font of warm water, similar to lowering the infant into a bassinet for a bath, there is certainly no danger to the child. A baby can be lowered into the water up to its breasts and held there by the parents, while the priest pours water and pronounces the formula. Especially for infants, this format allows the child to be totally washed without getting water into the child's nose. (Some commentators have pointed out that immersion does not necessarily imply *submersion*.)

- The temperature of the water is more crucial for infants than for adults. Among some Eastern Christians, it is the duty of the godmother to test the temperature of the water of the font before an infant is placed in it.

- Natural reflexes must be respected and precautions taken. In particular, it is not unusual for an infant to urinate when placed in warm water. Let nature take its course. Priests and deacons who have had little experience dealing with infants are forewarned about this possibility and should keep this in mind when holding an infant at the font. (Take some comfort in the fact that urine ordinarily is sterile.) Fonts with recirculating systems with water purifiers should be able to handle this problem with no trouble.

15. The Rite of Baptism for Several Children (Chapter I of the *Rite of Baptism for Children*) mentions several places where singing is desirable: n. 35 (opening song), n. 42 (procession into the church), n. 44 (liturgy of the word), n. 46 (after the homily), n. 52 (procession to the font), n. 59 (profession of faith), n. 60 (post-baptismal acclamation), n. 67 (procession to the altar), n. 71 (final hymn).

16. *Rite of Baptism for Children*, Introduction, n. 9.

17. *Christian Initiation*, General Introduction, n. 27. Rite of Baptism for Several Children, n. 32.

18. *Constitution on the Sacred Liturgy*, art. 26, 27.

19. *Rite of Baptism for Children*, Introduction, n. 10.

20. *Rite of Baptism for Children*, Introduction, nn. 12, 13.

21. *Rite of Baptism for Children*, Introduction, n. 11; *Christian Initiation*, General Introduction, nn. 12–14.

22. Cf. *Code of Canon Law*, canon 860 §1.

23. According to Robert Bellah, "individualism lies at the very core of American culture." Cf. *Habits of the Heart*, p. 142.

24. *The Milwaukee Symposia for Church Composers: A Ten-Year Report*, par. 53. This restates a point noted by the *Dogmatic Constitution on the Church, Lumen Gentium*, of the Second Vatican Council: "[God has] willed to make men and women holy and save them, not as individuals . . . but rather to make them into a people" (n. 9).

25. *Constitution on the Sacred Liturgy*, art. 26.

26. *Roman Ritual* (1614), Tit. II, c. 1, n. 10.

27. Cf. Gail Ramshaw-Schmidt, "Naming the Trinity: Orthodoxy and Inclusivity," *Worship*, v. 60, n. 6 (Nov. 1986), p. 492. Also see Duck, *Gender and the Name of God: The Trinitarian Baptismal Formula*.

In the fall of 1993, newspaper accounts carried a story of a Catholic priest in the New England area who had baptized infants using a non-traditional formula. Those baptisms were declared invalid by the bishop and the families were contacted so that the infants could be baptized validly using the traditional formula.

A significant problem with some alternative formulas is the tendency to identify one person of the Trinity with one specific external function. Although it is legitimate to attribute some activity to a specific person (for example, the Apostles' Creed states that the "Father Almighty [is] Creator of heaven and earth"), there has been a traditional hesitation in attributing some specific function exclusively with a particular person, for instance, in equating the external function of being Creator with the internal trinitarian reality of being the first person. Note that John's gospel states that through the Word "all things came into being" (1:3) suggesting a creative activity to the second person, and that a traditional hymn to the third person is *Veni, Creator Spiritus* ("Come, Creator Spirit").

28. In *Strong, Loving and Wise*, Hovda criticizes a booklet on celebrating baptism that "was full of suggestions about peripheral aspects of the celebration [but] said nothing at all about the actual bathing, the washing with water" (p. 30).

CHAPTER 5—THE GREAT MYSTERY OF CONFIRMATION

1. In *The Bible and the Liturgy*, Daniélou writes, "The history of the origins of the sacrament of Confirmation is one of the most obscure chapters in the origins of Christian worship." (p. 114)

2. Neunheuser, *Baptism and Confirmation*, Kavanagh, *Confirmation: Origins and Reform*, Fisher, *Confirmation: Then and Now*.

3. Hippolytus, *Apostolic Tradition*, Chapter 21.

4. *Constitution on the Sacred Liturgy*, art. 71, "The rite of confirmation is to be revised and the intimate connection which this sacrament has with the whole of Christian initiation is to be more lucidly set forth." Also see the 1971 apostolic constitution *Divinae consortium naturae* of Pope Paul VI promulgating the revised rite. In several places it clearly states that confirmation is the second sacrament of initiation, and that the entire initiation process is completed by participation in the eucharist: "the faithful are born anew by baptism, strengthened by the sacrament of confirmation, and finally are sustained by the food of eternal life in the eucharist. . . . [the faithful] after being signed by baptism and confirmation, are incorporated fully into the Body of Christ by participation in the eucharist." Also see *Rite of Confirmation*, n. 13, and *Rite of Christian Initiation of Adults*, n. 217 (U.S. edition) (n. 36, Latin edition). It is also presupposed by the 1983 *Code of Canon Law*, canons 842 §2 and 891, which prescribes the age of discretion for the reception of confirmation.

5. Kavanagh, *The Shape of Baptism*, p. 46.

6. *Code of Canon Law* (1917), canon 788.

7. That the reception of the eucharist constitutes the full incorporation into the Body of Christ, and thus the completion of initiation, is explicitly proclaimed in Paul VI's decree quoted in note 4. Also see the discussion in the *Newsletter* of the Bishops' Committee on the Liturgy (U.S.), XXVIII (May 1992), pp. 18–20.

8. Unfortunately, this approach still presents the problem that one

would have a single sacrament with two different "meanings"—one meaning
when celebrated with adults and unbaptized children of catechetical age, and
a different meaning when celebrated with young people who were baptized as
infants.

9. Cf. Botte, *From Silence to Participation*, p. 155. Kavanagh speaks
about "bending liturgy to serve . . . pastoral needs" and says that "good practice does not proceed from bad theology" (*Confirmation: Origins and Reform*,
pp. 63, 113).

10. *Rite of Christian Initiation of Adults*, n. 305 (U.S. edition).

11. See note 4 above.

12. *Code of Canon Law*, canon 1065, §1.

13. *Constitution on the Sacred Liturgy*, art. 71.

14. Unfortunately, too often there are odd objections raised about distributing communion under both kinds to children, oblivious to the fact that this
has never been an issue for Eastern Catholics who have never had the custom
of communion under the form of bread only—even for children.

15. Cf. *Rite of Confirmation*, n. 9. "The laying of hands on the candidates with the prayer, *All-powerful God*, does not pertain to the valid giving of
the sacrament. But it is still to be regarded as very important."

16. *Rite of Confirmation*, n. 5.

17. Similar thoughts also apply to the use of oil in anointing the sick.
See the relevant comments in Chapter 8 below.

18. *Pastoral Care of the Sick*, n. 107.

19. See Peter Mazar, "Oil," *Liturgy 80*, v. 19, n. 4 (May/June 1988), pp.
8–9 and v. 19, n. 5 (July 1988), pp. 8–11.

CHAPTER 6—THE GREAT MYSTERY OF THE EUCHARIST

1. Cf. Moloney, *Our Eucharistic Prayers in Worship, Preaching and
Study*, p. 15; Smolarski, *Eucharistia*, p. 15.

2. Cf. St. Justin Martyr, 1 *Apol.* 65.

3. Gregory Dix, in *The Shape of the Liturgy*, first proposed that the
structure of the liturgy of the eucharist was based on the four biblical verbs.
The General Instruction of the Roman Missal, n. 48, also uses the biblical
narratives to justify the structure of the liturgy of the eucharist, but highlights
three verbs. Contemporary scholars tend to be more nuanced about the exact
connection between the biblical texts and the ritual structure.

4. St. Jerome, *In Epist. ad Galat.* 2, *praef.*, PL 26:381; cf. Cabié, *The
Church at Prayer (Vol. II): The Eucharist*, p. 46.

5. The ten eucharistic prayers now permitted throughout the world are
as follows: the Roman Canon (Eucharistic Prayer I) taken with minor modifications from the Tridentine missal, three additional prayers published in the

late 1960s and included in the 1970 missal, two prayers for reconciliation and three for masses with children, published in the mid-1970s, and a prayer for special circumstances, a slight revision of the prayer issued for the Swiss Synod in the late 1970s. The eucharistic prayer for special circumstances has been included in Spanish, Polish, French and Italian sacramentaries, but as of 1995, only the Philippines had an approved English version. Certain countries have had additional eucharistic prayers approved, for example, Holland and England (for masses for deaf people).

6. *Rite of Christian Initiation of Adults*, n. 217 (United States edition); *Christian Initiation*, General Introduction, n. 2.

7. Power, *The Eucharistic Mystery: Revitalizing the Tradition*, p. viii.

8. Schmemann, "Theology and Liturgical Tradition," in Shepherd, *Worship in Scripture and Tradition*, p. 177.

9. Schmemann, *Liturgy and Life: Christian Development Through Liturgical Experience*, p. 60. Cf. Fagerberg, *What Is Liturgical Theology?* chapter 4.

10. General Instruction of the Roman Missal, n. 42.

11. Bishop John S. Cummins. "Twenty Years of Liturgical Renewal in the United States: Assessments and Prospects," in McManus, *Thirty Years of Liturgical Renewal*, p. 244. Cf. Botte, *From Silence to Participation*, p. 68. For suggestions for improving homilies, see *Fulfilled in Your Hearing*.

12. Much has already been written since the promulgation of the 1970 missal about the revised mass, both in global, historical, and academic terms and also in pastoral terms to help improve eucharistic celebrations. Cf. Emminghaus, *The Eucharist*; Cabié, *The Church at Prayer (Vol. II): The Eucharist*; Smolarski, *How Not To Say Mass*; Kavanagh, *Elements of Rite*.

13. Cf. Bugnini, *The Reform of the Liturgy: 1948–1975* for an in-depth commentary on the proposals of the Consilium and the compromises struck at the request of Pope Paul VI.

14. See *Notitiae*, v. 25 (1989), p. 266, p. 506 and v. 28 (1992), pp. 9 ff for notes on the *Liturgy of the Hours*. See *Notitiae*, v. 27 (1991), pp. 38 ff for a report on the discussion on the planned third edition of the *Roman Missal*. It has been acknowledged that some sections of the General Instruction of the Roman Missal (GIRM) need revision. For example, in the section concerning communion under both kinds (GIRM nn. 240–252), which was taken with very little change from the original document issued in 1965, two methods are described that are probably never used—communion via a tube (straw), or communion via a spoon. It is odd that the General Instruction does not mention the widespread custom of singing a recessional hymn. The GIRM also does not mention the rite of blessing and sprinkling holy water as an option for the opening rites, even though this rite is contained in an appendix in the *Roman Missal* and has been encouraged in subsequent Roman docu-

ments (see the Congregation for Divine Worship's *Circular Letter on Preparing and Celebrating the Paschal Feasts*, January 16, 1988, n. 97, and see the *Ceremonial of Bishops*, n. 133). There has also been discussion of simplifying the opening rites to avoid its duplications and of permitting the presiding priest to omit reciting silent prayers in order to join the assembly in song. Note that the Order of Mass is the only rite in which there are prayers prescribed for the presiding priest to be said privately.

15. *Ceremonial of Bishops*, n. 133.

16. 2. *Das Allgemeine Schuldbekenntnis kann entfallen, wenn eine besondere Festlichkeit des Gottesdienstes dies nahelegt.* "The penitential rite may be omitted when a particularly solemn celebration occurs." 3. *Die Vergebungsbitte kann entfallen, wenn das Tagesgebet eine solche Bitte enthält.* "The absolution can be omitted when the opening prayer contains a request for pardon." (rubrics 2 and 3 after the Penitential Rite and before the *Kyrie* in the *Messbuch.*)

17. See note 14.

18. *Constitution on the Sacred Liturgy*, art. 28; General Instruction of the Roman Missal, nn. 34, 66.

19. General Instruction of the Roman Missal, n. 276 (tabernacle), n. 272 (ambo), n. 271 (chair). *Introduction to the Lectionary* (1981 edition), nn. 32–34 (ambo). *Environment and Art in Catholic Worship*, nn. 70–75 (chair, altar, ambo).

20. Cf. Gilligan, *How to Prepare Mass*, pp. 85, 89–93.

21. General Instruction of the Roman Missal, n. 23

22. *Introduction to the Lectionary* (1981 edition), n. 28.

23. General Instruction of the Roman Missal, n. 283.

24. The focus of this chapter has been on the celebration of the eucharist. Hence, little has said about eucharistic devotions outside of mass. Yet, certain eucharistic devotions as well as prayer before the reserved sacrament in the tabernacle, if anchored in the celebration of the mass, can be beneficial in helping Christians appreciate the great mystery of the eucharist. Cf. Mitchell, *Cult and Controversy: The Worship of the Eucharist Outside Mass.*

25. Official documents list certain restrictions, such as at very large gatherings or at outdoor masses in stadiums. See *This Holy and Living Sacrifice: Directory for the Celebration and Reception of Communion under Both Kinds*, United States Catholic Conference, Nov 1. 1984, n. 22.

26. General Instruction of the Roman Missal, nn. 240, 56h.

27. *This Holy and Living Sacrifice*, n. 19.

28. General Instruction of the Roman Missal, n. 56i.

29. The General Instruction of the Roman Missal, n. 56j, explicitly mentions that priest and people may spend time in silent prayer, but it says that this should occur "after communion." The Latin text is more explicit:

distributione Communionis expleta, "when the distribution of communion is completed." When the extended period of silent prayer after communion is concluded by a communal hymn, some places have instrumental music during the recessional instead of yet another hymn.

30. The American bishops' statement, *Music in Catholic Worship,* mentions three considerations for determining the value of a given musical selection: the musical judgment, the liturgical judgment, and the pastoral judgment (nn. 25–41). Also see *Liturgical Music Today.*

CHAPTER 7—THE GREAT MYSTERY OF PENANCE

1. The history of the sacrament of penance can be found in various places. For example, see Crichton, *Christian Celebration: Understanding the Sacraments,* Chapter 11. Crichton mentions that the "form of penance, which we have come to regard as typical, was little used before the Fourth Lateran Council (1215) which decreed that all should go to confession at least once a year before making their Easter communion. . . . The council desired that people should approach communion worthily and that the custom of infrequent communions (once or twice in a lifetime!) should cease" (p. 222).

2. The 1614 *Roman Ritual* never required a confessional to preserve the anonymity of the penitent. The grating was only required when the penitent was female (for the sake of avoiding any hint of scandal between a woman and a priest). Also see the 1917 *Code of Canon Law,* canons 909 and 910. Over the years, anonymity became a presupposition in some countries, and most pre-Vatican II confessionals in the United States were built so that the priest could not determine the identity of the penitent on the other side of the grill. On the other hand, in some European countries the confessional grating is such that the priest and penitent can easily see each other.

In some Eastern Churches, there is no separate place for celebrating the sacrament of penance. Among Orthodox and Byzantine Catholics, penance is frequently celebrated before one of the icons of the iconostasis. For the prayer of absolution, the penitent kneels and the priest places the end of his stole over the penitent's head while imposing hands and making the sign of the cross.

3. Cf. Introduction of the *Rite of Penance,* nn. 5, 8.

4. *Rite of Penance,* n. 41.

5. Cf. Introduction of the *Rite of Penance,* n. 17; Rite for Reconciliation of Individual Penitents, the heading before n. 43. Sometimes a priest may have to adapt the order and offer some quotation from scripture as an initial response to the penitent's declaration of sins.

6. Cf. Chapter 3, note 5.

7. Cf. *Code of Canon Law,* canon 961. Many bishops in the United States have expressly prohibited the use of general absolution in their dioceses.

There are only a couple of minor differences in the order when general absolution is given in a communal celebration. After the homily or the examination of conscience, the deacon asks those who wish to receive general absolution to indicate their desire by some sign, for example by kneeling or bowing. Then the expression of sinfulness, litany and Lord's Prayer take place as in the other communal rite. There is no individual confession of sin, but immediately after the Lord's Prayer the priest pronounces the formula of absolution. In place of the standard formula for absolution, the priest may use a longer form, written in the style of a solemn blessing, with three preliminary sections before the final statement of absolution. To each of these sections the assembly responds Amen. After the absolution, there is a final hymn of thanksgiving and a final blessing but no concluding prayer between them. The rubrics also suggest that at the end of the homily (or before the deacon's invitation), the priest assigns an appropriate penance to those who will be receiving general absolution, to which "each individual may add something if he or she desires" (n. 60).

8. Cf. Crichton, *Christian Celebration: Understanding the Sacraments*, p. 246.

9. One alternative would be to allow confessions and absolutions to go for a pre-determined period of time, for example, 20 minutes. At this point, the communal service could be concluded in a usual fashion and the assembly be dismissed. After the communal dismissal, the priests would be available for those who were unable to see a priest earlier or who would like to spend more time receiving advice. This arrangement, though far from ideal, attempts to respect the communal nature of this form of celebrating the sacrament of reconciliation, while trying to address various concerns that affect modern society.

Chapter 8—The Great Mystery of Anointing

1. *Constitution on the Sacred Liturgy*, art. 73–75.

2. Cf. *Pastoral Care of the Sick*, General Introduction, nn. 40–41. Also see the various rubrics, e.g., nn. 121, 240. Also see the rubric in the Latin text (included in the 1974 translation) at n. 73: "The following litany may be said here or after the anointing or even, according to circumstances, at some other point. The priest may adapt or shorten the text." This rubric does not appear in the *Pastoral Care of the Sick*, which specifies the litany to take place at n. 121. In this position, this "prayer of faith" comes before the anointing in order to follow the sequence given in the Letter of James.

3. *Pastoral Care of the Sick*, General Introduction, nn. 38f, 39.

4. Cf. *Pastoral Care of the Sick*, nn. 104, 106.

5. *Pastoral Care of the Sick*, General Introduction, n. 19.

6. *Pastoral Care of the Sick*, n. 107.

7. *Pastoral Care of the Sick*, n. 124. Even if there are several priests and only one or a few sick individuals, the present Roman discipline is for a single priest to perform both of the anointings on each person. The formula is said once for each person, even if the person is anointed on several parts of the body. This is in contrast to the prescriptions of the Byzantine liturgy, used by many Eastern Catholics and Eastern Orthodox. In this ritual, the ideal is to have seven priests concelebrate the mystery of holy anointing. The principal priest blesses the oil, but each of the priests anoints each sick person on all the prescribed parts of the body, repeating the sacramental formula while anointing. From the Western perspective, it can be difficult to determine who is the minister of the sacrament and when exactly the sacrament is administered. However, such questions are foreign to the Eastern approach to liturgical theology.

8. Cf. *Pastoral Care of the Sick*, n. 124. "Depending upon the culture and traditions of the place, as well as the condition of the sick person, the priest may also anoint additional parts of the body, for example, the area of pain or injury. He does not repeat the sacramental form."

9. In practice, it would be difficult to "anoint" someone without some movement of the thumb, so tracing the cross is certainly an appropriate way to convey the anointing.

10. *Constitution on the Sacred Liturgy*, art. 26–27.

11. *Pastoral Care of the Sick*, General Introduction, n. 22.

12. *Pastoral Care of the Sick*, General Introduction, n. 21b, cf. 1983 *Code of Canon Law*, canon 999 §2; *Pastoral Care of the Sick*, n. 140. The Byzantine ritual assumes that the priest will bless fresh oil each time the anointing of the sick is celebrated. Among the Russians, the oil is provided by the family and a small bit of wine is added to it.

13. *Ceremonial of Bishops*, n. 654.

14. *Pastoral Care of the Sick*, n. 99.

15. *Ibid.*, n. 108.

16. *Pastoral Care of the Sick*, General Introduction, n. 8.

17. Huels, *Disputed Questions in the Liturgy Today*, p. 97. The quote from Glen is taken from: "Rites of Healing: A Reflection in Pastoral Theology," in Fink (ed.), *Alternative Futures for Worship: Anointing of the Sick* (Vol. 7), p. 60.

18. *Pastoral Care of the Sick*, General Introduction, n. 8.

19. *Pastoral Care of the Sick*, nn. 181, 193.

20. *Pastoral Care of the Sick*, General Introduction, n. 15. Also n. 263, and at the footnote to n. 269.

21. *Pastoral Care of the Sick*, Commendation of the Dying, nn. 212–222; Prayers for the Dead, nn. 223–231.

CHAPTER 9—THE GREAT MYSTERY OF MARRIAGE

1. In the East, St. Ignatius of Antioch (died around 107) wrote, in his letter to Polycarp, that it is desirable that a Christian couple obtain the "advice of the bishop" before marrying (Chapter 5). But no liturgical texts that date to the first two centuries have yet been discovered. Cf. Stevenson, *Nupital Blessing*, pp. 13ff.

2. Before the thirteenth century, it had been customary in some places for the father of the bride to place her hand into the groom's hand after the expression of consent, and this action by the father was sometimes construed as effecting the marriage. Some local rituals began to include this or similar formulas to indicate that it was the consent of the couple and the recognition of the Church that was significant, rather than the action of the father. The 1614 *Roman Ritual* included the formula that had been used for several centuries, but also permitted the use of other formulas from local rituals.

3. This general rite did not provide for a "double ring ceremony," although local rituals often provided for this option. Local rituals sometimes provided a formula to be used by the couple while placing the rings on each other's finger.

4. Not all Western theologians are comfortable with this formulation. For example, British liturgical author Msgr. J. D. Crichton writes that French liturgical scholar P. M. Gy

> thinks that the expression "ministers of the sacrament" as applied to the spouses is not very happy. He would prefer to say "the spouses themselves form the sacrament." The difficulty seems to lie in an understanding of what is meant by "minister." In a sense and whatever may be held as to who are the "makers" of matrimony, the priest, apart from the most exceptional circumstances, is the indispensable minister and with the couple does celebrate the sacrament.

Cf. La Maison-Dieu, n. 99 (1969), p. 134. Also see Crichton, *Christian Celebration: Understanding the Sacraments*, p. 138, note 24.

It should be noted that one would be hard-pressed to find the term "minister of the sacrament" used in reference to the bride or groom in official ecclesial documents, either. It is not found either in liturgical texts, for example, *The Order of Marriage*, or in conciliar decrees, for example, in the decrees of the Council of Florence in 1438 or of the Council of Trent in 1545, or in the *Constitution on the Sacred Liturgy* of the Second Vatican Council in 1963, or in the 1983 *Code of Canon Law*. It is not found in recent papal encyclicals about marriage (Leo XIII, *Arcanum Divinae Sapientiae*, 1879; Pius XI, *Casti Connubii*, 1930). In his 1943 encyclical on the Mystical Body,

Mystici Corporis, Pius XII did state that bride and groom "are ministers of grace to each other" (n. 20), a phrase that is not the same as "minister of the sacrament." The 1992 *Catechism of the Catholic Church* borrows the terminology of *Mystici Corporis* when it states: "In the Latin Church, it is ordinarily understood that the spouses, as ministers of Christ's grace, mutually confer upon each other the sacrament of Matrimony" (n. 1623), yet it must be realized that the *Catechism,* as a summary document, is not superior to the documents on which it bases its authority. Seemingly, until the 1990s, there is only one occurrence of the bride and groom being termed "minister of the sacrament" in papal writings, and that occurred in an allocution of Pius XII (March 5, 1941) to newlyweds. Such a private, sermon-like statement carries little doctrinal weight, however. It seems odd that so much emphasis is put in popular writings on the bridal couple being "ministers of the sacrament," when so little support could be found for this terminology in authentic church documents.

Certainly, the priest exercises an essential "ministry" in the celebration of the sacrament, since he must ask for and receive the consent of the couple, or else the marriage is rendered invalid. This is distinctly different than other ministries in the celebration of the sacrament, for example, the "ministry" of the two official witnesses, and the "ministry" of the bride and groom, who must also express consent, or else the marriage is also rendered invalid.

The problem with focusing too much on the expression of consent is that it raises problems with marriage as celebrated among other ritual traditions, for example, in Byzantine Churches (both Orthodox and Catholic). In the older usage in Byzantine Churches, there is no vocal expression of consent (no vow formula), and the theology of this mystery as expounded by Orthodox theologians insists that the priest's blessing is the essential moment in the celebration of the sacrament. See Searle and Stevenson, *Documents of the Marriage Liturgy,* p. 270, and *Catechism,* n. 1623.

Although the term "ministers of the sacrament" may not have occurred in official church documents, it was used by many commentators, for example, Jone, *Moral Theology,* p. 467.

5. *Constitution on the Sacred Liturgy,* art. 78.

6. *The Rite of Marriage* (1990 edition), n. 53 (penitential rite), n. 75 (prayer for peace).

7. *The Roman Ritual: Marriage—Ritual and Pastoral Notes,* Ottawa: Canadian Conference of Catholic Bishops, 1979, Pastoral Note 40, p. 41.

8. Nietzsche, *Human All Too Human,* quoted in Covino, *Celebrating Marriage,* p. 2.

9. Covino, *Celebrating Marriage,* p. 2.

10. Ibid.

11. *The Rite of Marriage* (1969 edition), n. 19. "At the appointed time,

the priest . . . goes with the ministers to the door of the church. . . . There he greets the bride and bridegroom in a friendly manner, showing that the Church shares their joy."

12. *The Rite of Marriage* (1969 edition), n. 20. "If there is a procession to the altar, the ministers go first, followed by the priest, and then the bride and bridegroom. According to local custom, they may be escorted by at least their parents and the two witnesses. Meanwhile, the entrance song is sung."

13. British rituals contain a special formula said by the couple before the "vows": "I do solemnly declare that I know not of any lawful impediment why I, N.N. may not be joined in matrimony to N.N." Both this formula and the formula of the "vows" have footnotes that state: "The attention of the priest is drawn to the requirement for the civil validity of the marriage."

14. California Family Law Code, §4206, states that "the parties must declare, in the presence of the person solemnizing the marriage, that they take each other as husband and wife." Thus, if a couple writes "vows" that do not use the words *husband* and *wife,* and instead use a circumlocution such as *spouse* or *life-companion,* the marriage would not be recognized as civilly valid.

15. *The Roman Ritual: Marriage—Ritual and Pastoral Notes,* Ottawa: Canadian Conference of Catholic Bishops, 1979, Pastoral Note 40, pp. 41–42.

16. *Constitution on the Sacred Liturgy,* n. 77; *Rite of Marriage, Introduction,* n. 14; *Code of Canon Law,* canons 1108 §2, and 1120.

Chapter 10—The Great Mystery of Order

1. Cf. Brown, *Priest and Bishop: Biblical Reflections;* McBrien, *Ministry: A Theological-Pastoral Handbook.*

2. Cf. Letters of Ignatius to the Trallians 2,3,7; Ignatius to the Smyrnaeans 8; Ignatius to Polycarp 6.

3. Translations become difficult when Latin texts include both *presbyter* and *sacerdos.* In an attempt to retain the biblical distinction, the translators of the ordination rites have used the word "presbyter" and "presbyterate" when referring specifically to the second order and "priest" and "priesthood" in other contexts (e.g., Old Testament figures, Christ, the Christian community). Such a distinction was not made in the older translations of the documents of Vatican II and, therefore, can make understanding certain statements difficult.

4. The consecratory prayer used at the ordination of bishops now has ecumenical significance, since it is essentially the same prayer found in the *Apostolic Tradition* of Hippolytus, which has been in common use in Byzantine Churches and other Eastern liturgical traditions.

5. Since priests now wash their hands immediately after the anointing, there is no need for the *manutergium*, which originally was merely a towel to keep the oil from dripping on the bishop's chasuble while the *traditio* of the chalice and paten took place.

6. St. Gregory the Great, Homily 17:3, 14, PL 76: 1139–1140, 1146. Cf. *The Liturgy of the Hours*, Office of Readings, Saturday of the Twenty-Seventh Week in Ordinary Time.

7. Based on this canon of Chalcedon, some might raise the question of the validity of ordinations of members of religious institutes who are not localized to one specific diocese, in contrast to older monastic orders whose members took a vow of stability. A common way of justifying such ordinations is to appeal to an understanding of "community" that transcends the geographical bounds of dioceses. Ordained members of religious institutes are certainly called to serve the Church, and in fact often do so very heroically in ways and places that diocesan clergy cannot. Yet we cannot deny that such ordinations do not fall into the explicit pattern envisioned at Chalcedon.

Perhaps this concern prompted the revision of the promise of obedience in the 1989 edition of the ordination rites. In the revised text, if a person who is to be ordained is a member of a religious order, he is asked whether he promises "obedience and respect" both to his own religious superior (who is his "ordinary") and, in addition, to the bishop of the diocese in which he will exercise his ministry. In the pre-Vatican II rite and in the first edition of the revised rite, the bishop was never mentioned in the promise by members of religious institutes.

8. *Dogmatic Constitution on the Church*, n. 28.

9. Ignatius of Antioch, Letter to the Trallians 2:1, 3:1.

10. *Ceremonial of Bishops*, nn. 18, 119. Cf. General Instruction of the Roman Missal, n. 59.

11. Cf. Brown, *Priest and Bishop*, pp. 11–12.

12. For details on the liturgical ministry of deacons, see Michael Gilligan, "The Deacon at Eucharist," *The Priest*, v. 50, n. 4 (Apr 1994), pp. 37–40 and v. 50, n. 5 (May 1994), pp. 29–32.

Chapter 11—The Mystery of Death and the Rites for the Dead

1. For an overview of Christian funeral rites, see David A. Lysik, "Death and Life in the *Order of Christian Funerals*," *Liturgy* 90, v. 21, n. 9 (Nov/Dec 1990), pp. 4–8, Rowell, *The Liturgy of Christian Burial*, and Rutherford, *The Death of a Christian*.

2. *Constitution on the Sacred Liturgy*, art. 81.

3. Introduction, 1969 *Ordo Exsequiarum*, n. 4, 8, 9, 21.

4. General Instruction of the Roman Missal, n. 308 d, e.

5. Introduction, 1969 *Ordo Exsequiarum*, n. 22.6.

6. In the 1971 U.S. *Rite of Funerals*, there was a text to be said by the priest while the pall was placed over the coffin (see n. 38), and it was permitted to carry the Easter candle in this entrance procession (see n. 37). Permission for the continued use of these options was denied when the revised translation was submitted to Roman authorities for approval in 1985.

7. Introduction, 1969 *Ordo Exsequiarum*, n. 6.

8. *Ibid.*, n. 10.

9. *Ibid.*

10. General Introduction, *Order of Christian Funerals*, nn. 35–38.

11. *Order of Christian Funerals*, n. 132 (U.S. edition).

12. General Instruction of the Roman Missal, n. 341.

13. *Order of Christian Funerals*, nn. 98–127 (U.S. edition).

14. *Ibid.*, n. 400.

15. General Instruction of the Roman Missal, n. 338.

16. Introduction, 1969 *Ordo Exsequiarum*, n. 15.

17. *Order of Christian Funerals*, n. 406, text 3 (U.S. edition). The British ritual contains a separate chapter for the committal of ashes with appropriate texts in place.

18. Introduction, 1969 *Ordo Exsequiarum*, n. 7.

19. See pages 432 and 433 of the Canadian edition of the *Order of Christian Funerals*.

20. General Instruction of the Roman Missal, n. 337.

21. St. Irenaeus, *Adversus omnes haereses*, 5.31.1 ff, quoted in Perham, *The Communion of Saints*, p. 2, and referred to in David A. Lysik, "Death and Life in the *Order of Christian Funerals*," *Liturgy* 90, v. 21, n. 9 (Nov/Dec 1990), p. 7. Lysik's article provides the background for this section.

22. Robert J. Hoeffner, "A Pastoral Evaluation of the Rite of Funerals," *Worship*, v. 55, n. 6 (Nov 1981), p. 483.

23. *Ibid.*, p. 490.

24. *Order of Christian Funerals*, n. 202 (U.S. edition), Prayer of Commendation, first option.

25. Irenaeus and Tertullian both suggested that, as an exception, the martyrs would be received into God's presence immediately after death. Cf. Perham, *The Communion of Saints*, pp. 3–4.

CHAPTER 12—THE MYSTERY OF BLESSINGS

1. Cf. Hippolytus, *Apostolic Tradition*, Chapters 5, 6, 31.

2. Bouley, *From Freedom to Formula*, p. 165, referring to Augustine's *De baptismo contra Donatistas*, 6.47.

3. For example, the United States bishops have included the old rite of blessing throats on the feast day of St. Blase, February 3, even though, interestingly, it is not included in the Latin *typica* edition.

4. *Book of Blessings*, General Introduction, n. 27.

5. A standard rite of blessing is a significant service, especially if singing occurs at the suggested moments. On some occasions, it might be more appropriate to integrate a blessing into a celebration of the liturgy of the hours, itself a liturgy of praise and giving thanks to God, rather than into a mass. The *Book of Blessings* and other liturgical books indicate that blessings associated with certain occasions, such as an engagement before marriage (cf. n. 199 in the U.S. edition) or the admission into the novitiate of a religious institute, should not be integrated into mass.

6. *Book of Blessings*, General Introduction, n. 13.

CHAPTER 13—OBFUSCATING THE MYSTERY

1. Kavanagh, "Reflections on the Study [of Parish Liturgy] from the Viewpoint of Liturgical History," p. 85 in Madden, *The Awakening Church: 25 Years of Liturgical Renewal*.

2. Often non-parochial priests are more prone to commit this "sin" than parochial clergy since they are frequently less familiar with what can be considered reasonable need and undue inconvenice.

3. Huck, *The Three Days*, p. 42.

4. *National Catholic Reporter*, Dec. 27, 1985, pp. 1, 17.

5. Cf. "Do not affect a loose informality," in Kavanagh, *Elements of Rite*, pp. 99–101.

6. Cf. Bob Hurd, "Liturgy and Empowerment: The Restoration of the Liturgical Assembly," Chapter 10 in Downey, *That They Might Live: Power, Empowerment, and Leadership in the Church*, p. 131.

7. Cf. *Roman Missal*, rubric before Masses for the Dead; *Directory for Masses with Children*, n. 51.

8. *Constitution on the Sacred Liturgy*, art. 22.3. This statement was based on a similar statement in the 1947 encyclical of Pope Pius XII, *Mediator Dei*.

As canonist John Huels states, "part of the context of this law is another norm from the Constitution which mitigates its uncompromising impact: 'Pastors must therefore realize that when liturgy is celebrated something more is required than the mere observance of the laws governing valid and lawful celebration' (*Constitution on the Sacred Liturgy*, art. 11)." See Huels, *One Table, Many Laws*, p. 33.

9. Cf. *Code of Canon Law*, canon 17. For an overview of liturgical law, see Huels, *Liturgical Law: An Introduction* and Huels, *One Table, Many*

Laws. Cf. Smolarski, *How Not To Say Mass*, "Do not take liturgical law too seriously nor too lightly," p. 26, cf. pp. 10–11.

A fundamental quality needed in liturgy is common sense. Not every question can be resolved by explicit reference to rubrics. For example, in some parishes immediately after communion the eucharistic ministers are given pyxes to take communion to the sick. This practice is not mentioned in our ritual books, but was mentioned with approval in the 1988 Vatican *Circular Letter on Preparing and Celebrating the Paschal Feasts* (n. 53).

In his *Spiritual Exercises*, St. Ignatius Loyola proposes an example of using common sense and of "reading between the lines." He offers some comments (in n. 299) about his meditation on Christ appearing to the Blessed Virgin after the resurrection. There Ignatius argues that even though this event is not mentioned in scripture, it is implied, since scripture says: "are you also without understanding?" (MT 15:16)

10. *Constitution on the Sacred Liturgy*, art. 28; General Instruction on the Roman Missal (GIRM), n. 34. In n. 66, the GIRM states that a reader should fulfill his functions even though higher ministers are present.

11. Cf. Day, *Why Catholics Can't Sing*, pp. 18–22. Day reports the story of an acquaintance who left a Catholic church, where congregational singing was encouraged, in disgust one day, complaining that it was "too Protestant."

12. *Music in Catholic Worship*, nn. 6, 23.

13. General Instruction of the Roman Missal, n. 19.

14. Robert Hovda, "The Amen Corner: Cautionary Tales About Liturgy's Verbal Parts," *Worship*, v. 61, n. 3 (May 1987), p. 247.

15. Gabe Huck, "Many Other Things: 'Be Careful of Words,' " *Liturgy 80*, v. 18, n. 4 (May/June, 1987), pp. 10–12.

16. Cf. Humes, *The Sir Winston Method: The Five Secrets of Speaking the Language of Leadership*, pp. 17–18.

17. Talley, *Worship: Reforming Tradition*, p. 85.

18. Cf. Smolarski, *Eucharistia*, pp. 67–70.

19. Leo the Great, *Sermon 13, On the Passion of the Lord*, 3–4. Cf. *Liturgy of the Hours*, Office of Readings, Thursday of the Fourth Week of Lent.

20. Taft, *Beyond East and West*, p. 16.

21. Cf. Dix, *The Shape of the Liturgy*; Stevenson, *Jerusalem Revisited*; Talley, "History and Eschatology in the Primitive Pascha," *Worship*, v. 47 (1973), pp. 212–221; Talley, "History and Eschatology," Chapter 6 of *Worship: Reforming Tradition*; Taft, "Historicism Revisited," Chapter 2 of *Beyond East and West*.

22. Stevenson, *Jerusalem Revisited: The Liturgical Meaning of Holy Week*, pp. 5–10.

23. In an address to the bishops of Abruzzo and Molise in April 1986 (quoted in the June/July 1986 *Newsletter* of the U.S. Bishops' Committee on the Liturgy), Pope John Paul II warned against mixing liturgy with popular piety. Pope Paul VI offered similar advice in his 1974 Apostolic Exhortation, *Marialis Cultus*. He wrote: "popular devotions must be subordinated to the liturgy, not intermingled with it" (n. 31). Cf. *Documents on the Liturgy: 1963–1979*, n. 3929.

24. Ryan, *Sourcebook for Sundays and Seasons: 1992*, p. 106. Cf. Jeffery, *A New Commandment*, pp. 52–58.

25. *Music in Catholic Worship*, n. 27.

26. *Music in Catholic Worship*, n. 26.

27. *Environment and Art in Catholic Worship*, n. 97. Also see nn. 34 and 67.

28. Cf. for instance, Simons and Fitzpatrick, *The Ministry of Liturgical Environment*, p. 10.

29. Cf. *Environment and Art in Catholic Worship*, n. 28. Also see Simons and Fitzpatrick, *The Ministry of Liturgical Environment*, p. 11, and Mauck, *Shaping a House for the Church*.

30. Cf. "Churches are not carpeted," in Kavanagh, *Elements of Rite*, p. 21.

REFERENCES AND READING LIST

Bibliographical Lists

There are several published lists of practical liturgical books for the pastoral minister. Those interested in building a collection for parish, school, or personal use might wish to consult the following entries or the bibliographies in some of the more recent books in the following section.

Fleming, Austin H. "A Liturgy Library for Your Parish," *Liturgy 80*, v. 20, n. 4 (May/June 1989), pp. 11–15.

Fleming, Austin H. "The Parish Liturgy Library: An Update," *Liturgy 90*, v. 21, n. 6 (Aug/Sept 1990), pp. 10–12.

Marrevee, William. "A Pastoral Liturgist's Library," *National Bulletin on Liturgy*, v. 20, n. 109 (May–June 1987), pp. 134–150.

Books and Booklets

Austin, Gerard, OP. *Anointing with the Spirit*. Collegeville: The Liturgical Press, 1985 (A Pueblo Book).

Baker, Robert A. (ed.). *A Stress Analysis of a Strapless Evening Gown: Essays for a Scientific Age*. New York: Prentice-Hall Press, 1963.

Bellah, Robert N. *et al*. *Habits of the Heart*. Berkeley: University of California Press, 1985.

Botte, Bernard, OSB. *From Silence to Participation: An Insider's View of Liturgical Renewal*. Washington: The Pastoral Press, 1988.

Bouley, Allan, OSB. *From Freedom to Formula*. Washington: The Catholic University of America Press, 1981.

Brown, Raymond E., SS. *Priest and Bishop: Biblical Reflections*. New York: Paulist Press, 1970.

Bugnini, Annibale, CM. *The Reform of the Liturgy: 1948–1975*. Collegeville: The Liturgical Press, 1990.

Cabié, Robert. *The Church at Prayer (Vol. II): The Eucharist.* Collegeville: The Liturgical Press, 1986.

Cabié, Robert et al. *The Church at Prayer (Vol. III): The Sacraments.* Collegeville: The Liturgical Press, 1986.

Casel, Odo, OSB. *The Mystery of Christian Worship.* Westminster: Newman Press, 1962.

Catholic Household Blessings and Prayers. Washington: United States Catholic Conference, 1988.

The Ceremonial of Bishops. Collegeville: The Liturgical Press, 1989.

Challancin, James. *The Assembly Celebrates: Gathering the Community for Worship.* New York: Paulist Press, 1989.

Chupungco, Anscar J., OSB. *Cultural Adaptation of the Liturgy.* New York: Paulist Press, 1982.

Chupungco, Anscar J., OSB. *Liturgies of the Future: The Process and Methods of Inculturation.* New York: Paulist Press, 1989.

Circular Letter on Preparing and Celebrating the Paschal Feasts, January 16, 1988, Congregation for Divine Worship.

Collins, Mary, OSB. *Worship: Renewal to Practice.* Washington: The Pastoral Press, 1987.

Cooke, Bernard (ed.). *Alternative Futures for Worship: Christian Marriage (Vol. 5).* Collegeville: Liturgical Press, 1987.

Covino, Paul (ed.). *Celebrating Marriage.* Washington: The Pastoral Press, 1987.

Cowan, Michael A. (ed.). *Alternative Futures for Worship: Leadership Ministry in Community (Vol. 6).* Collegeville: Liturgical Press, 1987.

Crichton, J. D. *Christian Celebration: Understanding the Mass.* London: Geoffrey Chapman, 1993.

Crichton, J. D. *Christian Celebration: Understanding the Prayer of the Church.* London: Geoffrey Chapman, 1993.

Crichton, J. D. *Christian Celebration: Understanding the Sacraments.* London: Geoffrey Chapman, 1993.

Daniélou, Jean, SJ. *The Bible and the Liturgy.* Notre Dame: University of Notre Dame Press, 1956.

Day, Thomas. *Why Catholics Can't Sing: The Culture of Catholicism and the Triumph of Bad Taste.* New York: Crossroad Publishing Co., 1990.

Dix, Gregory. *The Shape of the Liturgy.* Westminster: Dacre Press, 1945. (New edition with an updating appendix by Seabury [New York, 1982].)

Documents on the Liturgy: 1963–1979—Conciliar, Papal, and Curial Texts. Collegeville: The Liturgical Press, 1982.

Downey, Michael (ed.). *That They Might Live: Power, Empowerment, and Leadership in the Church.* New York: Crossroad, 1991.

Duck, Ruth C. *Gender and the Name of God: The Trinitarian Baptismal Formula*. New York: The Pilgrim Press, 1991.

Duffy, Regis A., OFM (ed.). *Alternative Futures for Worship: General Introduction (Vol. 1)*. Collegeville: Liturgical Press, 1987.

Emminghaus, Johannes H. (transl. by Matthew J. O'Connell). *The Eucharist: Essence, Form, Celebration*. Collegeville: The Liturgical Press, 1978.

Environment and Art in Catholic Worship, Washington: United States Catholic Conference Publication Office, 1978.

Fagerberg, David W. *What Is Liturgical Theology?* Collegeville: Liturgical Press, 1992.

Fink, Peter E., SJ (ed.). *Alternative Futures for Worship: Anointing of the Sick (Vol. 7)*. Collegeville: Liturgical Press, 1987.

Fink, Peter E., SJ (ed.). *Alternative Futures for Worship: Reconciliation (Vol. 4)*. Collegeville: Liturgical Press, 1987.

Fink, Peter E., SJ (ed.). *The New Dictionary of Sacramental Worship*. Collegeville: The Liturgical Press, 1990.

Finn, Peter C. and Schellman, James M. (eds.). *Shaping English Liturgy*. Washington: The Pastoral Press, 1990.

Fisher, J.D.C. *Confirmation: Then and Now*. London: Alcuin Club/SPCK, 1978. Alcuin Club Collections No. 60.

Fulfilled in Your Hearing: The Homily in the Sunday Assembly. Bishops' Committee on Priestly Life and Ministry, National Conference of Catholic Bishops, 1982.

Gilligan, Michael. *How to Prepare Mass*. Oak Park: American Catholic Press, 1972.

Guardini, Romano. *The Church and the Catholic and the Spirit of the Liturgy*. New York: Sheed and Ward, 1953.

Hippolytus, *Apostolic Tradition*, found in Cotone, Michael, OSC. "The Apostolic Tradition of Hippolytus of Rome," *American Benedictine Review*, v. 19 (Dec. 1968), pp. 492–514.

This Holy and Living Sacrifice: Directory for the Celebration and Reception of Communion under Both Kinds. Washington: United States Catholic Conference Publication Office, 1984.

Hopko, Thomas. *The Orthodox Faith: Vol. II—Worship*. New York: Department of Religious Education of the Orthodox Church in America, 1972.

Hovda, Robert W. *Strong, Loving and Wise: Presiding in Liturgy*. Collegeville: The Liturgical Press, 1976, 1985.

Huck, Gabe. *The Three Days: Parish Prayer in the Paschal Triduum*. Chicago: Liturgy Training Publications, 1981.

Huels, John M., OSM. *Disputed Questions in the Liturgy Today*. Chicago: Liturgy Training Publications, 1988.

Huels, John M., osm. *Liturgical Law: An Introduction.* Washington: The Pastoral Press, 1987.

Huels, John M., osm. *One Table, Many Laws.* Collegeville: The Liturgical Press, 1986.

Humes, James C. *The Sir Winston Method: The Five Secrets of Speaking the Language of Leadership.* New York: William Morrow and Co., Inc., 1991.

Jeffery, Peter. *A New Commandment: Toward a Renewed Rite for the Washing of Feet.* Collegeville: The Liturgical Press, 1992.

Jone, Heribert, ofm cap. *Moral Theology.* Westminster: The Newman Press, 1957.

Kavanagh, Aidan, osb. *Confirmation: Origins and Reform.* New York: Pueblo Publishing Co., 1988.

Kavanagh, Aidan, osb. *Elements of Rite: A Handbook of Liturgical Style.* New York: Pueblo Publishing Co., 1982.

Kavanagh, Aidan, osb. *The Shape of Baptism: The Rite of Christian Initiation.* New York: Pueblo Publishing Co., 1978.

Kay, Melissa (ed.). *It Is Your Own Mystery: A Guide to the Communion Rite.* Washington: The Liturgical Conference, 1977.

Keifer, Ralph A. *To Give Thanks and Praise.* Washington: National Association of Pastoral Musicians, 1980.

Kuhn, Thomas S. *The Structure of Scientific Revolutions,* 2nd ed. Chicago: The University of Chicago Press, 1970.

Lee, Bernard J., sm (ed.). *Alternative Futures for Worship: The Eucharist (Vol. 3).* Collegeville: Liturgical Press, 1987.

Liturgical Music Today. Washington: United States Catholic Conference Publication Office, 1982.

Madden, Lawrence J., sj (ed.). *The Awakening Church: 25 Years of Liturgical Renewal.* Collegeville: The Liturgical Press, 1992.

Martimort, A. G. et al. *The Church at Prayer (Vol. I): Principles of the Liturgy.* Collegeville: The Liturgical Press, 1986.

Martimort, A. G. et al. *The Church at Prayer (Vol. IV): The Liturgy and Time.* Collegeville: The Liturgical Press, 1986.

Martinez, German. *Worship: Wedding to Marriage.* Washington: The Pastoral Press, 1993.

Mauck, Marchita. *Shaping a House for the Church.* Chicago: Liturgy Training Publications, 1990.

McBrien, Richard. *Ministry: A Theological-Pastoral Handbook.* San Francisco: Harper and Row, 1987.

McManus, Frederick R. (ed.). *Thirty Years of Liturgical Renewal.* Washington: National Conference of Catholic Bishops, 1987.

Meagher, Paul K., O'Brien, Thomas C., and Aherne, Consuelo M. (eds.).

Encyclopedic Dictionary of Religion. Washington: Corpus Publications, 1979.

Metzger, Bruce M., Dentan, Robert C. and Harrelson, Walter. *The Making of the New Revised Standard Version of the Bible*. Grand Rapids: Wm. B. Eerdmans Publishing Co., 1991.

The Milwaukee Symposia for Church Composers: A Ten-Year Report, June 9, 1992. Washington: The National Association of Pastoral Musicians, 1992.

Mitchell, Nathan, OSB. *Cult and Controversy: The Worship of the Eucharist Outside Mass*. New York: Pueblo Publishing Co., 1982.

Moloney, Raymond, SJ. *Our Eucharistic Prayers in Worship, Preaching and Study*, Wilmington: Michael Glazier, 1985.

Music in Catholic Worship (revised edition). Washington: United States Catholic Conference Publication Office, 1983

Neunheuser, Burkhard, OSB. *Baptism and Confirmation*. New York: Herder and Herder, 1964.

Nietzsche, Friedrich W. *Human, All Too Human: A Book for Free Spirits* (transl. by R. J. Hollingdale). New York: Cambridge University Press, 1986.

Osborne, Kenan B., OFM. *The Christian Sacraments of Initiation*. New York: Paulist Press, 1987.

Perham, Michael. *The Communion of Saints*. London: Alcuin Club/SPCK, 1980. Alcuin Club Collections No. 62.

Power, David N., OMI. *The Eucharistic Mystery: Revitalizing the Tradition*. New York: Crossroad, 1992.

Power, David N., OMI. *Unsearchable Riches: The Symbolic Nature of Liturgy*. New York: Pueblo Publishing Co., 1984.

The Roman Liturgy and Inculturation: Fourth Instruction for the Right Application of the Conciliar Constitution on the Sacred Liturgy, January 25, 1994, Congregation for Divine Worship and the Discipline of the Sacraments.

Rowell, Geoffrey. *The Liturgy of Christian Burial*. London: Alcuin Club/SPCK, 1977. Alcuin Club Collections No. 59.

Rutherford, Richard, CSC and Barr, Tony. *The Death of a Christian: The Order of Christian Funerals* (revised edition). Collegeville: The Liturgical Press, 1990.

Ryan, G. Thomas. *Sourcebook for Sundays and Seasons: 1992*. Chicago: Liturgy Training Publications, 1991.

Schmemann, Alexander. *Liturgy and Life: Christian Development Through Liturgical Experience*. New York: Department of Religious Education, Orthodox Church of America, 1974.

Searle, Mark (ed.). *Alternative Futures for Worship: Baptism and Confirmation (Vol. 2)*. Collegeville: Liturgical Press, 1987.

Searle, Mark and Stevenson, Kenneth W. *Documents of the Marriage Liturgy*. Collegeville: The Liturgical Press, 1992 (A Pueblo Book).

Shepherd, Massey. *Worship in Scripture and Tradition*. New York: Oxford University Press, 1963.

Simons, Thomas G. and Fitzpatrick, James M. *The Ministry of Liturgical Environment*. Collegeville: The Liturgical Press, 1984.

Smolarski, Dennis C., SJ. *Eucharistia: A Study of the Eucharistic Prayer*. New York: Paulist Press, 1982.

Smolarski, Dennis C., SJ. *How Not To Say Mass*. New York: Paulist Press, 1986.

Smolarski, Dennis C., SJ. *Liturgical Literacy: From Anamnesis to Worship*. New York: Paulist Press, 1990.

Stevenson, Kenneth W. *Jerusalem Revisited: The Liturgical Meaning of Holy Week*. Washington: The Pastoral Press, 1988.

Stevenson, Kenneth W. *Nuptial Blessing*. London: Alcuin Club/SPCK, 1982. Alcuin Club Collections No. 64.

Taft, Robert, SJ. *Beyond East and West: Problems in Liturgical Understanding*. Washington: The Pastoral Press, 1984.

Talley, Thomas J. *Worship: Reforming Tradition*. Washington: The Pastoral Press, 1990.

Turner, Paul. *Confirmation: The Baby in Solomon's Court*. New York: Paulist Press, 1993.

Turner, Victor W. *The Ritual Process: Structure and Anti-Structure*. Chicago: Aldine Publ. Co., 1969.

Walsh, Eugene A., SS. *From Rubrics to Ritual: Celebrating the Difference!* Daytona Beach: Pastoral Arts Associates of North America, 1988.

Ware, Timothy. *The Orthodox Church*. Middlesex: Penguin Books Ltd., 1972.

Wilde, James (ed.). *When Should We Confirm?* Chicago: Liturgy Training Publications, 1989.

ARTICLES

Diekmann, Godfrey, OSB. "The Laying On of Hands: The Basic Sacramental Rite," *Liturgy*, v. 21, n. 1 (Jan. 1976), pp. 22–27.

Gilligan, Michael. "The Deacon at Eucharist," *The Priest*, v. 50, n. 4 (April 1994), pp. 37–40 and v. 50, n. 5 (May 1994), pp. 29–32.

Hoeffner, Robert J. "A Pastoral Evaluation of the Rite of Funerals," *Worship*, v. 55, n. 6 (Nov. 1981), pp 482–499.

Hovda, Robert W. "The Amen Corner: Cautionary Tales About Liturgy's Verbal Parts," *Worship*, v. 61, n. 3 (May 1987), pp. 243–248.

Huck, Gabe. "Many Other Things: 'Be Careful of Words,'" *Liturgy 80*, v. 18, n. 4 (May/June 1987), pp. 10–12.

Janco, Steven R. "What About a Youth Mass?" *Modern Liturgy*, v. 19, n. 3 (April 1992), pp. 15–17.

Koernke, Theresa F. "Toward an Ethics of Liturgical Behavior," *Worship*, v. 66, n. 1 (Jan. 1992), pp. 25–38.

Lysik, David A. "Death and Life in the *Order of Christian Funerals*," *Liturgy 90*, v. 21, n. 8 (Nov./Dec. 1990), pp. 4–8.

Mazar, Peter, "Oil," *Liturgy 80*, v. 19, n. 4 (May/June 1988), pp. 8–9 and v. 19, n. 5 (July 1988), pp. 8–11.

Ramshaw-Schmidt, Gail. "Naming the Trinity: Orthodoxy and Inclusivity," *Worship*, v. 60, n. 6 (Nov. 1986), pp. 491–498.

"Rereading the Constitution on the Liturgy," (U.S.) Bishops' Committee on the Liturgy *Newsletter*.
- *Baptism—Art. 67–70,* v. XXVIII (March/April 1992).
- *Confirmation—Art. 71,* v. XXVIII (May 1992).
- *Penance—Art. 72,* v. XXVIII (June/July 1992).
- *Anointing the Sick—Art. 73–75,* v. XXVIII (Aug. 1992).
- *Ordination—Art. 76,* v. XXVIII (Sept. 1992).
- *Matrimony—Art. 77–78,* v. XXVIII (Nov. 1992).
- *Blessings—Art. 79,* v. XXIX (Jan. 1993).

Searle, Mark. "Renewing the Liturgy—Again: 'A' For The Council, 'C' for the Church," *Commonweal*, 18 November 1988, pp. 617–22.

Talley, Thomas J. "History and Eschatology in the Primitive Pascha," *Worship*, v. 47, n. 4 (April 1973), pp. 212–221.

INDEX

absolution,
  funeral, 141–42
  general, 92, 94, 190–91n7
  penance, 19, 85–88, 90–94,
    182n5(Chpt 3), 191n9
  penitential rite, 76, 189n16
active (and conscious) participation,
  4, 15, 48, 50, 112–13, 136,
  159, 167, 177
  at the eucharist, 68–69, 74
adaptation, 8, 14–15, 75, 98, 111,
  135, 165, 179
  and baptism, 41, 43, 49–50
  ill-advised, 21, 24, 167, 170
  to local culture, 9–11, 27, 161,
  183n23
adults, initiation of, *see Rite of Chris-*
  tian Initiation of Adults
ambo, 62, 68, 70, 77–79, 120, 177,
  189n19
Anglican, 60, 170, 174
anniversary of death, 151–52
anointing,
  in baptism, 37–38, 42, 45–46
  in confirmation, 19, 34–36, 39,
  53–62
  in orders, 129
anointing of the sick, 1, 4, 19, 56,
  93, 136, 160, 164, 191n2,
  192nn7–9, 192n12

conditional, 104
  mystery of, 96–104
Apostolic Tradition (of Hippolytus),
  18, 34, 52, 128–29, 157,
  195n4
Athanasius, 180n1(Pref)
Augustine, 170, 176
authority of ritual, 31–32

baptism, 1, 4, 18, 26, 30, 70–71,
  86, 132, 135–36
  of adults, *see Rite of Christian Ini-*
  tiation of Adults
  of children of catechetical age,
  41, 56, 187n8
  of Christ, 34, 53, 106
  and confirmation, 36–38, 41–43,
  47, 52–55
  by immersion, *see* immersion,
  baptism by
  of infants, 4, 25, 37, 40–41, 43–
  47, 74, 163, 170, 183–86nn1–
  28, 186n4
  mystery of, 33–51
  second, 86
  and symbols at funerals, 138,
  144, 147–48, 154
  see also initiation, Christian
Bellah, Robert, 185n23
Benedict xii, 153

birkat ha-mazon, 65
bishop, 159, 165–66, 190n30,
    190n7, 198n3 (Chpt 12),
    200n23
  and baptism, 34, 43, 48
  and confirmation, 19, 54–62
  and the eucharist, 64, 66, 69, 75–
    76, 127, 136
  and holy orders, 19, 126–37,
    195n4, 196nn5, 7
blessings, 18, 65, 108–9, 112, 116,
    120, 198n5 (Chpt 12)
  mystery of, 156–60
  nuptial, *see* nuptial blessing
body language, 27
body of Christ, 20–23, 36, 49, 52,
    57, 66, 163, 173, 177–78, 179,
    186nn4, 7
Book of Blessings, 19, 156, 158–60
Book of Gospels, 132, 144–45, 148
Botte, Bernard, 15, 56
bread, 23, 28, 62, 65, 74, 158,
    163–64, 175, 187n14
  and wine, 18–19, 35, 64–65, 80–
    84, 132, 169, 171
breaking of the bread, 64–65, 73, 80
Bugnini, Annibale, 15, 188n13
burial, 26, 139–41, 145–47, 149,
    151, 161
Byzantine
  Catholics, 190n2
  Churches, 37, 42, 66, 82, 96,
    171, 177, 194n4, 195n4
  liturgy, 1, 53, 73, 75, 136, 192n7
  ritual, 192n12

candle, 28, 30, 67–68, 140, 143
  baptismal, 37, 43, 46, 123
  Easter, 25, 46, 62, 123, 143–44,
    151, 197n6
  wedding, 122–23
Casel, Odo, 180n1 (Pref)

catechesis, 15, 41
catechumen, 35–43, 54, 57, 121
catechumenate, 40–43, 56, 164
Ceremonial of Bishops, 76, 109,
    183n20, 189n14, 192n13,
    196n10
chair, presidential, 68, 70, 77–79,
    83, 120, 148, 177, 189n19
Challancin, James, 21
chapel of reconciliation, 91
children of catechetical age, baptism
    of, *see* baptism
choreography, 70, 78–79
chrism, 19, 34–35, 37, 43, 46, 53–
    54, 57, 60–62, 132
  fragrance, 17, 28, 62
chrismation, 52, 55
Church and eucharist, *see* eucharist
    and Church
Churchill, Winston, 172, 177
commitment, 15, 19, 40, 119, 125
  confirmation as, 55–57, 59
communal (dimension of liturgy), 3,
    14, 22–24, 30, 101, 159, 162,
    165, 168
  and baptism, 35, 38, 44, 47–49,
    163
  and the eucharist, 69, 74, 79, 82–
    84, 190n29
  and funerals, 147, 149
  and marriage, 113, 124
  and penance, 87–89, 91–94,
    191nn7, 9
communion
  first, 9, 30, 42, 54–55, 58, 122
  under both kinds, 60, 67, 69–70,
    74, 82, 148, 187n14, 188n14
  rite during Mass, 81–83
conditional anointing, *see* anointing,
    conditional
confession, 86, 91–94, 191nn7, 9
  see also penance

confessional, 86–87, 90–91, 190n2
confirmation, 4, 19, 30, 70, 93,
 101, 131, 186n1, 4
 mystery of, 52–63
 see also baptism and confirmation;
  commitment, confirmation as
Congar, Yves, 18
consent,
 in marriage, 19, 106–12, 118–
  21, 193n2, 194n4
 at ordinations, 131
Consilium, 74–75, 131, 188n13
Constitution on the Sacred Liturgy,
 2–4, 7–9, 47, 49, 78, 168–69,
 181n1, 192n10
 and anointing of the sick, 191n1
 and initiation, 41, 52, 59, 184n9,
  186n4
 and the eucharist, 64
 and funerals, 141
 and marriage, 108, 119, 121,
  193n4
convenience, 30, 47, 162–64
Council of Chalcedon, 133
Council of Florence, 129–30,
 193n4
Council, Fourth Lateran, 190n1
Council, Second Vatican, 2–5, 12,
 14–16, 32, 42, 164, 185n24
 and anointing of the sick, 97, 99,
  101–2
 and baptism, 37, 40, 184n9
 and blessings, 158
 and the eucharist, 67–68, 70, 77,
  81, 83
 and funerals, 140–42
 and holy orders, 131, 133, 135–36
 and marriage, 105, 107 8, 120,
  193n4
 and ongoing liturgical reform, 7,
  9, 11, 22
 and penance, 85–86, 93

Council of Trent, 9, 66–69, 97,
 193n4
covenant, 71, 105, 108, 112
cremation, 141, 145, 151
culture, *see* adaptation to local culture
Cummins, John, 73
Cyril of Jerusalem, 36

Damasus, 8
deacon, 11, 13, 19, 21, 25, 92, 166,
 169–71, 191n7
 and baptism, 34–35, 40–42, 47,
  184n14
 and the eucharist, 69–70, 73, 78
 and funerals, 146–47
 and holy orders, 126–37, 196n12
 and marriage, 110, 112–13, 116,
  121
death, 26, 29, 39, 53–54, 99, 102,
 124, 130
death, mystery of, and the rites for
 the dead, 138–55
death and resurrection of Christ, 1–
 2, 29–30, 95, 99, 106, 111,
 136, 161, 174, 179
 and baptism, 33–34, 38–39, 47
 and the eucharist, 64, 71, 80, 84
 and funerals, 138, 142, 154–55
 see also paschal mystery
Didache, 34
Diekmann, Godfrey, 18
Dies Irae, 140, 142
dies natalis, 138
Dix, Gregory, 174, 187n3
dying, 97–99, 102, 104

Easter, 26, 30, 53, 60, 62, 73, 93,
 111, 154, 158, 190n1
 candle, *see* candle, Easter
 season, 35, 43, 45, 76
 Triduum, 57, 77, 86, 154, 164

Vigil, 25–26, 35, 37, 41–42, 45,
   47, 57, 59, 70
Eastern
   Christians, 1, 39, 55, 62, 71,
      152, 170, 184n14, 187n14,
      192n7
   Churches, 36, 38, 55, 66, 82, 96,
      129, 190n2, 195n4
   see also Byzantine *and* Orthodox
education, 11, 12–13, 15, 56, 58,
   73, 157, 172
Egeria, 66
elect, 35, 41–42, 51, 138
entrance procession, 45, 47, 61,
   145, 148, 197n6, *see also* procession at marriages
*Environment and Art in Catholic
   Worship*, 176, 189n19
ephphetha, 37, 46
eucharist, 1–4, 18, 21, 29, 86, 93,
   160, 169, 171, 187n3, 188n12
   and anointing of the sick, 101,
      103
   and Church, 71–72
   and holy orders, 127–28, 132,
      136
   and initiation, 35–37, 41–43, 45,
      47–48, 51, 54–60, 70–71,
      186nn4, 7
   and funerals, 142–43, 145, 147,
      149
   and marriage, 109, 120–22
   mystery of, 64–84
eucharistic prayer, 19–20, 28, 65,
   67, 80–81, 120, 122, 148, 175
   special intercessions for, 76, 99,
      101, 110
   various options for, 69, 171, 187–
      88n5
eulogy, 140, 146, 148
exorcism, 35, 37, 42, 45
extreme unction, 97

faith, 2, 4, 7–8, 20, 24, 84, 100, 170
   and baptism, 35, 38, 40, 42–44,
      46, 48, 50, 163
   and confirmation, 56–57, 59
   and death, 141–42, 147–48, 152,
      154–55
   and marriage, 112, 114, 116,
      119, 121–22, 125
farewell, song of, 143, 149
final commendation, 29, 142–45,
   148–49, 151
flowers for Mary, 123
forgiveness, 34, 65, 85–86, 93–95,
   122, 141–42
funeral mass, 25, 140–41, 147–48
funeral procession, 26, 139–43,
   147, 149
funerals, 4, 25, 29, 74, 170, *see also*
   death, mystery of, and the rites
   for the dead

General Instruction of the Roman
   Missal (GIRM), 3, 70, 74, 79,
   81–83, 147–48, 151, 169–70,
   187n3, 188n14, 189n29
gestures, 1, 17, 88, 98, 104, 131,
   161, 166
   and imposition of hands, 17–20,
      60, 90–91
   during mass, 69, 79, 81, 175
   and posture, 27–28
Gibran, Kahlil, 124
godparents, 44–46, 51, 61
gospel, last, *see* last gospel
greetings, 20–21, 75–76, 166, 171,
   183n9
Gregory the Great, 133
Guardini, Romano, 180n3

handing-over ceremonies, 129
hands, laying on, *see* imposition of
   hands

healing, 18, 152, 160, 182n5(Chpt 3)
  and anointing of the sick, 56, 62, 96–97, 99–100, 103
  and penance, 85, 88–90
Hippolytus, 152, *see also Apostolic Tradition*
historicism, 174
homily, 14, 45, 70, 72–73, 80, 108–9, 120, 124, 177
  during funerals, 146, 148
  of Gregory the Great, 133
  of John Chrysostom, 73
  sample for presbyteral ordination, 136
Hopko, Thomas, 1
Hovda, Robert, 20–21, 23–24, 171, 186n28
Huck, Gabe, 164, 171
Huels, John, 103, 198n8
Hughes, Kathleen, 15

iconostasis, 177, 190n2
Ignatius of Antioch, 127, 135, 193n1
Ignatius Loyola, 199n9
immersion, baptism by, 18, 34, 37, 39–40, 42, 44, 46, 164, 184n14
imposition (laying on) of hands, 17–20, 34, 42, 45
  and anointing of the sick, 19, 96–97, 99–101
  and confirmation, 19, 53, 60–61
  and holy orders, 19, 128–29, 131
  and penance, 19, 86, 90–91, 182n5(Chpt 3)
incense, 17, 28–29, 70, 141, 143–45, 149, 151
India, 27, 114
individualism, 14, 19, 82, 185nn23, 24

infants, baptism of, *see* baptism
informality, 19, 166–69, 198n5 (Chpt 13)
initiation, Christian, 4, 29, 99, 131, 164
  and baptism, 35–37
  and confirmation, 52–60
  see also eucharist and initiation *and Rite of Christian Initiation of Adults*
interaction, 21–24, 66, 75, 87, 91, 104, 161, 166, 169, 173
International Commission on English in the Liturgy (ICEL), 4, 143
Irenaeus, 152, 197nn21, 25

Jerome, 8, 66
John XXIII, 3
John Chrysostom, 66, 73
John Paul II, 200n23
Justin Martyr, 187n2

Kavanagh, Aidan, 21, 161–62, 184n9, 198n5 (Chpt 13), 200n30
Keifer, Ralph, 21
Koernke, Theresa, 14
Krosnicki, Thomas, 20

lasso (at marriages), 111, 123
last gospel, 67, 69
last rites, 97, 103
laying on of hands, *see* imposition of hands
leadership, 18, 70, 126–37
lectionary, 4, 68–69, 72, 77, 80, 148
Leo XIII, 193n4
Leo the Great, 174
limbo, 44, 163
liminal rite, 24–26, 45, 117, 154

liturgia semper reformanda, 7–11,
    179

manutergium, 130
marriage, 4, 19, 25, 56, 59, 75–76,
    131, 136, 160, 165
    customs, 113–16
    mixed, 108, 121
    mystery of, 105–25
    see also posture of the bridal cou-
        ple
mass, *see* eucharist, funeral mass
McClory, Robert, 165
Mead, Margaret, 31
mediocrity, 176
metanoia, 7, 93
mimicry, 174–75
minister, ministry, 14, 66, 68, 79,
    107, 162
    non-integration of various minis-
        tries, 169
    volunteerism in lieu of ministry,
        172–73
    see also orders, holy
ministerial role of bride and groom,
    112
missal, *see Roman Missal*
month's mind mass, 152
music, 15, 160, 165, 170, 172, 176
    at baptism, 47–48, 50, 163, 170,
        185n15
    at the eucharist, 74, 83–84
    at funerals, 139–41, 146, 148, 170
    at marriage, 113, 117–18, 170
Music in Catholic Worship, 170,
    176, 190n30
myron, 54
mystagogy, 4, 15, 35, 43
mystery, 1–2, 4–5, 12–13, 17, 161–
    62, 179
    of Christ, 2, 40, 63, 84, 118,
        137, 174, 179

of the Church, 40, 63, 136–37,
    163, 178
    paschal, *see* paschal mystery
    *see also the individual chapters on
        the seven sacraments, on the
        mystery of death, and on the
        mystery of blessings*

Neunheuser, Burkhard, 36
Nietzsche, Friedrich, 115
non-scriptural readings, 124
nuptial blessing, 106–7, 109–11,
    120

offertory, 11, 67, 80–81, 130, *see
    also* preparation of the gifts
oil,
    blessing, 102, 157
    of the catechumens, 35, 37, 42,
        45, 62, 130, 132
    of chrism, *see* chrism
    of the sick, 62, 96–104
order and the Church, 134
Order of Christian Funerals, 4, 141–
    51
orders, holy, 19
    mystery of, 126–37
ordination, 4, 120, *see also* orders,
    holy
Orthodox, 1, 28, 39, 42, 59, 71, 82,
    96, 190n2, 192n7, 194n4, *see
    also* Byzantine *and* Eastern

participation, active, *see* active par-
    ticipation
paschal mystery, 2, 84, 99, 113,
    138, 155, 174
    and baptism, 33, 39, 47, *see also*
        death and resurrection of Christ
passover meal, 65, *see also* seder
Pastoral Care of the Sick, 4, 19, 62,
    97–104, 181n9, 191n2

pastoral notes, 10, 43, 98, 100, 111, 143
pastoral solution, 14, 164–66
Paul VI, 2, 69, 74–75, 77, 131, 186nn4, 7, 188n13, 200n23
penance, 19, 57, 72, 97, 99, 136
  mystery of, 85–95
Pentecost, 30, 33, 43, 63
perichoresis, 78
Pius X, 54
Pius XII, 129, 194n4
posture, 27–28, 69
  of the bridal couple, 119–21
Power, David, 71
prayers at the foot of the altar, 67, 69, 75, 78, 141
preparation, 48, 116, 162
  inadequate, 11, 168–69
  sacramental, 34–35, 48, 56, 89, 116
preparation of gifts, 26, 46, 80–81, 132
presbyter, 126–37
priest
  and presbyter, 128
  for the ministerial role of a priest see, for example, the individual chapters on the seven sacraments, on the mystery of death, and on the mystery of blessings
priesthood, 38–39, 128, 130
principles and practice, 12–16
procession, 11, 22, 25–27, 83, 164, 177
  at baptism, 45–46, 185n15
  at marriages, 107, 109, 116–18
  see also entrance procession *and* funeral procession
prose and poetry, 15

reception into full communion, 41, 50

reconciliation (sacrament of), *see* penance
reconciliation of penitents, 85
Red Sea (as image of baptism), 34
re-enactment (and remembrance), 173–76
reform, 7–11, 22, 56, 59, 66, 107–8, 120, 140–41
remembrance, 25, 29, 149, 150
  and reenactment, *see* re-enactment
rememorative piety, 174
representational piety, 174–75
Rite of Christian Initiation of Adults (RCIA), 4, 18, 41–43, 50, 52, 55, 70
ritual, 30–32, 166–68
Roman Missal, 4, 27, 66–80, 140, 152
Roman Ritual (1614), 72, 91, 157–58, 169, 190n2
  and anointing of the sick, 96–97, 101
  and baptism, 37, 41, 46, 49
  and funerals, 142, 144, 149
  and marriage, 107–9, 117, 119, 193n2
Ryan, Thomas, 175

sacramentary, 4, 69, 75–77, 170, *see also Roman Missal*
sacraments, 1–4, 9, 12, 17, 21, 24, 29, 48, 161–63, 165, 175, 178, 179
  and blessings, 157, 160
  and the imposition of hands, 18–19
  and music, 170
  widows as, 152, *see also the individual chapters on the seven sacraments*
salt, 37

satisfaction, 90
Schmemann, Alexander, 71
science and art, 12–16
scripture, *see* word (of God)
scrutiny, 35, 42
seal, 53
Searle, Mark, 11, 14, 180n4, 194n4
secondary, 5, 9, 43, 50, 58, 117,
    129, 131, 139, 168, 175–76
  elements in the eucharist, 67, 69,
    81
seder, 65, 173
sedilia, 78
sensory elements, 28–29
servant, 22–23, 32, 84, 126–28,
    132–37
Sexton, Anne, 171
sick, 14, 19, 47, 82, *see also* anoint-
    ing of the sick
silence, 22–23, 73, 79–80, 83, 91–
    92, 100–1, 107, 149, 165
sin, 34, 38–39, 43, 65, 122, 139–
    42, 153, *see also* penance
singing, *see* music
song of farewell, *see* farewell, song of
Spirit, Holy,
  and anointing of the sick, 100
  and baptism, 25, 33–34, 36–39,
    49–50
  and confirmation, 52–63
  and the eucharist, 65, 71, 80
  and funerals, 144
  and holy orders, 127, 132
  and marriage, 110
  and penance, 88, 91
sponsor (for confirmation), 61
sprinkling of water, 25, 60, 76, 104,
    141, 143, 147–50, 188n14
Stevenson, Kenneth, 174–75,
    194n4
stock, oil, 43, 61, 101–2

symbol, 15, 23, 25, 28, 30–31, 170,
    174–75, 177
  and anointing of the sick, 100
  and baptism, 34, 36, 39, 42, 45–
    47, 49
  and confirmation, 57, 60, 62
  and the eucharist, 65, 69–70, 81
  and funerals, 141, 143–45, 148–
    49
  and holy orders, 135
  and marriage, 116, 118, 121–22,
    125
  and penance, 91, 182n5 (Chpt 3)

Taft, Robert, 174
Talley, Thomas, 11, 31–32, 173–74
Tertullian, 28, 197n25
third penitential rite, 79
threshold rite, *see* liminal rite
time, 29–30
tomb (as image of baptism), 33–34,
    39, 57
touch, 17–20, 99–100
Tridentine, 14–15, 67–68, 70, 74–
    75, 78, 80–81, 140, 152, 168–
    69
Triduum, Easter, *see* Easter
    Triduum
Turner, Victor, 24

unitive piety, 174–75

viaticum, 97, 103
Vigil, Easter, *see* Easter Vigil
vigil service (for the dead), 145–47,
    149, 170
volunteerism, 172–73
vows (marriage), 107, 109, 111,
    115, 118–19, *see also* consent
    in marriage

wake, 74, 140, 142, 146, *see also* vigil service

Wayne, John, 27

wedding candle, *see* candle, wedding

wine, 13, 65, 106, 131, 158, 168, *see also* bread and wine

womb (as image of baptism), 34

word (of God), 159, 172
   and baptism, 35, 41–42, 45, 47, 50

and the eucharist, 64, 70, 72–74, 78–80

and holy orders, 130–31, 136

and marriage, 109, 120, 124

and penance, 87, 89, 92

words (human), 170–72

work, liturgy as, 177–78

worship space, 22, 74, 78, 177

Zaire, 27, 76